River of Fire
Conflict and Survival on the Seal River

The mind is not a vessel to be filled but a fire to be kindled.

- Plutarch

Library and Archives Canada Cataloguing in Publication

Wilson, Hap, 1965-

author
River of Fire: Conflict / Hap Wilson
ISBN 978-0-9958235-3-2 (paperback)
I. Title.

PS8607.O9274S66 2016   C813'.6   C2016-903184-5
Printed and bound in Canada on 100% recycled paper.

Book Design: Christine Lewis
Cover Design: Christine Lewis
Cover Photo: Chris Wilson

Published by:
Latitude 46 Publishing
info@latitude46publishing.com
Latitude46publishing.com

River of Fire
Conflict and Survival on the Seal River

by

Hap Wilson

LATITUDE 46
PUBLISHING

To the Sayisi Dene - People of the sand eskers

Acknowledgements:

As with any writing endeavour, it takes more than just the words of a writer to make things happen. Expeditions and explorations involve research and money. Needless to say, the time involved in research far exceeded any monetary donations, as is often the case. I would like to thank *Men's Journal Magazine* for sponsoring the expedition; The Explorer's Club and the Royal Canadian Geographical Society for their ongoing support for my geographical explorations; Canada Parks and Travel Manitoba to whom I am also indebted. Gratitude and thanks to my editors and publisher at Latitude 46 Publishing for accepting my manuscript.

I would also like to thank Allen and Mary Code and the Say-isi Dene people of Tadoule village for their hospitality and willingness to share stories and knowledge of the land. To Russell Kaye and Hodding Carter, my canoeing compatriots, I extend my heartfelt appreciation for your camaraderie and willingness to endure the unknown. Most importantly, I would like to thank my wife, Andrea, who is determined to love me no matter what.

Contents

River of Fire ~ Seal River, Manitoba

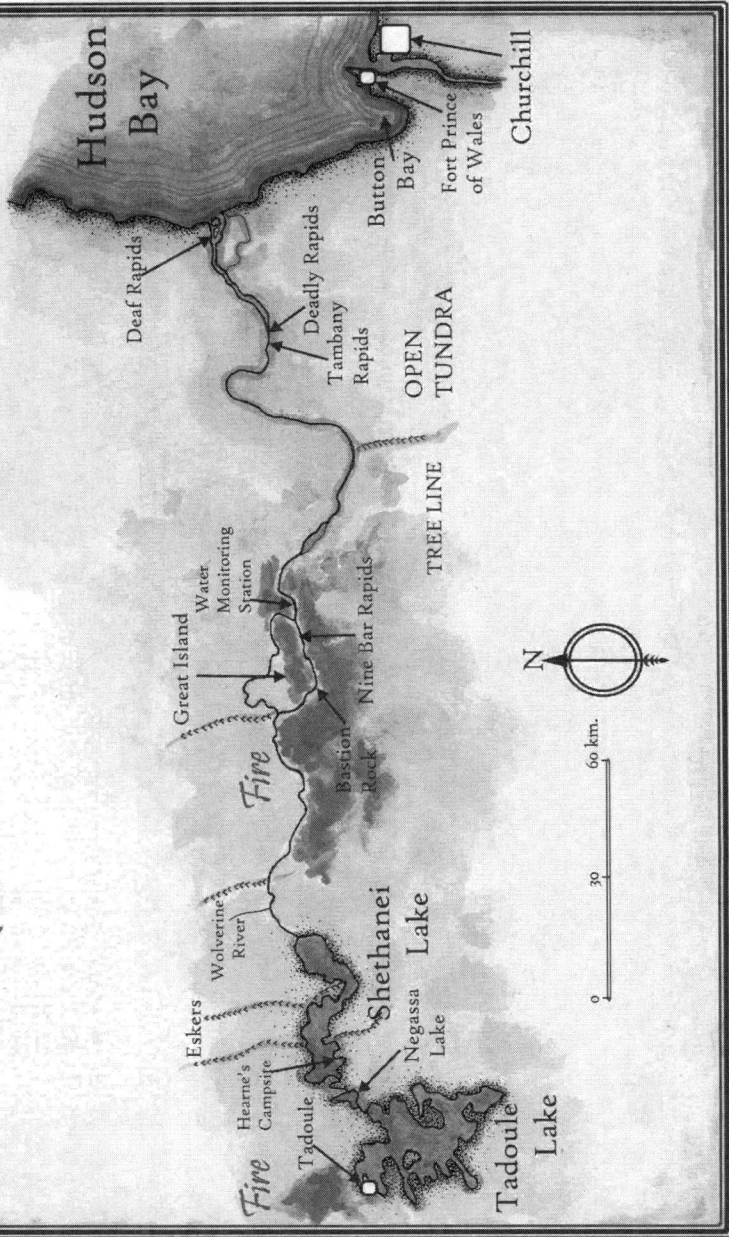

Hudson Bay

Churchill

Fort Prince of Wales

Button Bay

Deaf Rapids

Deadly Rapids

Tambany Rapids

OPEN TUNDRA

TREE LINE

Water Monitoring Station

Great Island

Nine Bar Rapids

Bastion Rock

Fire

Wolverine River

Eskers

Hearne's Campsite

Shethanei Lake

Negassa Lake

Tadoule

Fire

Tadoule Lake

N

0   30   60 km.

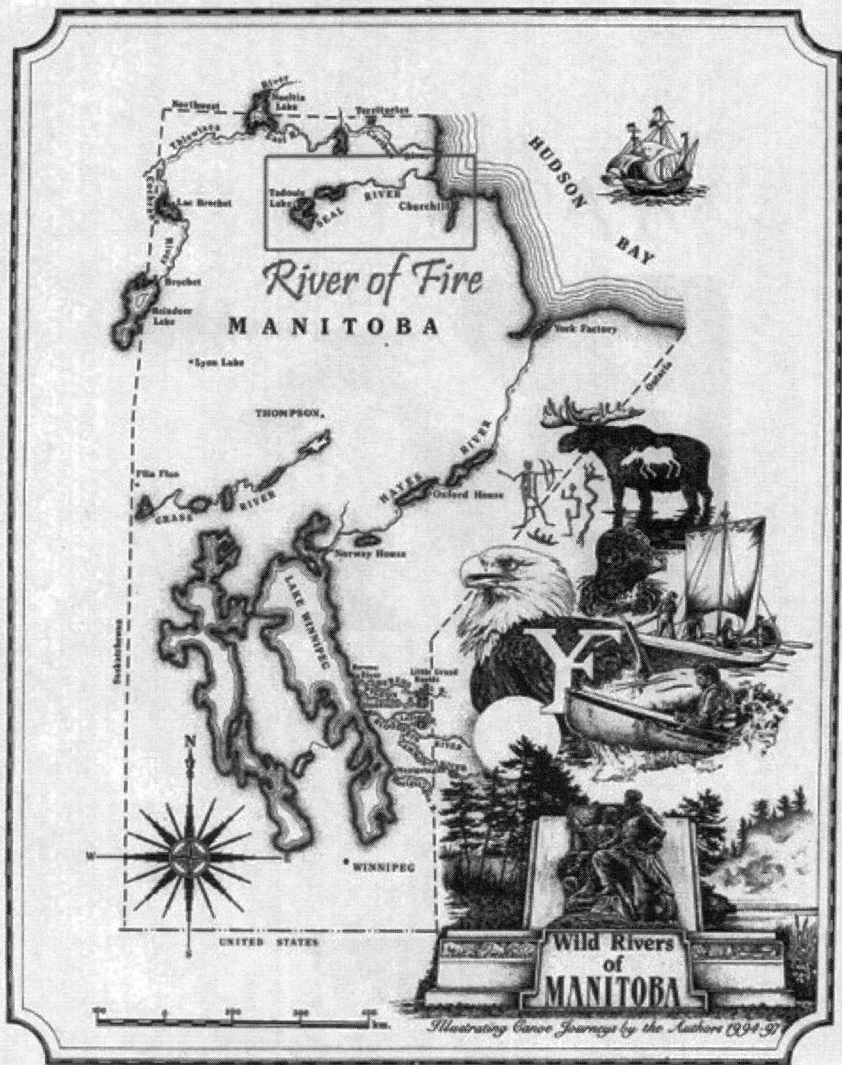

River of Fire

MANITOBA

HUDSON BAY

Wild Rivers
of
MANITOBA

Illustrating Canoe Journeys by the Authors 1994-97

UNITED STATES

Introduction

Anatomy of Exploration

"Visit the arctic barrens once and you write a book; go twice and you stay to live." This is an observation and sentiment defended by a canoeing acquaintance of mine. He is both scholar and explorer and no stranger to the canoe, or to the barrenlands of northern Canada. This assertion, though, seems somewhat critical of those tundra debutantes by inferring that their personal adventures, or misadventures, are perhaps trite and conspicuously vain. I have to disagree; not solely because *River of Fire* happens to be about my first journey to the northern barrens, but for historical and intellectual reasons.

Anyone who has ever travelled to that capricious tract of taiga for the first time has an individual tale to tell, dissimilar perhaps in circumstance and outcome, or maybe not quite the 'stuff' to transcribe onto the pages of a book; yet, who are we to exercise judgement over what is indelibly etched upon the mind and soul of an individual explorer? The mind's eye, for some voyagers, has that peculiar ability to open a portal for discovery and experience in short order, whereas it may take others incalculable time to visualize and articulate the same things, or to never actually see them at all. There have been great books written by veritable novices of the outdoors – first time adventurers – the likes of Dillon Wallace, who immortalized the Hubbard expedition in Labrador in 1903; and, of course, P.G. Downes: the school teacher from Vermont, who eloquently writes of his travels in his book, *Sleeping Island*, which took place in northern Manitoba in 1933. Even Farley Mowat, whose ventures into the far north were seasonal and temporary, and of suspect authenticity, brought us a plethora of classic northern stories. Not to be discounted too, are the journals of many an explorer: Champlain, Hearne, Thompson, and others who elected not to permanently live in the wilds of that they wrote about during their collective excursions, sojourns that chronicled them as historical heroes. Their writings, nonetheless, give us insight into a gloriously savage world few of us can ever really understand, comprehend or experience first-hand.

First encounters are often the most profound. Eyes are open wide to the nuances of discovery, challenge and mere survival. Who is to say that the narrative of a passive *visitor* is any less credible than one who has lived in the far north for many years? Personally, I find that a fresh view, cognizant of trail life upon a new path can be poignant and vibrant. Times have changed in the north. Few local northerners, Indigenous or white, spend the majority of their time on the trail. Methods of hunting game and wilderness travel have been improved through technological advancements, living conditions enhanced and even regular diets modified to adjust to modern times. That doesn't necessarily mean things are better.

Survival and necessity that once pinioned the First Peoples to the natural world are now mere pasttimes for sport and leisure. I'm speaking generally, but those of you who have travelled in the north will know this to be corroborated as a prognosis of development, both socially and technically. After all, post-contact Europeans have spent centuries cultivating this change. The assimilation of Canada's indigenous peoples to an archetypical capitalistic way of life has had an adverse effect on their social, cultural and spiritual potency and vigour.

And then there are those too who have perished on the northern trail: Hudson, Back, Franklin, Hornby – to name but a few historical figures. There have been mutinies, desertions, rebellions and murder within the ranks of early expedition parties. Time on the trail, especially for those unused to such an irresolute and unsympathetic host, has often tested the bounds of human endurance. Suffering amidst a veritable "Garden of Eden" indicated colonial man's inability to cope, or survive in a world they knew little about. The First People believed the natural world to be paradise – a land which provided everything they required for existence. As represented in this story, post-contact Europeans have regarded the natural world in terms of profit, often at the expense of Canada's First Nations and the sanctity of the environment.

Conflict on the trail is a by-product of fear and disassociation with the familiar parameters we construct as social, gregarious and dependent creatures. Remove the comfortable amenities of community existence, thrust the individual (be he or she uninitiated or imperious in character) into a world controlled by a whimsical god and the immutable forces of nature, and watch the true disposition of an individual unfold.

River of Fire takes place in 1994. Since then I have travelled several thousand kilometres across the barrens and arctic wilds by canoe and on foot; each exploration different from the next. I wrote this book two years after the expedition then put it on a shelf until I felt compelled to release it, perhaps because it is very personal.

Prior to my first venture to the arctic fringe in 1994, I had been guiding expeditions for over twenty years. These expeditions embraced the innumerable rivers and clear water lakes of the lower Canadian Shield; and through those adventures I was allowed to nurture a kindred relationship with the land upon which I travelled and lived for the greater part of the year. Guiding, as a profession, was incidental for me and something that burgeoned out of my distaste for urban living and my unquenchable love of the outdoors. I was certainly not 'corporate' material and aside from having reasonably accepted talents as an artist, I lacked any other skill other than those acquired through wilderness travel and exploration.

Wilderness guiding gave me the opportunity to explore how the human mind accepts, or repels the influences of a rather precarious and provocative trail existence. However short-termed most of these adventures were for the participants, the effect that wilderness life has on the personality, for some individuals, is as succinct and powerful a character modifier as hard liquor, mind enhancing drugs, or psychological trauma. Subjecting the client to the isolation of wilderness, I learned, could work as an elixir of restored faith, improved health and well-being, or as a conduit to the worst psychotic mind-shift imaginable. Wilderness could easily turn a person inward, where the sudden realization of one's own insignificance in the general scheme of life – one's vulnerability and mortality can abruptly, or subtly, turn a likeable saint into a sociopathic demon.

Guiding certainly has a romantic facade attached to it. Basic survival skills are fundamental; but if a person is to stay afloat in this oldest of Canadian professions they need to have a well-healed approach to personality disorders. Teaching greenhorns which end of the paddle went into the water is simple enough when handling the congenial mix of different and sometimes incongruous personalities; it soon becomes a job more for a psychoanalyst and not a backwoods guide. This realization as an expedition leader materialized on one of my very early organized canoe adventures when I unknowingly matched six marines from California with a group of gay-rights activists from Toronto.

A guide's reputation then, has to encapsulate a multitude of vocations; from chef, doctor/surgeon, entertainer, teacher, philosopher, musician and raconteur, to arbitrator and psychotherapist; none of which may deem the guide either qualified or professionally adept at any one ability. For a wilderness guide, living with clients in total isolation, and dealing with their sometimes peculiar and frightening character traits, is tedious and enervating work...and sometimes dangerous. Detecting aberrations in a client's mental character before he or she signs up for an expedition is not always an easy task. Personality disorders are often hard to discern but almost always likely to surface somewhere along the trail and the guide has to sort it out before it has a deleterious effect on group safety and morale. People suffering from manic-depression, schizophrenia, obsessive compulsive behaviour, paranoia, maladjustment and social dysfunctional disorders are more likely to confront the guide with their particular problem before exposing deviant social traits to the psychologist in the safe confines of an office.

And I've seen it all. But in most instances, it was recognition of the signs of trouble before it flared, knowing everyone's ability to cope with the extremes, their own limitations, and then addressing the problem with respect for the individual's privacy. Often it was just a reassuring word of comfort that was needed, or a break from the tedium of environmental conditions, getting out of the rain, away from biting insects, or the simple pleasure of a tea-break that would quell a potential flare-up.

But sometimes nothing works, as in the case of this story, relating the machinations behind exploration and the Canadian wilderness expedition profile, the blending and repulsion of personalities, confrontation – both on the personal side and one having to cope with some of the harshest natural conditions in the world - including the worst wildfire in Manitoba history.

River of Fire was written not so much as a narrative of adventure, but as an explanation of events that sometimes plague an ordinarily carefree occupation; more specifically, as an insight into the framework of the enormously expanding wilderness trade. The focus on the changing fabric of social existence in the Canadian north is also compelling where change is not necessarily a boon to the human condition, nor, as is often the case, beneficial to the scope of the environmental landscape. More obvious is the understructure of tension and disharmony when personalities collide and the sensibility and control becomes unglued.

Every incident in this book is depicted with care and accuracy, based upon my own daily journal notes, interviews and recollections. Some events that took place continue to haunt me; a reality bite into the human psyche and how far one will step to the outer bounds of self-discipline and self-control. The many facets of true wilderness exploration not only investigate hidden or remote places, but also navigate into the deeper recesses of the mind.

In 1994, New York's *Men's Journal Magazine* hired a studio photographer from Brooklyn, a post-master/writer from Thermond, West Virginia and two Canadian river guides to paddle one of the country's most dangerous whitewater rivers – the Seal in northern Manitoba - for the purpose of publishing the "quintessential Canadian adventure story". Add to this unlikely melange of characters, the possibility of capsizing in freezing water, seemingly endless canoe-eating rapids, one of Canada's worst boreal wild fires, the threat of polar bears and a midnight sail down Hudson Bay – *River of Fire* will carry the reader to the extreme edge of exploration.

PROLOGUE

Sometimes the soft underbelly of fate is exposed, uncovering the marrow of rational thought. It happened to me as a methodical event over time, like a jackhammer chips away at concrete, where pieces of your soul get broken up and scattered. Chaos appears like some hooded spectre in the fog, overshadowing even the remote possibility of order. I'm not sure if I was more ready to die in the cold ocean or to shoot the man who sat three feet away from me.

The coastline – if you could call it that – along Hudson Bay had disappeared. It was dark, save for a lone candle lantern hung from the rear shroud of our makeshift boat and the dim lights of Churchill far in the distance. Not even sure if they were the lights from Churchill or some grain freighter sailing north out of the village port. It was all pretty sketchy. Waves were starting to build up and roll lightly over the spray-decks; the spindly spruce poles lashing the two canoes together in a jury-rigged sailing catamaran creaked and groaned under the stress.

I was asleep; a deep, unconscious slumber, the kind of sleep born from weeks of exhaustion. Not just exhaustion but frustration and conflict. And so disposed, I was oblivious to the calamity unfolding and the peril that now confronted all of us. Fatigue *had* consumed me; it was my time to rest. The others were already asleep, curled up in the two bow seats, and now they were shouting at me to do something.

I heard myself say it, at first, and I couldn't believe that it came out of my mouth. I just wanted to sleep. *Don't bother me, let me sleep for Christ sake,* I thought, trying to form the words in my brain.

"I don't care," I said softly, more to myself than to the two distressed men in the front of the canoes.

"What?" the two men stared at each other then at me. At first I had no idea where I was or what was happening. *I don't care* was not the answer they were looking for. And then it happened; the slap of reality in the face. *What the fuck am I doing? This was my job, to look after things.*

I looked to my right, at my assistant guide, Dawson, who was steering the canoes. "DAMMIT DAWSON...YOU WERE SUPPOSED TO STAY ON COURSE DOWN THE COAST!" I shouted. No response. Dawson leaned harder on the ruddering paddle propped under his right armpit, a sardonic grimace on his face. Hours earlier we had argued about the crossing of Button Bay – a deadly stretch of open water thirty kilometres across to the town of Churchill. I told Dawson that it wasn't an option; people had died attempting the short-cut. The coastline was safe enough, except for polar bears, but with an offshore breeze the waves would only get bigger the farther from shore we sailed; where we were now. Reluctantly, Dawson had agreed to hold the course while I caught some much needed rest. Once everyone was fast asleep though, he turned the boats directly away from the sanctity of the shore and headed us towards the lights he thought were from the town and bore down on his steering paddle, propelling our flimsy craft deep out into the ocean.

The canoes were now running with a brisk offshore wind and waves began piling up over the bow. "DO SOMETHING!" came a cry from the front of the boat. I dug in hard with my own paddle to try and turn us but it was futile – we were going too fast and we were picking up speed. Suddenly we were all yelling at the crazy man but he just smiled, gripping his paddle even harder.

"PUT UP YOUR DAMN PADDLE!" I screamed, more than once. No response; Dawson just smiled defiantly. I quickly thought of all my options of which there was only the one; that option made my stomach turn. *Fuck this*, I said aloud - *this is insane!* I had no other choice. I yelled at my two companions up front to take down the sail, reached under the spray-cover in front of me and gripped the stock of the Mossberg 12-gauge shotgun and thumbed the safety off.

Hap Wilson
Spring 2017

Chapter One

New York City

"April is the cruelest month, breeding
Lilacs out of the dead land, mixing
Memory and desire, stirring
Dull roots with spring rain."
T.S. Eliot

In retrospect, it is difficult to comprehend that this adventure actually began in downtown Manhattan, New York City. It is plausible to note that great scholars agree that nothing worthwhile is obtained from something too easily acquired. So it might be fitting then, that one of the most calamitous wilderness adventures of my life was to take root out of the depths of such a prominent urban community. I had little fear of the vast Canadian territories that lay beyond the last vanguard of rail and bush track, but the abject thought of being ensnared within the grimy clutches of such a huge and consuming metropolis pared a gaping hole in my armour. The patent distaste I had for the city – any city for that matter, was legendary amongst my peers.

I had been to New York City on two other occasions, once in 1987 while attending an ill-conceived outdoor adventure show, and then again in 1991 when I was to meet a friend prior to a sailing trip in the British Virgin Islands. Each time I was duly entertained by all the consummate profanities of human existence possible; everything from a recent outbreak in subway murders, arbitrary muggings of visiting tourists, throngs of inhospitable citizenry, a thwarted fist fight with two armed security guards, to a bizarre attempted suicide from atop the Empire State building – a sorry soul who had vaulted to a certain death only to be cheated by fate to be blown by a gale wind through a window just three floors down from the precipice.

I had even attempted to drive into New York during rush hour only to succumb to my own diffident driving skills and became hopelessly lost under the Brooklyn freeway, stranded amidst derelict shells of burned-out cars and roving gangs of pipe-wielding punks. The most gregarious inhabitant of the Big Apple turned out to be a city rat I met huddled in the door way of Macey's Department Store before opening hour. I sat on the step beside the rat commiserating on the state of our affairs.

Dawson and I had taken the train to New York from Toronto, thus avoiding the angst of driving in a city where road rage was an acceptable social exchange. I could relax on the train and not have to worry about the negative aspects of driving again to a city of such renowned culture trapped within a matrix of complicated streets, tunnels, bridges and pedestrians. Just in case, though, I had slipped a twenty-four inch hickory axe handle down a hidden sleeve in the back of my pack that could be extricated quickly if the need arose. Not that I was looking for trouble; whenever I found myself in the city, trouble seemed to tackle me to the sidewalk.

Amid the din of sirens, traffic, blaring horns and the

cacophony of daily Manhattan commerce, my compatriot and I found an oasis of calm in a hotel on 47th St. and Lexington Avenue called the Roger Smith. It was one of those small, unobtrusive but elegant boutique hotels, like the Royalton, Paramount or Chelsea. You wouldn't remember it unless you were mugged on the sidewalk out front, or had chanced to stop at Lily's for an espresso – the Roger Smith's street-level cafe.

The hotel was owned by Jim and Sue Knowles, friends of Dawson's, going back to his Camp Keewaydin days on Lake Temagami in northern Ontario. Jim had been a canoe tripper there in the 1970s and had met Dawson some time later. At the time Dawson was guiding the long trips to James Bay while his brother worked in the camp store. Dawson had slipped his foot in the door of the fraternity of ex-campers; the almost Masonic bond between old Keewaydinites was solid.

North America's oldest canoe tripping camp had always leaned towards building the characters of rich, mostly east-coast prep-school boys whose fathers sometimes flew them directly to the camp dock in their own floatplanes. The camp was morally strict, where honour and respect among fellow man/boy was literally beaten into them through a rigorous lifestyle along the wilderness trail. Hard adventure in the Canadian backwoods, hefting antiquated cedar-canvas canoes and wannigan boxes crammed full of tinned food, created an inseparable union amongst campers that followed them into adulthood.

Keewaydin had its beginning in upstate Maine in the late 1880s when there was still wilderness to be found and the rivers ran clear and fresh from the uplands. At this same time, Henry Rushton, a cedar boat builder from Canton, New York, began cranking out the first commercial "Canadian" recreational canoes for a burgeoning market of weekend paddlers. Gregg Clarke, a Harvard graduate, in 1893 founded and directed the first camp which was then known as "Kamp Kah Kou", an Abenaki word for 'large white gull.' To simplify things, Clarke abbreviated the name to "KKK" despite the obvious inference to the Ku Klux Klan – a secret organization begun in 1866 to conduct a campaign of terror against newly enfranchised African Americans. The camp flaunted the KKK acronym by emblazing the letters onto the canoes.

As the solitude and peace of the Maine woods deteriorated, and after having shot an albino deer out of season, Clarke had thoroughly strained relations with local authorities. As a result he moved his camp northwest to the unexplored regions of Lake Temagami, in isolated northern Ontario. The new camp was established on Devil's Island and the camp name quickly changed to "Keewaydin", the Ojibwe word for 'northwest wind.' One of the three "K's" was dropped from the camp brand. Since then little has changed aside from the addition of girls to the roster of campers. Keewaydin continues to adhere to strict Puritan values and military strictness, offering parents the right stuff in which to prepare their boys and girls as future doctors, lawyers, bankers and politicians.

The Knowles had been up to my Temagami cabin the previous fall. Dawson had made all the arrangements. They flew in as paying clients; a nostalgic visit to old haunts for Jim and a welcomed rest from the hectic hotel business for Sue. It was also an opportune time for Dawson and I to secure lodging in New York for the following April.

Earlier that year, Dawson and I formed the "Wild River Company", a venture pandering to the adrenalin appetite of yuppie executives who, in turn, would be voluntarily thrust down some of the wildest rivers in the Canadian wilderness. Setting the company up cost us a paltry $25.00 for a business registration fee and a few dollars for printing off some inexpensive brochures.

At the same time I was attempting to get my feet back on solid ground after having endured a rather long crusade against logging companies and myopic bureaucrats bent on clear-cutting and selling off old-growth pine in Temagami. After working as a government interior ranger for several years I had been operating a successful canoe outfitting company in Temagami – a northern logging town that was obsessed with the eradication of remnant ancient red and white pine stands. The granite hills, crystalline waters and fervent cataracts of the Lady Evelyn River were as much my home as any place had ever been. After the Ontario government proffered up prime forests to local logging companies, I took a front-line position and my outfitting lodge became command central for the environmental crusaders. As a seasoned guide I was accustomed to the worst physical abuse induced by the hand of nature, yet in no certain way was I prepared to combat the cruelties inflicted upon myself, my customers and employees, from the wrath of an industry town scorned. Tactics were dirty, cowardly and emotionally debilitating. And it wasn't your ordinary brow-beating at a town meeting; it regressed to saloon-style fisticuffs, death threats, vandalism, theft, bullying from the local constabulary, rape threats towards my staff, customer intimidation and public humiliation.

The whole affair, after the eco-warriors returned to the city, had left me tattered around the edges, alone and dangerously despondent. Now, three years later, I had rekindled most of my energy and enthusiasm for exploration, yet still remained overtly cautious and guarded about partnerships or relationships. My grandmother once told me that "partnerships were rocky ships". Wisdom I didn't fully appreciate until the Wild River Company was born.

Dawson was another story. He too was a by-product of the "Temagami Last Stand", having acquired his kudos by mounting a tree beside the window of the Ontario Premier's office at Toronto's Queen's Park, demanding (by cell-phone) that the government curtail its support of clear-cutting old growth pine forests in Temagami. It was a grandiloquent two-day stunt that gained him much press for the movement and deserving praise from green crusaders. But, like me, Dawson was useful for the edgy contra-mainstream antics that nobody else would do. We were expendable as front-line activists often are, especially when any legal ramifications come into play.

The 1980s enviro-movement did create a strong post-conflict support group made up of front liners and burned-out directors of the Temagami Wilderness Society – the group I had co-founded – to consolidate International support to protect Ontario's symbolic provincial tree. Temagami was home to the largest, last stands of big pine; some trees topping the age scale at 400 years. A lot of us gave up a good part of our lives back then. The camaraderie was iron-clad; like old war veterans or seasoned cops. Most of us were pretty fucked-up by then but our abhorrent personal idiosyncrasies were generally overlooked.

Dawson was a good tripper, or so I was led to believe, having guided for Camp Keewaydin for several seasons. But he portrayed definite social dysfunctional tendencies that made him unreliable and extremely unpredictable. He had the full six-pack but lacked the plastic thingy that held it all together. His social deviance, I assumed, might not be such a bad thing if his energy could be focused on something productive...like the Wild River Company. Still, reluctantly, I buckled under peer pressure and ignored my gut feeling (or my grandmother's sage advice) and took him on as a business partner.

Mutual friends agreed that the Wild River Company was a good idea for the both of us. Having tripped with Dawson the previous summer unfortunately did not instill the sense of confidence in a partner that might be called upon in a life-threatening situation. He wanted guidance from me, being his senior by twenty-years, yet he accepted even helpful criticism poorly and needed constant supervision. I gave him the opportunity to guide four regular customers of mine on a river expedition in Quebec. When I drove the eight hours to the pick-up location after the trip, only Dawson was there, having left the customers many miles upstream. He hitched a ride out on his own along a bush track, fell asleep in the stranger's truck and couldn't remember the route back to where the customers were waiting. Needless to say, the clients were miffed when we finally found them and Dawson refuted any responsibility for the incident.

Dawson's brother and several of my close associates from the movement persuaded me to give him the opportunity to prove himself - again. Dawson too, did everything to convince me that he was a worthy partner and friend. I folded. But then I was prone to giving people more than the token one chance; for the movement, I convinced myself, was a worthy enough gesture of faith in the human spirit. It turned out to be a huge mistake.

Dawson was an adept charmer. He could get his foot into any door. Whether he was schmoozing a woman or an affluent high-roller, he was a perfectionist. He had that swashbuckling, cavalier good-look that could melt candles when he entered a room. And it was Dawson who first made contact with the editors of *Men's Journal Magazine* in New York. He had told them about the Wild River Company, about my reputation as a guide and explorer, and the idea of doing a story about the Canadian wilderness. It was his attempt at reviving the Wild River Company and gaining back my favour as a senior partner. He knew that the Men's Journal idea wouldn't steam under his own power. Okay, this could work, I thought. Now that I was hooked and yanked into the boat, I felt compelled to drift along with it.

As it turned out, the editors agreed to consider sponsoring a northern river expedition piece for the magazine. The editors opted to have their own writer and photographer join us in Canada. Men's Journal would pay us $8,000 US for the expedition but they first wanted to get some details about the budget, and to meet us personally before signing the cheque. Dawson trimmed up immediately. I had renewed faith that this could highlight the company and my relationship with my business partner. Dawson even agreed to seek psychotherapy for some of his previous abhorrent antics inflicted upon other individuals. He never went. A date was set for April, 1994, the following spring, to meet with the editors of *Men's Journal Magazine* in New York.

*   *   *   *   *

From Central Station it was a fair hike to the hotel; but it was April and the walk felt good on my cramped winter legs. I was a fast walker and people had often told me that my "portage" gate was quick and steady but I could barely keep up with the stream of traffic milling along the sidewalk. Everything was moving in perpetual fast-motion, everywhere, charged with a nervous energy braced on caffeine and ambition. I was in Manhattan, scared shitless that I was going to die there, trampled by the horde of briefcase wielding money-brokers or crushed between endless lines of horn-blaring yellow cabs, profanities spilling out the windows in a multitude of languages. Trying to cross a busy street was like scouting a boulder-strewn rapid, looking for a safe passage, only these rocks were constantly shifting. It was a nasty stretch of dangerous current, embarrassingly obvious that I was an out-of-towner. Dawson, having grown up in the city, seemed to weave in and out of traffic with an inordinate sense of grace.

At the Roger Smith the Knowles delighted at our arrival, a

little surprised that we didn't portage a canoe down Lexington to the hotel. We were ushered to our room which, I presumed, would be a vacant housemaid's quarters in the basement. Instead, we were treated as royal guests and given the penthouse suite, replete with kitchen (not that we could afford to buy food to cook), a loft, balcony and rooftop garden with a barbecue.

James, himself, was an eccentric artist who had inherited the 136-room, depression-era hotel through his in-laws. He adorned the Roger Smith with abstract bronze sculptures, whimsical murals and ever-changing exhibits by young artists. It was this inherent idiosyncrasy of hotel and owner that had attracted a great many actors and musicians, among them singers Nanci Griffith and Lyle Lovett. The Roger Smith was also the haunt of Pete Seeger, Arlo Guthrie and Jim Croce. It wasn't unusual to see members of the bands Los Lobos, Midnight Oil and Soul Asylum, wandering the halls at any hour of the day or night. We were in good company, both past and present. The owner's eclectic interests had helped them establish a comfortable niche in the New York hostelry trade. It may have been predicated too by the Knowles' penchant for paddling in the Temagami wilds.

Dawson and I felt quite at home in the penthouse and my own nervousness about the city seemed to drift away. So long as I didn't leave the room I thought I'd be okay. It was a world far-removed from the lingering echo of the loon and frenzied bite of mosquito. As for myself, as an artist and photographer, I appreciated the ambiance and winsome quality of the hotel. James had proclaimed that the Roger Smith certainly entertained an "art bias".

"More than anything," Jim admitted, "I want this hotel to be a place where good ideas can occur."

I took these words to heart. The Wild River Company had a good idea brewing and there was provocative energy within the stone walls of the Roger Smith. If our canoe expedition story was going to fly, it would be here.

We were lodging in a $300 a night suite but it cost us almost nothing to stay in New York aside from the few evening meals and bus fare. Breakfast at Lily's was complimentary and both Dawson and I treated it as if it were an all-you-can-eat endless pantry. After Lily's the first morning, we waddled down to the Avenue of the America's and the offices of *Men's Journal Magazine*.

Jann S. Wenner, of Wenner Media Incorporated, had created *Rolling Stone Magazine* some years back; the highest accolade a performer or singer could receive was to have their mugshot on the cover of Wenner's rock and roll rag. *Men's Journal* was fashioned after *Rolling Stone* and was just starting to make a name for itself with well-scribed articles, sexy ads merchandising TAUGeuer sport watches and Lexus automobiles. It even had a mildly trashy personals section flaunting the wares of Dr. Bross's Penis Enlargement Systems, sexual enhancement supplements and hypnosis for men having erection problems. It was a hip men's magazine that appealed to the up-and-coming Wall Streeters, anyone who aspired to break away from the mainstream corporate crowd. What better place to flaunt a Canadian adventure story! With its oversized, trendy format, *Men's Journal Magazine* certainly stood out on the vendor's shelves.

We sat in the visitors lounge looking a little out of place. On one side were the offices of *Rolling Stone*, on the other – *Men's Journal*. Young men and women breezed past us as if we weren't there, dressed and manicured appropriate to the job; various and obviously expensive colognes and perfumes filled the waiting room.

"Geez Dawson, do you think we're overdressed," I said jokingly. We had decided to wear our bush duds just so we looked like Canadian guides to the editors but the way people were looking at us I was starting to lose my self-confidence. Dawson didn't care; he was too busy eyeing the pretty girls flashing by in front of us.

Peter Griffen, the features editor along with the editor-in-chief, John Rasmus, met us in the lobby and escorted us to the editorial offices.

"How was your trip down to New York?" Griffen asked as he pushed two chairs towards Dawson and me.

"Good, uneventful. Far better than driving," I said. Griffen and Rasmus laughed and nodded agreeably.

"Yes, New York can be a nightmare for drivers coming into town, not the easiest city to navigate," Rasmus said, flipping through a folder containing some of the maps I had sent.

"We're excited about the expedition, the whole staff…great idea and the location looks perfect," Griffen beamed. Rasmus nodded, still looking through the folder.

The meeting was brief, succinct and informative. We had already discussed the location setting for the article. It was to take place along the Seal River in northern Manitoba. It was selected for various reasons, one of them just pure gut feeling. As throngs of Gore-Tex clad adventurers headed out to the high arctic to hallmark collectible rivers such as the Nahanni, where the increasingly heavy traffic was regulated and the experience engineered by numerous outfitters, we opted for one of the more obscure and lesser known waterways. The location had to have the correct formula for adventure isolation, cultural history and unparalleled aesthetics; not to mention hair-raising white-water rapids and the element of extreme danger. Intrigue was the catch-word; unusualness the general theme with at least one or two animals that resided above humans on the food chain, like polar bears.

The Seal River, located along the boreal fringe and sub-arctic tundra of the Manitoba northland, easily fit the criteria we were looking for. It was one of those notorious rivers either too difficult for most paddlers to run safely, or too expensive to fly in and out of without having to hock the family heirlooms. Sheth-tie-eye-desay, the Chipewyan name for the Seal River meaning "river that flows out of", had attained Canadian Heritage status in 1992. It had gained this status because of its 7,000 years of pre-history and unique earth-science features and the fact that harbour seals cruise upriver more than two-hundred kilometers from Hudson Bay. But in typical provincial or federal practices, Heritage status means almost nothing when it pertains to protection efforts and such rivers are generally chosen for their paucity of conflict issues; an easy sell to politicians who aspire to conform to national and world conservation trends without raising the ire from local corporate interests. Still, it had been identified as a Canadian river that stood out for obvious reasons.

Just reading what I could find out about the Seal River presented a myriad of concerns for me as an explorer. It was obvious that the only people plying the endless rapids of the river were a few Churchill band Chipewyans, or Sayisi Dene (Den-aye) who were based out of the relatively new village at Tadoule, near the headwaters. And most of that travel was in the winter when everything was frozen, or for hunting forays to harvest caribou, carried out by aircraft, All Terrain Vehicles (ATV's) or snow machines. The Seal lay more than three-hundred kilometers north of the nearest settlement and it flowed into the tenacious and unpredictable Hudson Bay whose ragged coastline was revered as one of the most inhospitable environments in the world.

There was no doubt that the Seal was wild and dangerous. It was considered one of the last great wild rivers in Canada and the only northern Manitoba river that wasn't dammed for hydro-electric power. We would start at the Dene village of Tadoule, and paddle 310 kilometers to Hudson Bay. I had calculated that the river dropped 247 meters (741 ft.) over that distance, or roughly two and a half feet every kilometer. Since there were no navigation maps for the river I had to assume that there would be substantial drops at key rapids along the way. It was a perfect choice for the *Men's Journal* article and the editors certainly liked the sound of it.

I had to admit that I was disappointed when the magazine editors introduced Dawson and I to their selected writer and photographer, in absentia of course as we weren't actually to meet up with them until the trip in June. I was a bit miffed because I had both the experience and credentials to do the job as writer/photographer myself. Hodding Carter, the chosen writer, worked a day job as the post-master in Thermond, West Virginia. His father was a big name in the political arena, but it was Hodding's sister who shone brightly as an up and coming Hollywood star, playing Kevin Bacon's leading lady in the 80's sci-fi flick "Tremors". Hoddings own notoriety hailed from a recent book he had published retracing the moccasined steps of Lewis and Clark across America, only Carter had followed their route in a motorboat. The photographer, Russell Kaye, was a studio freelancer from downtown Brooklyn. He accepted the job because the magazine had agreed to pay him well for his time and buy him a full camping outfit, the best in fact, including a $700 North Face all-weather rain slicker – the preferred choice of the New York City drug dealers, or so I was informed.

As it turned out, neither Hodding Carter or Russel Kaye had any canoeing experience whatsoever. Apparently, there wasn't a surplus of journalists willing to endure the isolation and harsh conditions of a northern Manitoba canoe trip, let alone put their lives in the hands of two wily Canadian bush guides.

I eventually did warm up to the plan, convincing *Men's Journal* editors that there would be sufficient time to pass on the required skills to Hodding and Russell. Many of my clients who signed up for whitewater adventures or tagged along on mapping explorations in the past were virtual greenhorns. It was oftentimes easier to teach a newcomer new skills then to wrestle bad habits from a self-acclaimed 'seasoned' paddler. This could work, maybe, but I had no idea what I was up against venturing far north of my comfortable niche in the woods of Ontario and Quebec.

The deal was clinched and the cheque would be mailed out in two weeks. We now had a major sponsor for the expedition! We invited the editors to the hotel for an evening slide show of some of my past adventures, places I had guided trips over the past twenty-five years. They agreed to come. Roger Smith's curator was none other than Molly Barnes, a well-known New York and Los Angeles gallery owner, art critic and the author of "How to get Hung." She had the 18th floor reception room prepared for the event.

"This was Buckminster Fuller's room in the 1930s," Molly commented rather proudly. "He was destitute and needed a place to stay so the hotel gave him free accommodation here, in this room, without a bed." You could tell Molly loved telling this story, how Fuller had gazed up at the room's cove-ceiling, accented with tiny triangle-patterned bas-relief, and was inspired to invent the Geodesic Dome – choice of architecture for many reclusive hippies and draft dodgers of the 1960s.

The hotel had a non-institutional air about it. A few weeks ago at their once-a-month "brown-bag art lunches", where artists, critics and gallery owners convened to discuss their work, SoHo gallery owner Ivan Karp showed up, along with Barbara Toll, famous art dealer, with artists Philip Perlstein, Mark Kostabi and Joseph Digiorgio in tow. There was no shortage of personalities meandering through the halls of the Roger Smith. Oddly enough, I found myself wearing Fuller's shoes; looking for inspiration, furnished with a free hotel room and about twenty dollars left to my name. Molly Barnes extended every courtesy to Dawson and me as if we were Canadian celebrities.

Guests filed in to the elegant reception room that evening; mostly hotel patrons and staff, lights were dimmed and the slide show was executed without a flaw. Griffen and Rasmus didn't show up until after the show and had brought along their assistant editor Kristina Harvey whose good looks and solid features were not unnoticed by either Dawson or myself. Dawson moved in quickly suggesting to Rasmus that *Men's Journal* send Harvey along on the expedition. It was a cheesy suggestion delivered with overt charm that prompted polite smiles but I could tell that Kristina Harvey thought Dawson to be a bit of an asshole. She was physically stunning, cultured and smart enough to parry cheap and insincere male advances from the likes of Dawson.

With a couple of days to kill we quickly discovered that there was no shortage of things to do or see in New York, most of which didn't cost anything. So we hung out in Central Park and watched a musical roller-blade derby where athletic women, shrink-wrapped in spandex, orbited with deft moves, spins and jumps around a funk band. The Bronx zoo was strangely empty of patrons; an oddity for a city of over twelve million people, but it was on Dawson's list of things to do in New York. When he had something on his mind that he wanted to do, that was it, he would commit to it even if there were other places we were obliged to go at the same time. He was like that and it bugged the hell out of me.

I was down to my last few dollars. The downside of the seasonal tourism industry positioned April as the low-point on the income scale, unless deposits were received for scheduled expeditions which were sometimes hit-or-miss. It looked to be a rather lean year, other than the Seal River exploration. Dawson never seemed to have two nickels to rub together so we were forced to budget for the remaining meals. We filled up at Lily's in the morning, pocketing a few buttered buns to be eaten later in the day. I felt pretty good about our trip to New York; the *Men's Journal* deal was set and I'd be back in the bush and up to my cabin in Temagami very soon. And as we sat in our New York City penthouse suite, eating stale buns and cheap salami bought with my last five dollars, life in general had few discordant edges. The prevailing sense of euphoria wasn't to last.

Chapter Two

Packing and Planning

The cheque from *Men's Journal* magazine finally arrived, only I never laid eyes on it. Dawson had phoned the editor and told him to have the money sent directly to him. This was extremely distressing news since Dawson had absolutely no concept of money management and any Wild River Company funds were to go through me to be deposited directly into the company account. What I did begin to realize was that it was part of a control complex my assistant nurtured, insidious but relevant to his need for constant self-assurance. Dawson was still living with his parents and it was his mother who suggested the redirection of company funds. His mother was the ruling matriarch of the family.

"DAMMIT, Dawson – you had no right to do this," I scolded. "Why would you do such a thing?"

"It was my mother's idea," Dawson replied defensively.

"What?" I was pissed. "She doesn't work for the company." I knew the argument had hit a wall and there wasn't much recourse now that the expedition funds ended up in the wrong bank account.

Rerouting the much needed exploration funds was underhanded. Dawson maintained that the cheque had been deposited into the account, but I was soon to discover that two-thousand dollars was missing. My assistant guide had taken the liberty to upgrade his personal camping and outdoor attire. All this put us behind schedule another two-weeks since *Men's Journal* had to track down the cheque through their accounting department and put it through various channels before it could be released and mailed. We had little time left in which to make the necessary expedition purchases and to ready our outfit for the trip to Manitoba. Supplies had to be bought, maps ordered and canoes fitted with skid-plates and spray-covers, all of which was put on hold until the funds arrived. It was initially agreed that whatever was left after expenses we would divide between us as wages earned for guiding the expedition.

The Manitoba government kicked in some expense money for bush flights under their author/writer program, sponsored by the Ministry of Tourism. This kept our costs down to basic travel, supplies and return train fare from Churchill on Hudson Bay. The train would bring us back to Thompson where I would leave my truck and where we would pick up Hodding and Russell at the airport. Old Town Canoe Company was one of my sponsors and they donated two seventeen-foot "Tripper" *Royalex* expedition canoes for the Seal River exploration. Still, it was going to be an expensive expedition to outfit.

Aside from the sponsored canoes, I had supplied all of the gear, most of which were remnants of previous expeditions, and it would be my vehicle used for the 6,000 km road trip to Thompson Manitoba and back. It was an aging Isuzu Trooper with over 200,000 kms chocked up on the odometer; roadworthy but pushing the limit for both tires and brakes. It was starting to cost me money but I loved this truck and had spent many a night in the back or sprawled out in my sleeping bag on the roof while parked off the highway on remote bush roads. It would be a three-day road trip to Thompson from southern Ontario.

Dawson was left with the responsibility of ordering the topographic maps and picking up knee pads, which were to be epoxied into the two canoes. On the day we were to leave he had only accomplished the packing of his own personal gear, which took up space in two canoe packs, instead of the agreed one pack per person. He forgot about the knee pads and failed to order the expedition maps.

"I gave you simple tasks to do Dawson and you screwed up," I said, outraged and unforgiving. Dawson looked stunned; not that he couldn't understand what I just said, but because I was angry for no reason whatever.

"So, no big deal," Dawson chimed. His total lack of concern just made me angrier.

"We have no maps!" I barked at him. "Isn't that a big deal?"

"Okay, I'll get on it, maybe tomor..."

"It's too fucking late!" I cut him off waving my hands in the air. "It takes three weeks to order maps and we're leaving in a couple of days. WHAT WERE YOU THINKING?"

Luckily I had a friend who had contacts in Ottawa who would personally pick up our maps and have them couriered to Thompson in time for our flight north to the Seal River. I should have known better. We were off to a bad start and the Dawson I thought had begun to shape up was actually regressing into the old fickle knucklehead. I was honestly doing my best at trying to forget his constant screw-ups but couldn't help thinking of the incident the previous summer when he had joined me on the Missinaibi River in Ontario. Our first trip together, and he had the responsibility of buying all the fresh meat for the three week expedition. He was to hitch a ride with a client, making sure that the meat was frozen and packed in an ice chest for the road trip north to our start point. It was an all day drive in hot weather. When he arrived at the rendezvous location, the meat had simply been shoved into plastic bags and stored in the trunk of the car. After forty-eight hours in a hot trunk the meat had seriously fouled and had to be pitched in the bush for the bears and ravens. Over two-hundred dollars worth of meat had been wasted. Our bland diet now consisted of meatless pasta and rice dishes.

For longer expeditions any meat that wasn't double-smoked (like bacon or salami), was typically cooked and then frozen, then packed appropriately before the start of the trip; smoked meat being wrapped in vinegar-soaked cheesecloth. I had planned to cook all the raw meat Dawson had brought during our first night out.

All of the inept things that Dawson had perpetrated previously rolled around in my belly like a ball of maggots. The old unreliable goof seemed to have returned. There was little I could do at this point and I wasn't about to cancel the expedition. At this juncture I was banking on hope springing eternal but there was just enough doubt in my mind to keep our relationship on a prickly edge. I was running out of patience.

After returning to Canada from New York I headed straight to my cabin in Temagami. It was my sanctuary and my only permanent home after leaving the outfitting business behind. I had a lot to think about. Mutual friends had encouraged Dawson to embark on a solo canoe trip, something he had never done, and perhaps to do some serious soul searching. He agreed. Unfortunately he ended up bunking in with a mutual friend for three days and tallied up a three-hundred dollar phone bill. He had a new girlfriend: an artist, pretty and talented and seriously naive. I felt bad for her and hoped this expedition would smarten him up, at least for her sake.

I had just spent the winter in a log cabin north of the small community of Michipicoten on the shore of Lake Superior, completing a guidebook for the Missinaibi River. It was a three-year project in which I investigated the over thirty deaths along the river over a fourteen year period. I first descended the upper Missinaibi in 1990 with my future wife, Andrea, who at the time was assisting me in running the outfitting business. We were initially investigating the river for potential canoe tours for the company but the emphasis changed the more we delved into its bleak history as a recreational waterway. Like the Seal, the Missinaibi River was nominated as a Canadian Heritage River; it was also branded as a provincial waterway park. Yet, every branch of the government, including the federal map office, failed to recognize the multiple inaccuracies on the topographic charts. As it had turned out, more than 17 deaths had been attributed to faulty maps: waterfalls and rapids either not marked or portages indicated on the wrong side of the river. I had spent two gruesome days at the Ontario Coroner's Office in downtown Toronto, going over police and third-party reports about the deaths, photographs of young paddlers stretched out over stainless steel gurneys, lifejackets still on, bodies contorted and twisted in death.

Andrea and I had even paddled over the body of a man wedged in the rocks below the surface on a small rapid while the Search and Rescue team assembled on the shore. At the time we thought nothing of it, believing it to be a field exercise of some nature but when we reached the town of Mattice at the end of the trip, people were talking about a recent drowning on the river.

But there was more to my self-banishment to a lonely Michipicoten beach cabin than writing a guidebook. I had fallen hopelessly in love to a beautiful young woman with whom I lived for three years while running the outfitting business. And then

she was gone; too young to be corralled into a longer relationship, and I was too naive to think that she would stay. I was devastated, morose, prone to taking chances, pushing myself physically in order to forget her. I never would. Andrea came back
into my life eighteen years later.

Throughout the long, harsh coastal winter, living on the
Lake Superior beach, I had the opportunity to get my life back
together. The Missinaibi River project kept me busy during the
day and long evenings. The protracted nights had induced sleep-
lessness and bouts of depression that, as the winter deepened,
caused the melancholy to drift slowly into the far recesses of my
soul; unrequited love lingering, still, but somewhat abated. The
Seal River expedition was percolating on the back-burner and
that guaranteed some semblance of personal recovery, at least to
keep my mind off other personal matters.

*   *   *   *   *

Having explored thousands of kilometers of wilderness over
the past twenty-five years I had concluded that more guidebooks
were necessary for safe navigation. Topographic maps were not
intended for this type of remote recreation and the majority of
trip reports and journals were not up to date or accurately field-
truthed. Many of the country's wild rivers were also being investigated for hydro power; the lack of watershed protection was
also on my mind to include in any future explorations for guidebooks. People generally, and moreso as the interest in wilderness
travel grows, prefer to know as much as possible about where
they are going. The unwritten but practiced tenets of wilderness politics dictates that if the adventuring public doesn't use
it, the developers will. With that in mind I had approached Parks
Canada and the Canadian Heritage River Board in Ottawa about

doing a guidebook for the province of Manitoba.

My Missinaibi guidebook had been sent off to the publisher just prior to the New York venture. Ottawa liked my work and supported the Seal River exploration by offering me an illustrating job for another book publication about Heritage Rivers. They wanted to see what I could do with the Seal River, as far as updating maps and producing a field-friendly guide. Later that year, the Heritage Rivers book would win the Natural Resources Council of America Award for best environmental book of 1994. Although I was not to write the article for *Men's Journal Magazine*, or offer my photographic work, I had manufactured my own agenda based on the idea of exploring a virtually unexplored river for cultural and recreational values and to include the Seal in a book about Manitoba rivers.

I knew nothing about Manitoba except from what I had seen out of a car window as a child while driving the monotonous Trans-Canada Highway across the south end of the province on a car ride with my parents. I remembered it to be very flat, boring, and the horizons spiked with grain elevators. I was so wrong.

That's the lustre of exploration – the requisite obligation to do the research, to study maps, collect whatever published data is available, talk with locals. With Manitoba there was a great visual deception. There was much more to greet the eye than an endless plain of wheat fields and grain elevators; a person just had to do some exploring to find a vastly diverse landscape.

Chapter Three

On the Road

I was on a high and nothing could stultify the feeling of elation and freedom I was enjoying. I drove to Oakville to pick up Dawson. The canoes were strapped to the roof, gear was stowed in the back, the gas tank was full and I had a bit of cash in my wallet. As with any pack and prep for an expedition, especially on a time constraint, the process was exhausting. The outfitting business I left behind where I had back-to-back canoe expeditions and whitewater clinics, primed me for efficient packing, but back then I had staff to help out. The only thing that made the Seal River expedition wearisome was Dawson and his inability to concentrate on any of the tasks presented to him.

Once we were on the road to Thompson I thought to myself that all this nonsense with my assistant was trivial and unproductive. *Maybe I was just acting trite and over-sensitive.* By the time we reached Sudbury, five hours into the drive west, I had changed my mind again. It was a road trip only Stephen King could write about. All the objectionable mannerisms literally poured out of Dawson as if they had been stored too long in an undersized trunk. He would cat-call young teen girls through his window at street stops, begging them to come along, only to receive the worst visceral looks imaginable and a constant reprimand from me.

"What the fuck...do you know how bad this looks," I scolded Dawson after the mother of two very young teen girls gave us the finger.

"I'm just having fun," Dawson replied, as usual, thinking nothing of the consequences.

"Our company name is on the side of the truck you idiot!" I said trying to hold it together. He just laughed and shrugged his shoulders.

Dawson had his driver's license revoked; why, he wouldn't tell me but I was stuck with all the driving. He slept most of the time. I just figured that constant offensive behaviour must be tiring. About every two hours I had to pull the truck over to the side of the road so that he could take a piss, like a dog marking his territory, not draining his bladder all at once but spot-pissing on popular shrubs, fence-posts and garbage cans. When it came time to stop for a roadside meal Dawson would be dressed in a thread-bare pair of dirty shorts, no shoes, no shirt and sported a fuck-you-if-you-don't-like-it attitude. The restaurant owner would throw him out, either for improper dress or for smoking in a non-smoking designated area. And these were not five-star eateries. It was embarrassing for me, not that I was an angel of principles. I had my own share of bad habits, but I did know when to extend certain courtesies if only to secure good service in gas-bar restaurants.

He was also a chain smoker. Whenever we stopped for gas he'd always light up, right there at the pumps beside the sign that said NO SMOKING. With his window down Dawson would hang his butt-hand out and flick his cigarette ashes onto the ground between the pumps, and each time I would yell at him for doing it. "It's your car," he'd retort then go on to something else equally annoying. More than once I had considered leaving him behind on the road, just drive off and run the expedition on my own. But that wouldn't work – we needed the fourth person and it would be impossible to conscript a replacement in that short order. And I would remember our friends back home and how they counted on this expedition, on me, to pull Dawson together; how heavily my peers relied on me to carry it off. *Piss on that*, I thought. I was no damn martyr.

In Winnipeg we stopped briefly to pick up some supplies and helpful field information about the Seal River from Rick Wilson who worked for the provincial parks service. The information was sketchy at best but it was all he had. Dawson had forgotten his rain pants and managed to liberate a pair from Rick. They were Gore-Tex, expensive, and he never returned them. But he was like that. Once he had something in his possession it immediately became his property.

We arrived in Thompson on the 29th of June, late in the evening, tired from the long drive north from Winnipeg. Dawson had slept all the way. We had a full day, ample time to pick up fresh provisions, pack, ready the canoes and to meet Hodding and Russell at the airport the next evening. I had booked us into the Mystery Lake Hotel: Thompson's poshest motor hotel, perched in the middle of town and a stone's throw from every watering hole in the community. Next morning my assistant disappeared and I was left alone to make preparations. Final packing was routine for me; but very time consuming having to make sure food was portioned out for each day, double waterproofed and labelled, going over check-lists, making any repairs to gear.

Selecting food and working out a month-long menu was always a lot of work. Meal portions had to be precise and configured as to how much food four men would consume during high activity. I had already packaged some of the basic dry foods such as rice, pasta, flour mix for bannock bread, labelled and readied it all to be blended with any fresh ingredients which I would buy locally. Each meal was carefully planned per day, with generous portions and culinary considerations for chopping and dicing, lots of spices, desserts that could be baked in the reflector oven, chocolate, and I had enough good coffee to last for at least the first week, even fresh eggs and salad fixings to last a month. A healthy bush salad could be made using cabbage, carrots, onions, garlic, sunflower seeds, ginger, balsamic vinegar and spices – all ingredients that would last the trip.

I was actually enjoying the space from Dawson and looking forward to meeting the other guys. We had spoken briefly a week before and both were enthusiastic about the expedition but a little worried about their inherent lack of canoeing skills. I assured them that my assistant guide and I would teach them the skills needed to get them down the river safely. I had anticipated a more chastened attitude from Dawson once our American paddling partners appeared.

Although Dawson was nowhere to be found, I did expect him to be around when it came time to pick up the Americans at the airport but he wasn't. I went alone to meet them at the small airstrip outside of town. They were easy to pick out from the assemblage of people filing off the Air Canada commuter from Winnipeg: Hodding was tall, wiry and self-assured while Russell actually looked like a studio photographer from Brooklyn who suddenly found himself way out of the box, intense and wide-eyed. Both were in their early thirties. They were surprised that my assistant guide wasn't there and I made up some excuse that he was in town doing some last minute preparations. We grabbed the packs from the luggage conveyer and I noticed right off that there was far too much gear. I told them I'd help them sort out the absolutely necessary items for the trip; the rest could be left behind at the hotel.

I still had four-weeks of provisions to pack that evening but I asked Hodding and Russell to meet me in the hotel bar once they had booked into their rooms. Dawson still hadn't shown his face and I began to get concerned, thinking he had done something stupid and was thrown in the Thompson jail. In the bar Hodding seemed relaxed but Russell was on edge about the trip. Russell had met up with Hodding for the first time at the Winnipeg airport. While on the flight to Thompson, Carter had shown Kaye an article from *Outside Magazine* that expounded on the deaths of several well-known guides in the United States (not to mention more than a handful of paid clients). The article was about taking chances, living on the edge, the adrenalin charge, bad judgement and cocky, over-confident guides pushing their limits. No wonder Russell was already a little white-knuckled about the expedition. With a couple of beers and my best at-tempt at assuaging any trepidation the Americans may have had about the canoe trip, I assured them that they were in the hands of responsible guides.

"Hodding, Russ, I know you're a bit nervous about the whitewater," I had said, "Dawson's a reputable paddler: Between the two of us we can teach you what you need to know."

"I'd like to meet the assistant guide, still...talk to him...it would make me feel a lot better," Russell announced, nursing his beer slowly, eyes prying deep into my own.

"He'll show up. He had a list of things to do," I lied, "and we don't have a lot of time left before we head out tomorrow."

We had just started to enjoy each others' company, tell-ing stories, talking about what to expect along the Seal, and of course the question about polar bears came up. I had little to offer about the great white bear so I shared experiences I had with black and grizzly bears, even relating the fact that more people were mauled and killed by black bears than any other species but only because we've fractured and reduced their natural habitat, increasing the chance of confrontation.

"But we're still in black bear country, right?" Russ questioned. I suddenly realized that any talk of bear attacks wasn't a good thing at this juncture in our newfound relationship.

"Sure," I parleyed, "but they are only dangerous in close proximity to communities or well-traveled parks like Algonquin in Ontario."

The second beer didn't seem to quash Russell's apprehensions about the trip, about bears, about paddling whitewater. To make matters worse, Dawson suddenly showed up stoned and obnoxious. He wavered over the table gibbering about meeting several local Cree Indians behind the Legion Hall and sharing a can of Finesse hair-spray with them. *Hair spray of all things!* It was obvious that the alcohol laden contents weren't destined for the scalp. Dawson was completely swacked on the stuff; no doubt fused with whatever grog he could panhandle, along with a joint or two. Russell stood up, "I'm getting the fuck out of here," he blared, obviously pissed at Dawson's condition. Hodding and I tried to console Russell and I again reassured him that he would be in the canoe with me and not my assistant. He calmed down, somewhat, sat down and pushed his beer away as if it would add to his anxiety if he finished it. Hodding didn't seem to be phased by Dawson's condition. I told my partner to meet me back in the room and I walked out of the bar.

Flopping out on his bed, Dawson was puzzled why I was visibly upset.

"Don't you get it?" I kicked the bed.

"Get what?" Dawson replied with the usual defiance.

"Don't you think first impressions are important? These guys are greenhorns. They need to trust us!" I was starting to raise my voice. I was pissed.

"Chill out...I was just having fun...they don't care."

"What? Russell was about to hop on the plane back to New York you idiot!"

"You're too serious about this stuff...relax...what's wrong with a bit of fun?"

"FUN? YOU JUST ABOUT SCREWED THIS UP!" I kicked the bed again. This time Dawson sat up and looked at me.

"Fuck this," Dawson whispered and stormed out of the room.

"PICK UP A PIZZA OR SOMETHING!" I yelled at him, "I'll be packing up without your help...," my voice trailing off in a whisper against a slamming door.

Asshole, I whispered to myself as I heard his footsteps fade down the hallway.

I finished the packing and helped Hodding and Russell sort through their gear. I hadn't had the chance to eat anything all day. Dawson came back three-hours later with a half-eaten, cold pizza under his arm. I blew up. I wanted to throttle him but knew it wouldn't change a thing. "What's your fucking problem!" he retorted, turning my own anger against me. I was in a spot and he knew it. I couldn't actually dump him now when we were to fly in to the Seal River early the next morning. The knots in my stomach twisted tighter.

It was close to midnight when we started arguing about personal gear and what was to be left behind to lighten our load. Because Dawson had two personal packs he then encouraged Hodding and Russell to do the same. But even with all their extraneous stuff they still had the designated one pack each. Russell did have an extra fifty kilograms of specialized photography equipment which I had agreed was needed and we'd make room for. Dawson insisted that his oversized Keewaydin wannigan be included as part of the kitchen appurtenances. It was a rather large wooden box and no Keewaydin guide would be seen without it, apparently, along with the full-size Keewaydin splitting axe. I already had a kitchen wannigan and a steel-handled pack-axe, both sufficient for our needs. I reached an impasse with Dawson so we compromised; I didn't feel like arguing anymore and I was bone-tired – his axe would stay but he was allowed to bring his wannigan.

Our total camping equipage included: two wannigans, five personal canoe packs, one gear pack containing tents and related base camp cog and two very weighty food packs. Miscellaneous gear consisted of four personal day packs, camera cases, tripods, life-jackets, six paddles and spray-covers for each canoe. How all of this was going to fit into two seventeen-foot canoes was a mystery yet to be solved.

I left the hotel around 11:00 pm and went for a walk around Thompson. I had to clear my head and stretch my legs. Normally, packing for an expedition was a thoroughly satisfying, albeit tiring occupation; this trip was overwhelmingly tedious and frustrating. I had never in my life experienced such discourse with either client or assistant. At this point, things could only get better.

The northern mining community of Thompson, Manitoba, seemed to come alive about this time with another sort of enterprise – heavy drinking. Bars stayed open late, along with the liquor stores. Video lotto terminals, or VLT's, lined the walls of the watering holes and every seat was taken, sucking money from mothers on welfare, whites, natives and anyone fool enough to believe they could beat the machines. For those addicted, Health and Welfare put up a toll-free help number above every machine.

I stopped in for a beer and sat at a table near the machines; the sound of a steady flow of coins being drawn into the void. The criminal element here was the fact that the Manitoba government's take was 80%! Seemed like a vicious cycle – steal from the poor then put the money back into their pockets through social subsidies. Cynical? Maybe, I just don't understand the government's illicit marriage with the corporate industry towns in the north.

The dust from working in the mine, the VLT's, social malaise, long winters and isolation must play a heavy toll on the general temperament of the town. I had been to a lot of northern mining towns during my travels, lived in one for years myself, and there was always a lingering sense of impermanence. Like Sudbury, in northern Ontario, Inco built Thompson out of the Manitoba wilderness in 1957 after discovering a huge nickel ore body lying beneath the boreal forest. It flaunts its presence in tourist brochures, taking up most of the space on the shelves of the local Chamber of Commerce: "Romantic images of exploration and adventure in virgin wilderness are part of the heritage of mining." In the mid 1970s Inco in Sudbury built its "super-stack" and commenced pumping out 1% of the world's total pollutants. My own home wilderness of Temagami, lying in the path of the fallout, suffered greatly from acid deposition, killing vast populations of lake trout. In 1993, Inco descended upon the virgin boreal coastal turf at Voisey's Bay in Labrador, despoiling the earth with thousands of test pits and disturbing the migrations of geese and caribou over Innu and Inuit homelands. Yet, Inco Limited, in their base headquarters in Toronto, had one of Canada's largest art collections owned by a single corporation; art depicting the beauty of untrammelled wilderness, native culture and history. The contradiction and hypocrisy goes unnoticed in Thompson, even after the downsizing of the community from a boom of 25,000 people to 15,000. Company infiltration of the community social dynamic is a requisite part of the corporate strategy: money is pumped into social programs, the construction of shopping malls, playgrounds, arenas for hockey and curling, creating the right facades to mollify the needs of the people and keep them from leaving. And that seems to work fine for a sunset industry and a mine ready to pack up and leave once the market hits a low or the mineral asset loses its global potency.

The Thompson populace bought into the corporate promise of forever jobs. It even had a golf course, zoo and ski hill. Nobody talks about the eventuality of the mine running out of ore, or the fact that there are over 500 one-industry ghost towns littered across northern Canada. You just don't talk disparagingly about the big corporate brother, the provider of all things good.

There were various groups gathered about the bars and in scattered pockets along the main street; some panhandled but others were too drunk to get a sentence together. Aboriginals, who came to town to shop talked quietly in their own language, shopping bags in hand, waiting for rides that would take them back to their respective reserves. Like any northern town, Thompson had its seedy side, a collecting pot for down-and-outers and the occasional lost soul off the reserve, mostly Cree from as far away as Garden Hill, Shamattawa and God's Lake. There were also Chipewyans from Churchill, Tadoule and Lac Brochet. The Cree were traditional enemies of the Chips, and from time to time, that age-old animosity erupted into fights behind the local Wal-Mart or Pizza Hut, keeping the Thompson constabulary busy until sun-up.

Walking around town helped to consolidate my own philosophy about life and how we've managed to screwup the environment and rob the First Nations of Canada out of their land, culture, language and ultimately their dignity. I couldn't wait to climb back into the canoe and get away from this place, to purge the dirty feeling of social unease, toxic mine effluent and prevailing despair. Travelling with Dawson didn't seem so bad after-all.

Not everything about Thompson was bad, and my heart went out to those who worked hard every day to raise their families in the north. They weren't a part of the corporate or bureaucratic ruse, just the manipulated pawns. There was the Burntwood Diner and it served the best breakfast north of Winnipeg. That's where we met up with Tom Ellis and his companion Blair the next morning. Tom was a Chipewyan whom I managed to track down, as he had some knowledge about the Seal River. He lived in town for the most part and made extra money as a guide and outfitter. He knew a lot about the native cultural features and didn't mind sharing some of its secrets with us.

"What about the Bay?" Tom asked in a heavy tone. "How are you going to get across to Churchill to catch the train?" This was a big concern for us. We had two choices: either hire a fellow by the name of Jackie Bastone and have his boat pick us up at the estuary of the Seal, or paddle down the coast of Hudson Bay.

Tom shook his head. "It's a tough paddle...some canoeists have died trying to take a short-cut across Button Bay, you know." Hodding and Russell perked up. Dawson of course jumped in and explained that we could do it easily because we were prepared to latch the canoes together and use spray-covers, turning them into a seaworthy catamaran. Tom looked doubtful and Russell looked grim. Breakfast arrived and we concentrated on eating. I noticed Russell pushing the food around on his plate and not eating. I could tell he was still having second thoughts about the adventure.

I reflected on Tom's skepticism. I recalled the research I had just completed on my last book about the Missinaibi River where half the drowning incidents occurred from misreading maps or trusting maps that were inaccurate. For novice map readers it only takes one slip-up, a simple miscalculation, and the world can unfold quickly. At Thunderhouse Falls on the Missinaibi River, a cartographer had arbitrarily marked a portage on the wrong side of the river on the topographic chart. As a result, five canoeists lost their life trying to access a portage that didn't exist. It was a big story. I wanted to embarrass the government who had failed to provide the necessary 'duty-of-care', to at least have travel-friendly maps available for public consumption. The Ministry of Tourism in Ontario had even taken out expensive full-colour ads in American magazines, touting the Missinaibi as a Canadian Heritage gem where one could paddle from Lake Superior all the way up to James Bay and only cross two roads. After leaking the story to the press, it immediately hit the front page of the *Toronto Star*, headlining the Missinaibi as the "River of Death." The resultant story brought a deluge of phone calls and letters to the reporter's desk: paddlers who had close calls at Thunderhouse, even a group of rafters that went over the falls and had survived. The reporter later told me that this story hailed the most feedback than any other story he had written.

It was an axiomatic truth that canoeists, and their guides, have perished and for reasons not always associated with faulty topographic maps or government short-sightedness. Adventurers have designed their own failures with peculiar regularity since first stepping foot on Canadian soil centuries ago. Our disassociation with the outdoors in general has all but erased any rational sense of order in the wilderness. Views are often anthropocentric, born from a white-European colonial mentality that saw nature and wilderness (and its indigenous tribes) as something to be conquered and subdued; almost the same inference used by resource administrators today who use computer-generated paradigms to "protect" or sell-off the remaining chunks of wilderness in this country.

Travelling in the wilds demands an unbending and resolute respect for the land, its aboriginal peoples, and nature's inherent peculiarities. Those who challenge nature, see it as something to beat or conquer, always lose. The lack of reverence will often lead to mishap, and sometimes death. Mistakes are made, bad judgements stubbornly carried out with astonishing acquiescence. Reading through the Coronor's reports had rattled my own psyche. Someone had gotten drunk and backed over a precipice behind a campsite and fell into the rapids at night while his buddies were too inebriated to save him; another neglected to wear his lifejacket while running a set of rapids. His body was found three days later after his wife had walked 50 kilometers through bug-infested bog to inform authorities; and then there was the body that Andrea and I had inadvertently canoed over that turned out to be a one-armed man who had failed to put on his lifejacket, capsized and got pinned against a rock underwater. It was almost a week before his body was recovered.

Another trip down the lower Missinaibi, shortly after two Americans drowned at Thunderhouse Falls, I had found their waterproof camera floating in a pool above the cataract and handed it over to the reporter later on. With permission from the family the reporter had the pictures reproduced, two of which were printed in the paper along with the article. Four guys from Ohio having a good time on a wild river, planned for months, relying on topographic maps for navigation thinking that the Canadian government wouldn't release erroneous maps, made a fatal mistake one day that saw half their party disappear over the lip of a treacherous waterfall.

"Hap, you're not eating your breakfast!" Tom exclaimed, catching me off-guard in a delirium of abstract thought.

"Mind's going a mile a minute," I said. "A lot to think about; Hodding and Russ don't have a lot of experience in a canoe."

"I have a bit," Hodding piped up, "not really much in fast water though, but I can catch on quick, I'm sure it can't be that hard."

Russell said nothing, perhaps a bit sheepish as he had little experience to share at all. Tom's mouth dropped slightly.

"It's better this way; trying to break bad habits is one thing, teaching new skills always works out for the good. These guys look strong." I gave Russ a light punch in the arm to try to lighten him up a bit but it didn't work.

"I don't know about this," Tom lamented. "This isn't like the south woods up here...a lot can happen."

As we listened to Tom talk about the harshness of the land we were about to travel in, and about the dangers of trying to navigate Hudson Bay, I again recalled a particular tragedy that took place in 1984, ten years earlier.

I had first read about it during my Missinaibi research at the Coroner's office; a tragic story of four young canoeists who had died while trying to paddle the James Bay coast from Fort Albany to Moosonee. While attending the Toronto Canoe Symposium as a speaker, arctic paddler George Grinnell launched his book, *A Death in the Barrens,* his account of a fateful canoe odyssey on the Dubawnt River in 1955 where the leader, Arthur Moffat died of hypothermia after an upset in the cold water. The remaining five in the canoe party barely survived the trip. Grinnell's book is also a rather compelling autobiography. It wasn't until I read the book that I learned that it was his two sons, a nephew and a girlfriend that had lost their lives in the frigid arctic waters of the Bay. It struck me that I was privy to information George Grinnell probably didn't even know about from having scanned police and coroners' reports depicting the final events of the incident.

They were young but not without some canoeing experience gained from previous family trips. The four Americans had just completed a forty-day expedition down Ontario's longest wild river – the Albany which empties out into James Bay – the large southern bay off Hudson Bay.

George's two sons were just drying out from a bout with drugs and alcohol, deciding that such a wild river trip would straighten out their lives. When they finally arrived at Fort Albany, a Cree village at the estuary of the river, the regular boat haul to Moosonee that their father had told them about was no longer in service. It was either an expensive flight to the railtown that would take them back south to Cochrane, or a dangerous 150 kilometer paddle down the James Bay coast. Local Indian guides had offered to take them to Moosonee by boat but the four ignored the voice of wisdom and experience. They decided to save themselves the few dollars it would have cost them. They were also amply warned about the dangers of the coast. But they struck out anyway. Four days later a severe storm battered the James Bay coast. Two weeks later, three bodies and miscellaneous gear and canoes were recovered but there were no survivors.

All of these graphic pictures flashed through my head at breakfast. I shared none of this with the others. Maybe it wasn't such a good idea after all to sail down the coast. There was still enough *Men's Journal* money left to hire Jackie Bastone's barge for a pick-up. I did want to explore the coast, to paddle amongst the beluga whales and play the tides to our advantage. The only way to do this was in a canoe, not a motorboat.

The four of us discussed the options back at the hotel. We made the decision to have Bastone pick us up at the estuary on a set date. I made the call and arranged for pick up. This pleased Hodding and Russell immensely. The two greenhorns must have been calibrating their odds at surviving this expedition and whether or not if they actually made it as far as the Bay, why should they push the negative side of the probability factor any further.

*   *   *   *   *

Shortly after noon we boarded Skyward Aviation's E-110 BAN-
DEIRANTE, C-GSKD or, in short, the "Bandit": a twin-engine
prop work horse used by the air service to make supply runs
to the outlying Cree and Chipewyan communities. The interior
passenger seats, save four for human baggage, were removed to
make room for the two canoes and the mountain of gear. That
pushed the load to the max according to the base manager who
packed the plane.

Ron, the pilot, informed us that we'd be flying at 10,500 feet
and it would take us a bit more than an hour to get to Tadoule
from Thompson, a distance of 275 kilometers. I was used to
flying in bush floatplanes but barely above tree-top level, seldom
above a thousand feet. I asked the pilot why we were traveling
at such high altitude and his reply was not at all what I wanted
to hear.

"To clear the smoke from the fires," Ron exclaimed, "a bad
year for fires...they're everywhere." We all passed a look of dread
around like a hot potato. *Fires? Just great,* I thought to myself, *as
if there wasn't enough work cut out for me as expedition leader. It's a huge
province, maybe we'll skirt by them.* I sat back in my seat and tried
to relax.

Once in the air the sudden realization that the expedition
had actually begun seemed to untangle some of the knots of
angst in my gut, save for the disconcerting notice about fires.
That was the axiomatic thing about expeditions, when you could
finally get into the headspace of where you were going and how
you would carry it off; when there was no chance of turning
back, no opportunity to purchase stuff you may have forgotten, no chance of telling the pilot to turn around because you've

changed your mind. The exhaustion and prep-work that had consumed my life for the past month was behind me.

By now Dawson had straightened out somewhat and he was getting along great with Hodding. It was that errant charm that made Dawson likeable, an energy that was contagious if you hung around him enough. Channeling that energy in a positive way was often elusive; half the time he was good company while the other half I was devising ways of getting rid of him. I did try my best not to judge him too harshly and I was prone to giving him several chances at making amends for his intolerable behaviour. It was that damn, lingering sense of camaraderie borne out of the environmental front lines that allowed me to give in, soften, continually testing the level of my tolerance. I didn't know how long my patience would last.

Flying north of any rail or road, beyond the ramparts of the civilized world, always instilled an immediate sense of aloneness and solitude in me. And here, now, the furthest north that I've explored by canoe amplified those feelings. I was in my element; not really knowing what lay ahead, or really caring. I would be in the canoe and on the river was all that mattered. Aloneness, for me, doesn't purvey a notion of abandonment. More specifically it's a lack of the things I try to purposely leave behind; going to a place where I'm most at home.

There was a great comfort in knowing that during the years past my own apprenticeship in the outdoors had prepared me reasonably well for the challenge of living contentedly in the wilderness. A survivalist at heart, the precept of "survival" in the wilds for me had given way to something less combative. I had been doing this for so long now that terms of my own existence was measured in being "out there" as often and for as long as possible. To do this I had to accept the fact that nature wasn't my enemy. I simply had to make adjustments. There was an art to it.

Endurance and survival on my own personal level was gauged at my inability to conform and total incapacity to dwell in the mainstream with any level of success. My heart and soul just wasn't in it. Out here it was another story.

I suppose what ruined me for the corporate or mainstream world was being too involved with the prevalent insensitivity to the land, to humankind in general, wrought by institutions, countries driven to elevate a protracted standard of living that the earth could no longer afford. I had given up good paying jobs and numerous opportunities in order to maintain my freedom. Money meant little to me. In reality, if there was any one thing others envied most was another person's freedom. Not money. In that sense I was a rich man. And to live solely by wits and ingenuity outside the safe parameters set by mainstream order was restitution enough, challenge enough, and the value of soulful compensation incalculable. Fighting for the earth too was always a noble and worthwhile undertaking, no matter how great the enemy. It was the right thing to do.

Self-banishment and my own philosophies were predicated by hard adventure; an affirmation that life anywhere other than the wilderness path was totally and irreversibly fucked up. The green movement has a way of pushing you towards an apocalyptic inspection of life. All the deleterious information pours across your table on a daily basis, like an effluent pipe from a pulp mill spewing waste and mercury into a river and then trying to deal with it. People with their collective heads buried in the sand start to call you a cynic. Throwing rocks at the corporate bad guys didn't always work in favour of the green movement; the browns had the money to hire good lawyers and, as is often the case, they own the press. Still, I try my best at keeping the faith in humanity. That being said, I accepted Dawson as a challenge, perhaps in some obtuse way representing the humanity I have faith in, or hope, or some such bullshit, or maybe he is just another victim of humanity gone awry.

After about twenty minutes in the air, bound for the Seal River, I could see the curtain of smoke choking the horizon from myriad wild fires burning unchecked. We flew through it at 10,000 feet, the Bandit pitching against a strong headwind. Soon enough, the acrid smoke from the fires below crept into the hold of the plane. The burnt smell of spruce clung to the insides of my nostrils and I did my best to suppress a gag and an overwhelming feeling of vertigo. The pilot did his best to keep clear of the smoke. I suspected the plane had no way to circulate fresh air inside the hold.

We flew along the top parameter of the smoke with the blue azure sky suspended above, clouds seeming to float on the brown fire haze like a sea of great ice hummocks. There were at least a dozen or more spot fires burning around Indian Lake, apparently moving quickly south with the prevailing early summer wind. The Chipewyan settlement there had been evacuated, children and elders flown to Churchill while the able-bodied men stayed behind until the last moment. The Manitoba government allows these fires to burn themselves out on their own; the boreal tracts are a fire-dependent ecosystem. But the real reason the bureaucracy stands back is motivated more by the fact that the timber isn't marketable that far north, not even for pulp. They'll instigate an evacuation, at the last minute if the fires encroach upon a First Nations settlement.

The air finally cleared and I could see land again. The percentage of water appeared to equal that of the earth, presenting a crude, patterned mosaic of black spruce, open lake and fenland. Crests of low hills and eskers were topped with sand, sporadically manged with gnarled, wind-whipped birch, stunted evergreens, wiry sedge and twisted willow. There were no roads.

We flew over the immense hydro dam that suspended Indian Lake above the brown effluent of the once mighty Churchill River, now sullen and uncertain. It made me think of T.S. Eliot's poem, *the dry salvages*, where he describes the river as a "strong brown god...almost forgotten by the city dwellers in cities-ever, however, implacable, keeping his seasons and rages, destroyer, reminder of what men choose to forget. Unhonoured, unpropitiated by worshippers of the machine, but waiting, watching and waiting."

To be perfectly honest, I had no idea what to expect of northern Manitoba. People I had encountered, both fellow paddlers and strangers, even those Manitobans living in the Winnipeg urban sprawl, had little notion of what lay beyond the great prairie veldt. To me it was another different type of wilderness that few have known, save for the sporadic explorations of the industrial provocateur and the occasional foray by First Nations. And that was the lure of exploration – the unknown. Few places on the planet were left unexplored. Canada has a great majority of unexplored territory. The power of the Seal River, its intimidating features and the lack of information rendered the isolated waterway too dangerous for most canoeists.

There were several fires burning about eight kilometers north of the village of Tadoule. They were not yet a threat, presumably, moving slowly southwards as it seemed likely the nature of the landscape and the number of lakes caused the fires to branch out and run helter-skelter on their own accord. Luckily, the smoke drifted high and off to the southeast away from the village. The town itself seemed to be conspicuously perched along the apex of a long esker in no particular order of house arrangement. An esker is a long, sinuous, steep-sided, narrow-crested ridge consisting of cross-bedded sands and gravels, laid down by glacial meltwater. Northern Manitoba is criss-crossed by eskers of impressive length and height. Esker formations are as much a part of the Dene history and culture as the caribou.

The landing strip lay beyond the few rows of houses and about a kilometer away from the lake. The "fasten your seatbelt" sign flashed on at the front of the passenger hold. A thin partition of aircraft aluminum and grease-stained fabric separated us from the pilot and co-pilot. The Bandit circled once to check the wind-sock then put down gracefully on the packed sand and gravel tarmac and wheeled up to the small, tin shack that served as the Tadoule airport terminal. As we were landing I had noticed several trucks and all-terrain vehicles heading up to the landing strip from the village.

The gear was quickly dropped to the side of the plane and the canoes hauled out and placed alongside the mountain of camping equipment.

"You're not putting all that stuff in those two canoes are you?" the pilot queried with an obvious trace of amusement. "There's plenty of room," I lied, without letting on that his humour and our predicament were verifiable. To maintain the comedy of it I added the fact that we would simply swim alongside the canoes if we ran out of room for passengers. Everyone laughed except me.

"Do you guys have an ELT?" The pilot asked us if we carried an Emergency Locator Transmitter. "No, we'll just have to keep our wits about us," I answered sheepishly. Search and Rescue frowned on the use of ELT's by canoeists because they were being accidentally set off in packs or people would engage them hoping for a rescue pick-up for the flimsiest of reasons including running out of toilet paper. (*Global Positioning Systems or GPS would not be available to the public until 1995). We had enough gear to haul along with us.

"Good luck!" the pilot shook his head and walked back to

the Bandit. The four of us stood by the pile of gear, a little bewildered, while an audience of expressionless Chipewyan men
watched from beyond the compound fence.

Chapter Four

Tadoule

As soon as we had stepped off the plane we were greeted by a frenzy of "bull dogs". Bull dogs were horse flies, vexation of the barrenlands and they had the bite of a junkyard dog. They were quick and resolute on feasting on some fresh city meat. The horse flies, in fact, were so bad that we failed to notice how terrible the black flies were.

Behind a chain-link partition that kept vehicles off the runway, several men from the village loitered about just watching us, waiting for something. They spoke in a language totally unfamiliar to me, a dialect so primitive it seemed incongruous to watch them mill about and tinker with their ATVs and beat-up trucks. I had studied Ojibwe and Cree languages but there was absolutely no commonality between the Algonkian and Chipewyan (Dene) dialects. I presumed that most could also speak English and that they had come up to the airbase to make a few bucks shuttling our gear down to the lake. Since there was almost no other commerce amongst whites and Chips, or any need of for that matter, any man owning a track-worthy vehicle showed up at the airstrip. But they just stood there waiting for us to make a move first. There was no vying for position like airport cabbies, or fighting amongst themselves as to who was there ahead of the other, just a calm intercourse that bore a curious resemblance to men watching a rather tedious game of checkers.

I walked casually over to a fellow by the name of Anderson, Andy for short he said. He would drive us to the lake or wherever we wanted to go, "as long as it isn't Thompson," he added with a pleasant chuckle. There actually was a winter road to Thompson that was driveable for almost two months each winter – the only time Tadoule was connected with the rest of Manitoba except by air transport. I gave Andy twenty dollars to haul our gear to the far end of the village in his battered pick-up. I had made earlier contact with Tadoule residents, Allan and Mary Code. Allan was a white man who had married into the Dene clan at Tadoule. Mary, or *Ma Si Cho*, was the chief's daughter. Allan was a cine-matographer and Mary was a historian; their combined talents produced a visual and written record of the Churchill Dene.

We rode in the back of Anderson's truck, all the while try-ing desperately to keep the canoes from bouncing off onto the road. It took two trips to get all the gear the short distance to the Codes' house and by then we were well coated with a layer of Tadoule dust, fine as talcum-powder. Once there we were greet-ed amicably by Allan who quickly directed us down a path at the edge of his house to a small clearing where we set up our tents.

The four of us sat and talked with Allan for a short while, extracting what information we could about the Seal River. As it turned out, Allan had accompanied the Canadian Heritage Riv-ers Systems study team down the Seal in 1985. He was able to produce some footage for his film about the Sayisi Dene people during this expedition.

After being nominated for heritage status by Parks Can-ada, the Seal never gained official acceptance into the system until 1992. The creation of new parks and reserves, it seems, is never absent of some controversy, usually stemming from extractive-based resource factions: miners, loggers, developers and the hunting and fishing groups who claim that protected spaces will defrock them of their constitutional rights. Despite the protracted heritage status, the recognition means very little except by title within the government's own resource documentation about the Seal River, produced in 1990, it clearly states that:

"In the event that a hydro-electric or major mining resource development is proposed that exceeds the conditions for maintenance of heritage values and heritage status, all options for river use will be reviewed. If the province of Manitoba determines that provincial interests are best served by other resource uses, heritage river status will be removed if necessary."

It was a blatant 'no-balls' approach to protecting Canadian cultural and ecological resources. I had brought along the report. It was mildly helpful, full of riverine data, written with all the typical government rhetoric and impersonality. The maps were of no use at all. Even Allan couldn't tell us much about the rapids except that they were "voluminous and very long."

"The few people who run the river generally use motorized rafts," Allan informed us.

"Our expedition canoes are equipped with nylon spray-skirts and we can easily manage up to Class IV whitewater," I explained, although at this time did not really know how efficient spray-covers actually were. I did know that a Class IV rapid was one classification over the maximum limit for open, recreational canoes. The International River Grading System uses a scale of one to six – anything over grade four, for a stock canoe, was pushing the odds considerably.

"The water's cold, never warms up," Allan remarked, "and the ice just went off the lake here a few days ago so the river will be running high and as cold as winter itself."

"We all have wet-suits just in case there is an upset in the rapids," Dawson said proudly. You could tell Allan was skeptical; he knew as well as I did that even with that thin layer of protection you would still have to get out of the river quickly before hypothermia set in. If the rapids were as long as Allan said they were, an upset could be fatal. I could tell that Allan wasn't buying everything we were telling him.

I asked about the village, about Tadoule. It looked as if it had been thrown together on a whim. Buildings were prefab plywood structures, basic and bereft of character and no sign of any cultural fixtures one would normally see in most other First Nations communities. Something was missing. Luckily, Allan was glad to share his knowledge of the people he chose to live with. I wasn't about to feign my reasons for exploring the Seal River but did let my host know that our group was there under honourable intentions. *The Men's Journal* article was mildly accepted by Allan, questioned for its general purpose but not embraced.

I made it clear that at some point during our visit we would like to partake in a pre-voyage ceremony under the edification of a Tadoule healer or shaman; that it would invariably illustrate our respect for the Dene by asking permission to travel through their homeland. Allan agreed that it would be a good gesture.

"In fact," Allan remarked, "there just happens to be three visiting Navajo healers here in the village. They're coming for dinner, you'll meet them."

"Navajo?" I said confused, "what are three Arizona shamans doing three-thousand kilometers north in Dene land?" I asked.

Allan gave me an abbreviated history according to regional archaeologists. Indication of human habitation along the Seal River dated back to at least 4,000 B.C. As glacial waters contracted and the environment became increasingly favourable for caribou and fish harvesting, the Shield Archaic cultures moved north from the plains into the north-east. Caribou were markedly easier game to bring down by primitive methods than were bison. Although seasonal hunting forays were made into the barrenlands, it was unlikely that the "Taltheili" people expanded permanently into northern Manitoba until 500 A.D. It was these people who formed the historic eastern Athabaskan nomads.

The Navajo were evidently from the same gene-pool as the caribou hunters; northwest Canadian Athabaskan stock who drifted down into the southwest around 1300 A.D. They were fierce nomadic raiders, closely related to the plains Apache. The Navajo terrorized the sedentary corn-planting tribes of the Arizona region. The Pueblo Indians called them *Apachu*, meaning "enemy strangers." This led to the mixed Tewa and Spanish "Apaches de Nabahu," which ultimately shortened to become just "Navajo". Today the Navajo are the largest and wealthiest Indian nation in the United States.

The northern Athapaskans, or present-day Sayisi Dene, and the Navajo, share distinct anthropological and ethnological traits; they just live in disparately different environments with almost a whole continent separating them from each other. Both nations refer to themselves as Dene (Din-eh) meaning "the people". Linguistically, their language has assumed geographically induced modifications but they are still able to communicate in the old tongue. Religious faith is strong, built upon a foundation that worships the winds and waterways, and a close relationship with the Earth Mother. Ceremony is very important to the Dene and it seems as if the visiting Navajo healers play an integral role in preserving that faith and maintaining ancient customs.

The northern Dene make a point of resenting their anthropological label as "caribou eaters", so-called by their traditional enemies as "Edthen-oedeli-dene". They much prefer Sayisi Dene which translates into "People of the Rising Sun." The Dene were also known as Chipewyans, derived from the Cree word *wichip-wayaniu*, meaning "pointed fur people", referring to their pointed winter coats.

Allan's passion for these people was obvious. You could read it in his energy when he talked about them. He refers to himself as their "watchdog", often acting on their behalf as intermediary in tribal affairs, dealing with white-man's often fickle laws and policy. Who better to translate white-man rhetoric than another white-man? And there was never a shortage of issues to attend to between Winnipeg bureaucrats and Federal Indian Affairs officials.

"You can't help but get involved," Allan said solemnly. "You live with these people and you see things differently...through their eyes and you can feel the torment they've been through; not just in recent times, but from early days of starvation and hardship. The hardship is written on their faces."

"Are things getting any better for them here, now, I mean between the government and the band," I asked.

"Not really," Allan answered rather bitterly.

"Why not?" I kept pushing Allan for more information.

"They don't trust anyone from the government. They don't trust whites."

"They trust you," I asserted. After all he was married to the Chief's daughter.

"It took a while, at first; with anyone, really, it takes time and you have to prove yourself."

"Prove yourself?"

"Yes, that you aren't trying to screw them over. They know when you're honest and when you're trying to fuck with them. Of any Canadian Indian band, the Dene have probably suffered the most."

On that note we let the conversation lapse into momentary silence. Mary gifted me with a copy of the transcripts from her writing about the Dene Nation and I read through it that night in the tent. It was easy to see where Allan's ardour emanated from and his enthusiasm to help the Tadoule Dene in any way he could. It was also evident that he was very protective of the people that adopted him into the community; his suspicions of us and our intent were neatly concealed. I could tell he was, in a kind enough way, testing us.

The history of the Churchill Dene is suffused with tragedy and misfortune, and a misguided irony that has left the people with deep scars and a sour taste in their mouths when it comes to white-man logic; and any logic is purely accidental in their eyes. When the white-European colonials built Fort Prince of Wales in 1717, near present-day Churchill, the Dene and Inuit were immediately encouraged to trade with the Hudson's Bay Company; animal furs in return for trinkets, faulty muskets and other cheap stuff. Reluctant to enter into Cree territory, trade with the Dene remained sporadic at best until inland posts were erected much later on, at Reindeer Lake near the Saskatchewan border, and at Caribou and Little Duck Lakes, north of the Seal River. In the 1780s, a smallpox epidemic decimated nearly nine-tenths of the Sayisi Dene population, a direct result of the interaction with the whites at Churchill and a ready supply of disease-ridden blankets purposely distributed amongst local tribes. Many "Company" provocateurs believed that the "reduced population would weed-out the undesirables, put less pressure on the local game reserves, and make survivors more dependent on trade with the Hudson's Bay Company."

But unlike the Cree, both the Dene and Inuit remained aloof and independent. So dependent upon the movement of caribou were the Chipewyans that the hunt always took precedence over the fur-trade, much to the frustration of the HBC stationed at Churchill. This was the deciding factor for establishing posts nearer to Dene home-grounds.

Although the coastal region and delta of the Seal River was known to the Chips, the general environs were better known to the coastal Inuit hunters. These whaling people effectively exploited whale, seal and other sea-mammals, not only for themselves, but also later for the HBC, albeit on an irregular schedule. Further inland the Dene utilized the unique esker formations as overland travelways, several of which etched across the Seal River landscape.

Allan Code was conspicuous about his devotion concerning the people with whom he now lived. His anger at the "feckless system" was patent and he made no bones about pointing an accusatory finger at the Manitoba government for various well-founded reasons. Our conversation returned to the village of Tadoule where Allan disclosed much about the plight of the Dene. I was able to piece together a more objective chronology over the years since our meeting in Tadoule in 1994.

The very existence of the Dene revolved around the caribou migrations. There was a time not so long ago, in fact, when hundreds of thousands of these tundra animals occupied the Seal River corridor. The caribou belonged to the nomadic Kaminuriak herd, which was centered around Baker Lake in the Keewatin District of the northwest Territories (now Nunavut). Up until 1970 the herd would typically range south, well into and beyond the Seal River during the winter, seeking the shelter of the boreal tree-line. In the summer they would again migrate north back to the open tundra-lands. Quite suddenly, however, the herd failed to extend into the transitional forests. The reason for this shift in range is not known for sure...at least by Manitoba government speculation and conjecture. The bureaucrats and the Dene people each have their own axe to grind if the word caribou ever comes up in a conversation.

In 1929, the Hudson's Bay Company established a post at Caribou Lake, north of the Seal River. Sydney Augustus Keighly worked the post as the factor for ten years. In his memoirs entitled, *Trader, Trapper – the Life of a Bay Man*, first published in 1989, Keighly talks about the indiscriminate hunting practices of the Sayisi Dene:

"Let one of them sight a caribou, and he will immediately set to work to kill it, whether there is a need for meat or not. Similarly, when either of these native groups [Inuit and Dene] sees a herd, they will slaughter until there are no survivors, even if much of the meat has to be abandoned. Cree, on the other hand, only hunt when they want food, and take only what they will actually use, either immediately, or in the coming weeks."

Even previous to Keighley's observations, Warburton Pike in 1917, in a book entitled, *The Barren Ground of Northern Canada*, exclaims that;..."when Indians [Dene] or Eskimo get among a number of caribou only one thing stops or limits their killing, lack of ammunition". This annihilative killing contradicts even Dene moral and ethical laws governing the conservation of game. In his book entitled, *Yamoria, Dene elder, George Blondin*, writes:

"...one of the Dene laws about living off the land is to never over-harvest an area..."

In Mary Code's own retelling of the Dene history, about the legend of "how caribou came back to the Dene", she claims that the Dene respect for the caribou was paramount. In the words of the elders:

"...people had to struggle to survive...survival was the way of life. Our life was that of deprivation and hardship...but we knew the land and where to find food. We knew how to adapt to

54

the environment and harsh climate. We were solid as the natural elements."

According to Dene mythology, the caribou, had been put on the earth for the exclusive use of the Chipewyans. Regardless of the ease with which caribou were exterminated upon the introduction of firearms, long periods of starvation and hardship endured by the people seem to exonerate them from their lack of conservation ethics.

P.G. Downes, a Boston schoolteacher who made historical recreational trips into the barren-fringe in 1939, writes about the Dene Chief Kasmere's reaction to criticism about over-hunting from the government Indian agent at Brochet. He says:

"Who is this white man who presumes to talk about what is ours. The next thing we know we will be told how to treat our wives and children. The caribou are ours, they have been given our forefathers and to us forever. Who is this king that will send a man to talk like this? How dare this creature even use the word idthen in his mouth?"

Like any religious faith, whether Christian, Muslim, Hindu or Chipewyan, morality and principles are sometimes led askew by a zealous ownership of liberal idealizations. Carl Jung proclaimed that: "anthropologists have often described what happens to a primitive society when its spiritual values are exposed to the impact of modern civilization. Its people lose the meaning of their lives, their social organization disintegrates, and they themselves morally decay."

The fact then that the over-killing of caribou could be construed as a 'quality' learned from the whites upon first exposure is a distinct possibility...*a probability!* Colonial attitude, guided by a Christian faith that expounded on the virtues of subjugating nature and usurping its bounty may have, in all likelihood, mislead and confused the northern tribes into believing that excessive slaughter was somehow ordained and sanctified by a higher power. After all, the Dene too perceived the whites to be driven by greed and excess as if it were decreed the norm.

But there is another stone to be overturned here. After the closure of the Caribou Lake HBC post in 1941, another was established at Little Duck Lake, about ninety kilometers north of present-day Tadoule. To the Sayisi Dene this was a traditional hunting and fishing site, a place where caribou crossed the Wolverine River in great numbers. Once the post was erected, the Dene attempted to carry out normal lifestyles that awkwardly blended with the commerce and religion of a white, capitalist society. Children were sent to white residential schools where Dene customs and language was strictly forbidden. Chief Kasmere's worst fears materialized.

In 1956, the Manitoba government relocated the Dene to the mouth of the North Knife River, just south of the Seal estuary on Hudson Bay, near the town of Churchill. Families never even had the opportunity to take their personal belongings with them. The Knife River was an unfavourable location, unproductive, game-poor and too close to the foul coastal climate of Hudson Bay. The relocation site was soon abandoned and people began filing into the port town of Churchill in search of food and shelter. Crude houses were built from waste lumber and cardboard liberated from the town dump. It wasn't long before a Dene "shack-town" rose up from the discards of white affluence. Apathy and misery led to alcoholism, crime, suicide and family abuse. The lame attempt by Indian Affairs to assimilate the Dene to a "better life" culminated in the almost complete annihilation of the eastern Sayisi Dene people.

Mary Code asserts that the move from Little Duck Lake to Churchill was instigated by the Department of Natural Resources working through Indian Affairs. Of course it seemed natural that the Department would blame the Dene for the decrease in the caribou herd. The Manitoba government did want a quick assimilation of the Dene into white society for other reasons as well, as I was to find out later through further investigation.

The Great Seal Prospecting and Developing Syndicate began mineral exploration in Dene country just three years prior to the relocation of the people to Churchill. Along certain geographic sections, the Seal River crosses a "Greenstone Belt": a geological term representing a large volcano-sedimentary basin, important for its crustal evolution. Actinolite and epidote impart a green colour to the massive metamorphic mineral base. Needless to say, greenstone has a medium to high mineral potential, namely gold. Prospectors had discovered the huge nickel reserves at Thompson at about the same time, and low-grade discoveries were turning up along the Seal River. By conveniently relocating the Dene people and removing them from the equation it would be easy to develop the resources along the river. It was already common knowledge to wildlife specialists that such operations and disturbances to the natural environment would affect the migrations of caribou. Although the core-sampling turned up results showing less than 40% metallic iron content, too low a concentration to warrant full-scale mining activity, the damage had already been done. A plethora of survey and mining camps had been established along the Seal, close to sensitive caribou crossings. Wherever the caribou entered the water, the Dene deemed these as sacred places which were to be left untouched. These *ben-kah-dah* were easily disrupted, particularly by white interlopers through mining exploration and the proliferation of aircraft traffic over the tundra.

There were also other factors affecting the shift in the caribou herd migration. Immediately after the Dene were relocated to Churchill in the late 1950s, the Natural Resources Department began to carry out caribou-tagging operations at Duck Lake. Sigurd Olsen, the well-known author from Minnesota, had accompanied the government technicians as an observer. In his book, *Runes of the North*, in a short essay titled "Caribou", Olsen doubted the actions of the government tagging operation when it was measured against the historic use by the Dene Nation for millennia. Olsen laments, "Had we now reached a point in our conquest of the earth when, because of our expanding population and human depredations, there was no longer an opportunity for other forms to live undisturbed?"

As a first-hand observer, Olsen also writes:

"But now, with the caribou population seriously depleted, killing more than is actually needed for food and clothing does make a great difference, and with the advent of the motor-driven canoe it is far easier to run down all the members of a band of swimming caribou and spear them before they can reach the shore. Not many years before, during a good migration, the shores of Nejanilini were piled high with bloated and unused carcasses. While the rifle may have increased the kill in certain areas, ammunition is still too costly to use where more primitive methods suffice. The tundra was covered with bleached antlers, snow white and beautiful...there were hundreds of them, possibly thousands, as the killing had gone on for many years."

Mining activity, increased flights over the tundra and the government tagging operations may have had an accumulative and deleterious effect on caribou migrations – a short-sighted meddling by an opportunistic bureaucracy. Add to this the effects of global-warming and the subsequent increase in boreal wild fires and the caribou really had no chance of maintaining a modicum of peace.

The Dene people back in 1956 never stood a chance against an ostentatious, self-serving bureaucracy. There was no environmental or cultural movement in Canada at this time and certainly no accountability or transparency expressed by governments or by industry. In the public eye the Dene were not blamed for the decrease in caribou; they were blamed for their own near demise and lack of fortitude by not assimilating to the white community of Churchill. By 1973 the Dene had had enough. The almost total collapse of their society prompted an unsolicited move back to their homeland. Unassisted by the Manitoba government, the Dene erected a village at *tehs-heh-oo-lee-tuat*, or "floating cinders lake", now known as Tadoule Lake.

Many years ago, when the Dene traveled to that part of their traditional territory, they would often camp along the shore of this lake. Upon leaving the campsite they would toss the still-burning wood from their campfire into the water. Others traveling the lake would then see the floating cinders. The Dene had chosen Tadoule Lake because of the excellent lake trout fishing. Traditionally, they would come here whenever the caribou hunting was poor. The present community site is known as *thay-nu-tuay*, meaning "rock reef bay", after the odd pile of rocks that form a solitary island just offshore, east of the village, marking the open expanse of Tadoule Lake.

*   *   *   *   *

Allan seemed to carry a bitterness towards whites that was historically induced and plausible, emphasizing the strained relations between the Manitoba government and his adopted people as I was reluctant to inform him that I had intentions of charting the river for inclusion in a river guidebook for Manitoba, as any attempt at explaining this to Allan may have compromised my attempt at putting an environmental strategy to work. He may have perceived the concept as a vain attempt by me to exploit the river for my own gain. The "use-it-or-lose-it" dogma that faced Canadian wilderness was not a new awakening set to storm the country. The notion of developing adventure, eco-based or cultural tourism was only just breaking out of its hard shell and too easily misinterpreted by the bureaucracy.

Like most large provincial rivers in Manitoba, the government realized their potential for hydro-electricity development; certainly a marketable commodity. Locking up tracts of land or protecting watersheds wouldn't put dollars into the government coffers. Even though the Seal River was now a Canadian gem, the title and notoriety could not protect it from the grasp of Manitoba Hydro. They had already established seven potential sites for dam construction along the Seal in 1965. The total head available for hydro development was an impressive 600 vertical feet calculated at 88% efficiency. But it remained too isolated to develop. The Seal River remains as the last great undeveloped river in northern Manitoba. Government bureaucracies, generally, at this time, focused on the tangible, dollar-value assessments of natural resources. Rivers included. Any marketable natural resource was gauged on a consistent use and a direct remuneration for the province. During this period in Canadian developmental history, the damming of rivers and lakes for logging or hydro-power was carried out with immunity. Aboriginal cultural sites and pre-contact archaeology was often flooded out, people displaced and wildlife populations disrupted – not to mention the huge release of methane from dam reservoirs that contribute to global warming and climate change.

My own strategy for marketing rivers to the burgeoning adventure-travel tourists, in the past, had helped to instill public awareness of watershed ecosystems, their cultural history and importance as part of the collective Canadian identity. Working within the bureaucracies of Parks Canada and Manitoba Tourism

I had hoped to identify all the threatened rivers in the province. The guidebook was more than just a safe, field-friendly assist to visiting paddlers, it could also surface as an effective environmental tool.

I wondered if the Dene today ventured very far from the new village. Their nomadic history certainly seemed to be remiss of any cultural need to take from the land. This proclivity was addressed to Allan. He was quick to remark that after their [the Dene] relocation to Tadoule, and with the resultant paucity of caribou along the Seal River, the Dene had kept mostly to the lake upon whose shores offered some semblance of village autonomy, except for the regular shipments of white-man's supplies via air from Thompson.

"The fishing, mostly lake trout, is exceptional," beamed Allan, and I could tell that he spent many an hour with the rod tipped to the depths of Tadoule Lake. In fact, Allan was about to guide the three visiting Navajo medicine men on a fishing safari designed to secure dinner to which we were all cordially invited.

*   *   *   *   *

After setting up their makeshift village on the nape of an esker at Tadoule, the Manitoba and Federal governments were embarrassed into recognizing the Dene determination for independence and self-esteem. Autonomy and pride is one thing; accepting government money was not turned down when it was finally offered. But life had certainly changed since the 1950's. A drastic vacillation between cultures had, and still was taking place amongst the paltry number of Churchill shack-town survivors.

It was evident that Tadoule town life emulated a sort of Native suburbia. Houses were simple, newly constructed and even numbered. Not that I was expecting the Dene to live in hogans or teepees, but it was obvious that the modest structures were simply facades, and that upon closer inspection I was elated to see that portions of the Dene culture *had* survived the transition. It was just tucked neatly within the pseudo-white, plywood quarters, or rambling around on ATVs and disintegrating pickup trucks. Their spirit was strong - how else would they have been able to accomplish such a remarkable revival? Snippets of the ancient tongue and customs that nurtured pleasure and entertainment became more obvious while customs born of survival and of the hunt no longer seemed to apply here, at least in any obvious way. The facets of white culture they had chosen to meld with their own were arbitrary and eclectic. Snowmachines had replaced dog teams once used for caribou hunts and winter travel. Community organized hunting that was once practiced at common caribou crossings, employing the use of "deer" fences, now entails the use of aircraft to transport hunters and their ATVs to a particular site as observed from above. Caribou are quickly rounded up and the harvest is quick and efficient, the animals dispatched, gutted and shipped back with the hunters on the airplane. Fat tundra tires allow the plane to land and take-off on stretches of open tundra.

Overland travel by foot is no longer a consideration. Long gone are the days of trekking along hot, sandy eskers, to bury the dead, and following the caribou along the same sinewy vales. In fact, according to Allan Code, the hunting of caribou had, to some degree, been offset by the hunting of harbour seals. Somewhat of an ecological anomaly, this gregarious marine mammal works its way up the Seal River as far as Tadoule Lake: a distance of over 250 kilometers. The harbour seal, a coastal salt-water creature *(phoca vitulina)* has adapted to the freshwater environment and remains an interesting and little understood deviation from their normal habitat traits. In the spring they migrate up the river feeding on the resident grayling population and the occasional crayfish, returning usually, but not always, to Hudson Bay in the fall before freeze-up. The name of the river affirms this odd occurrence in nature.

Seal meat actually tastes quite wonderful. I knew this from having purchased and eaten it sometime ago while visiting Labrador, before I realised baby seals were to become one of the planet's iconic animals to be saved from extinction. Seal meat has the texture, taste and smell that resembles a gelatinous blend of liver and tuna; not for the bon vivant with a weak stomach. The Tadoule Dene made the occasional foray downriver to Shethanei Lake by boat in search of seals to kill. It's as much a sport to them as it is a cultural morale booster.

It was hard to determine the actual population of Tadoule, or at least the number of registered Dene actually living there. According to Rick Wilson, Natural Resources bureaucrat in Winnipeg, there are 500 people living in the village, relating directly to the number of government cheques issued. Allan claims there were only about 250 to 300 Tadoule Dene. By government standards, unemployment was at a static 90%. It was true that the Dene wanted control of their own resources which could be good news or very bad medicine: good, if they developed an eco-tourism or cultural tourism strategy that catered to guided raft runs on the river, receptive to the growing market of Europeans looking strictly for First Nations village experiences; bad medicine if they had carte blanche and total managerial rights to wild game and hydro-power resources; unless, of course, they were managed with ecological integrity.

It was at that moment during our conversation that Allan and I hit an impasse and although no words were spoken, it was that uncomfortable moment of silence that imparts unease and tension. I was mildly suspicious whenever I encountered native rights activists who espoused "motherland" ownership and resource stewardship, be they white or aboriginal. There are success stories, certainly, but there are also sell-outs and mismanaged lands and waters and deals that have embraced corporate greed and profit. Governments at this time were just beginning to enjoy this strategy of land division because it pitted the environmentalists against native groups. Most city-based eco-mainstreamers who still envision Canada's First Nation people as good stewards still living off the land won't dare touch such a sensitive issue as native land stewardship, even at the cost of despoiled, mismanaged or depleted resources.

Allan was skeptical about our intentions, worried that throngs of Gore-Tex clad adventure seekers and self-provisioned outfitters would flock to Dene-land, should we publish the *Men's Journal Magazine* article.

"I'd like to run my own trips down the Seal," Allan remarked proudly, "and it would be Dene owned and operated."

"I think that's the way it should be," I told Allan. "Most canoeists wouldn't be able to afford the air fare anyway, or have the required skill to run the river, by the sounds of it."

"It sounds like it would be a great river for people just to read about," Hodding added.

"And with the Dene history; maybe something all Canadians should know more about," Russ said.

"Perhaps," Allan agreed, "so long as it was told in the right way."

Allan never showed us disrespect, or made an attempt at dissuading us, nor did he openly criticize our expedition. After all, Allan was one of us; not just white, but also in the media business and he liked the fact that we went out of our way to make an effort at communicating with the Dene Band before setting out downriver. Apparently, as Allan told us, the few canoeists who pass through seldom stop to talk with anyone, seem timorous of any contact at all with the Dene; and the Dene accept this as a direct insult. But then, as I've noticed, people are generally uneasy around native Canadians; they don't know what to say or how to act. Be it guilt or just plain white arrogance, it doesn't help bring the two cultures any closer together.

According to Allan's account, some kayakers had flown in to Tadoule and were making their way quickly down to the lake when they were followed by a rather piqued group of Dene elders. As the whites hurriedly lugged their gear from the airstrip to the beach, amidst a hail of terse words, Dene phrases and wild gestures, the kayakers feared for their life, loaded up quickly and set off down the lake without a word. The elders placed curses over the kayakers as they pulled away from shore. As it turned out, the Dene elders had mistaken the kayakers for their traditional Inuit enemy because of the style of watercraft. In this particular case, white unsociability had little to do with attitude. It was simply a case of mistaken identity and an age-old conflict with an enemy.

Unfortunately it is often like that in the Canadian north for a white visitor, regardless of good intentions or courtesies bestowed or explicit respect. Unless whites have business to attend to, or an obvious need for native services, the welcome mat is sometimes rolled up tight. I can hardly blame them, although when it happens to me I tend to roll with the punches and let it ride, and quite often it works in my favour. Their nature too, sometimes embraces the sublime game of matching wits, making fun of and taunting the "tourist", which in a lot of cases can be mistaken for malicious antagonism when it's simply their instinct to have fun with no harm implied at all. Whites are accustomed to their own cultural communicative gestures. First Nations people have been gifted with an extra sensory perception when it comes to understanding the land and how to communicate their feelings, passion and playful teasing in a non-combative way that is often misunderstood. Still, there is an understandable tension that bleeds through if they feel threatened by white deceit and government rhetoric.

We had the remainder of the day to wander at leisure around the village. Allan said we could stay over for the upcoming sweat-lodge ceremony if we helped to cut the poles required for the teepee. We agreed to help and made plans to stay an additional day in Tadoule. I was nervous about the expedition, about having too much gear, about Dawson and about Hodding and Russell and their lack of experience. In all respects, the conversations so far projected the Seal River as a formidable technical challenge in high water – water that was just above freezing. I felt strongly that without some kind of ceremony we might invoke bad luck; superstitious, yes, I've seen too much over the years not to believe in a greater power.

Tadoule was built on sand, a deep, powdery dust that blew about in mini-storms whenever someone drove by in a truck or ATV. Even if somebody passed by on foot you would be engulfed in a furious, enveloping cloud of particulates that would find their way into every conceivable orifice. I solved part of that problem by wrapping my bandana around my face. Camping on sand was distasteful enough but I had a hard time trying to fathom how these people could enjoy living on it day after day. I supposed that after such long winters, a couple of months of warm, airborne sand was not something to complain about.

As I walked along the main trail that skirted the beach I noticed the smoke rising from the bush fire only a few kilometers north of the village. It was closer. It was also noticeably more intense, broadening, eating up the horizon with its voracious and consuming appetite. It was disconcerting. Thankfully, with the evening calm, the wind would subside and the energy of the wild fire would diminish with it. I walked on.

Most of the vehicles in Tadoule looked as if they had been scrounged from the auto-wreckers in Thompson. No reason to have anything else, given that there were no roads to anywhere except around the village. But there were also some rather new service vehicles such as road graders, and a GMC Jimmy that I had walked by, parked conspicuously on the beach. The government "Indian Affairs" logo was emblazoned on the door panels. Someone had commandeered the truck and then left it on the beach, incapacitated with its wheels buried in the wet muck. Kids had crawled through the open tailgate window and had switched on the headlights so the battery would go dead. The tires were all flattened. It was symbolic.

A huge diesel generator hummed in the distance, powering the isolated community. Satellite dishes scooped in the latest Hollywood gobbledygook; Indian Affairs' answer to the social calamity facing remote reserve towns. There was a small trading post, the "Northern Store" but it was closed for the July 1st weekend. That was also symbolic. I wondered why the Dene would even bother to celebrate such a holiday after Canada's mistreatment of them. But I suppose it was an excuse to shut down the village's singular commerce for the day. No fireworks display had been planned. Instead, the focus was on a traditional sweat-lodge ceremony with the visiting Navajo medicine men.

A convenience store, the size of a department store change-room, sold junk-food and rented movies. Among the few flicks on the shelf I did notice Graham Greene on the cover of *Clear-cut, Indian kicks white man's butt mixed with a sad projection of native mysticism*. I bought a coke and sat on the steps. People moved about appearing to have nothing in particular to do. Other than the store there were no other signs of commerce to be seen. Kids played down by the beach and small groups of adults just hung out, mostly watching us, glancing casually, joking, stealing the odd glare. There was a latent bitterness to the air and it wasn't because of the fire, or the probability of evacuation to Churchill. Ill feelings towards whites ran deep like the esker sands and until we proved ourselves not to be a threat, or blatantly too white, we would be standing on precarious testing ground.

During the evening, after having consumed the wonderful catch-of-the-day with Allan, Mary, the three Navajos, and our crew, I walked alone over to the community centre; a longish, uninteresting plywood shell erected in the middle of the Tadoule dust bowl. There was much activity in and about the entrance, like a bees' nest that senses an intruder. Mounting the steps I passed by shy-faced kids and teenagers who just looked away, any of my "hellos" vanishing into thin air as if not spoken at all. The adults leaned against the porch railings and stared distantly beyond the fringe of the village while others paid no attention at all. Our eyes never met. I walked through the door and for a moment I just stood there, transfixed as if suddenly entering another dimension. I felt stupid, standing at the entrance with my mouth open, realizing that I had just passed through a portal into a different time and it took several seconds to make the decision either to step forward or retreat.

What confronted me was so incongruous to anything I had observed so far that I was more than dumbfounded. Up until now I had seen nothing of Dene culture save for hearing a few scattered phrases in Chipewyan, even then mixed with English. There emerged a sort of prevailing lethargy around the village as if they were waiting for something to happen and I assumed it must have been the approaching fire.

In the community centre I had stumbled into a National

Geographic travelogue. There was no quiet drama taking place here. More human electricity coursed through that room than kilowatts pumped out in the generator shed. I stepped forward slowly while my eyes adjusted to the dullness of the large room.

There was a drum beat and it resonated up through the floor boards and into the soles of my feet and from there it pulsed someplace deeper, perhaps into my soul. And it wasn't the raucous thrashing of a rock band, or the improv ramblings of a jazz quartet, but the steady, rhythmic and spirited tempo of the Dene handgame drum. The energy inside that room was communicable and potent. It drew you in as if by some magic trance, like stepping closer to the edge of the precipice to get a better look, a little nervous but hypnotized by the alluring curiosity.

There were at least two dozen men playing at one of the oldest gambling games, "odzee", or simply *handgame*. A square piece of carpet had been laid out on the floor upon which several of the men were now sitting in an oval; two groups opposing, facing each other sitting cross-legged. These were the players. Only men were allowed to play handgames. At a table near the entrance of the hall, some distance from the game, sat a bevy of women working earnestly on various quilts and garments and crafts, talking amongst themselves and paying little attention to the men's gambling enterprise. It was a certainty, though, that the exuberance of the handgame players' antics, charged by the drum music, breathed more than just a little smoke into their own engines.

Handgames, an ancient Dene gambling competition, was as old as the very metavolcanic soil upon which the village stood. Bets for money were modest; not like the old days when one tribe would play another, betting precious personal belongings, weapons, and even dog teams. Back then, up to forty players or more would start betting everything they owned, and sometimes the game would last several days, the men stopping only for brief moments to eat or relieve themselves.

Odzee is initiated by two people who determine which side will go first. The players take an object small enough to hide in the hand – a piece of bone, a cartridge shell or a small stick and then put both hands behind their backs. The closed hands are then displayed in front again, hiding the object in one hand. Both players attempt to guess in which hand the object was concealed. The one who guesses wrong forfeits the chance for his side to begin the game. The game now begins and the drum beats a fast tempo, usually in pace with the player who has the floor. On one side three men squat while a small object is passed around between them, concealed from view but held tightly in the fist. Players often flip the object into the air, wave their hands wildly, hide their fists under their coats, tuck them under their armpits, or pound them on the floor for effect. All the while the drum is beating out a steady charge, keeping up a pulse affixed to the men's rising energy; and the opposing team, some standing, exchange up to thirty hand gestures to signal the whereabouts of the hidden object until guessed. Points are counted on a wooden board, holes drilled to accept several pointed sticks used as markers. There is little pause between guessing episodes and hardly a drum beat is missed as the turn passes. I was caught up in the energy myself. Drawing nearer I found a spot to sit just beyond the thick ring of spectators.

The drum is one of the world's oldest and most widely used percussion instrument. Many aboriginal people refer to drumming as the "heartbeat of the earth". Science tells us that the electromagnetic resonance frequency of the earth is, in fact, tuned into the same frequency range as the drum beat used to induce shamanic trances – at 7.5 cycles per second. Drumming aligns brain waves naturally with the pulse of the earth. Drum beat frequencies are produced in the alpha and theta ranges, in contrast to the beta waves characteristic of ordinary conscious- ness. Pulses increase in the right hemisphere of the brain: that portion of grey-matter devoted to creativity, lucid imagery and states of ecstasy. Drums used other than those used for sha- manic trance work still induce a higher plane of consciousness and excitement and, because drum beats are of low frequency, it means that more energy can be transmitted to the brain than those of higher frequencies. This is possible due to the ability of the low frequency receptors of the ear to resist damage, un- like the delicate high frequency receptors that trigger pain rather quickly. Drumming does produce changes in the central nervous system and that rhythmic stimulation directly affects the electri- cal activity within the multitude of sensory and motor receptors of the cerebral mass, not ordinarily affected otherwise. The way this works is due, in part, to the fact that the solitary beat of a drum contains many sound frequencies and accordingly it simul- taneously transmits impulses along a variety of nerve pathways in the brain. The drum beat in the Dene handgame activated both nervous and creative energy and those not directly partici- pating in the game were also drawn into the "trance". I was taken in completely by the magic of it, science aside.

It was up to the gallery of onlookers to motivate the players, somewhat like the spectators at a hockey game; a low energy crowd, or poor drummer, could render a mediocre game action. That wasn't the case here. I felt like an intruder though; a tour- ist, and not by any other notion but my own paranoia about cultural separation. I felt embarrassed about taking a couple of photographs. I wanted to join in on the game and be a part of the laughter, but they were in their own element, their own world; an old world, untouchable, unmoveable, proud. I closed my eyes and allowed the drum beat to whisk me away to another dimension; the obscurity helped to move my soul just a little closer to the people in the room, and there was finally a great comfort in the semi-darkness and I no longer felt alone. Soon enough, other spectators joined the milieu and I was enveloped within the folds of people, sharing a moment in their pleasure.

*   *   *   *   *

Early the next morning, Allan took us to meet Geoff Bussidor. Geoff looked more French-Canadian than Dene, was soft-spoken, hard-working and was held in high esteem as a leader in Tadoule. Geoff would soon be Chief of the Tadoule Band. He was to meet Hodding, Allan and myself across the lake where we would cut several twenty-five foot spruce poles for the sweat-lodge while Dawson and Russell were to peel off the bark once we brought the poles back to Tadoule. As we pulled away from shore in the boat and headed south across the lake we could see the immensity of the fire directly behind the village. Billowing plumes of grey-black smoke consumed the entire horizon, like an incoming storm of gargantuan proportion. Luckily, the smoke did not settle over the landscape but rose skyward, thousands of feet into the air and levelled off as if pushed against a ceiling and trailed off eastward and safely away from the village.

"Things could change quickly," Allan barked over the sound of the outboard, "there's been talk of evacuating the elders and children." Even so, many of the villagers were reluctant to go, or even to talk about leaving. The last place on earth some of them ever wanted to revisit was Churchill. There were still lingering memories of the Dene shack-town.

We had the poles cut and hauled out of the thick spruce bush in short order and loaded them into Geoff's boat. The sweat-lodge ceremony was planned to go on through the night.

There was even talk of peyote being passed around to help speed up trances. Unfortunately, the encroaching fire would put it off all together. The government had evacuated sixty elders and children that afternoon and had them flown to Churchill, three-hundred kilometers to the east. We sat in Geoff's kitchen waiting for him to come up from the landing. The coffee in Geoff's percolator sat on his propane stove and was boiling down to thick oil. I took the liberty of turning the heat down to a simmer. When Geoff walked in he immediately wondered who had tampered with his coffee pot and cranked the brew up to a vigorous boil.

"Anyone want coffee?" Geoff beamed. We all said yes. I asked if he had any cream and sugar and everyone stared at me as if I had just cursed God. I drank the coffee, black as sin and bitter.

I asked Geoff if it was alright to have gone into the community centre to watch the handgames and take a few pictures. "Sure," he said, "nobody really minds. Sometimes Germans come here and that's all they do, so they're used to it." That put me at great ease, at least in my own head space. We talked briefly about the fire, about our planned trip down the river and we listened intently to some of their own stories about life in Tadoule, government screw-ups (a most popular topic), and about the future.

"What about Hudson Bay?" Allan asked, "What do you plan to do when you get there?"

"We've made arrangements for Jackie Bastone to pick us up in his barge," I paused mid-sentence, "and if we hit the Bay early we might just try to sail down the coast."

Allan and Geoff gave us the *Holy Shit* response that we could have done without and, like Tom Ellis back in Thompson, they related the story about those who had died trying to cross

Button Bay, trying to reach Churchill. We thanked them for their advice. *Were they selling us short,* I wondered? Maybe they thought we were too full of bravado and not enough common sense. We were after all, southerners. They didn't know my qualifications, or Dawson's and they knew the two Americans had never done any whitewater paddling at all. It all stacked up, and not in our favour. Added to the stew pot of doubt was a forest fire that loomed over the village.

The rest of the day carried no commitments so the four of us decided to further explore the village. We met several captivating individuals whose lives portrayed the intensity of the remote lifestyle and the harsh environment. There was young Clayton whose father had been shot by a Band council-member in a drunken brawl. Most of his father's left forearm had been blown clean away by a shotgun blast at close range. Caroline, one of the still remaining elders who refused to leave, made the most beautiful tanned moccasins while her husband illustrated them with ornate beadwork. She did not speak English but I was able to communicate the notion of purchasing a pair of moccasins for a friend back home. She smiled a toothless grin at my hand gestures, probably thinking I'd be a good contestant at the handgames; Caroline nodded and confirmed the sale with a happy nod.

Roger, the village constable, kept a rag-tag team of huskies out the back of his house, all in various degrees of summer mange, panting in the afternoon sun, most of them friendly. And then there were those with attitudes, probably lead dogs who had gone the distance, fought the fights and couldn't give a rat's ass about a pat on the back of the neck. Roger patrolled Tadoule at night on his ATV and sold joints to anyone who was willing to pay the price. Dawson hung back and bought five cigarettes for fifty-dollars using company reserve funds. I was able to find out a few days later after I asked him where he picked up the smokes.

Tadoule was a "dry" village, but like most other liquor-free reserve towns there was always local hooch available, along with an assortment of drugs. Most of the people we met were generally friendly, some withdrawn, and others just avoided us. We walked the long esker that snaked north from the village toward the oncoming fire and came upon the town's cemetery. A white picket fence identified the perimeter of the graveyard, with several lesser pickets framing individual plots inside the boundary. It was alarming how large the cemetery was for such a short history of human occupation at Tadoule. Many of the graves were adorned with plastic flowers and gifts. Some plots looked fresh as if just interned. Three Dene were making a tobacco offering to one of the deceased. I stayed back in a show of respect but Dawson barged right in and started chatting them up. They were visibly pissed and told him to fuck off and in no uncertain terms. He just shook his head in disbelief and retreated, muttering "what's their problem?" I walked the other way, eventually teaming up with Hodding.

Evening came, which looked no different from the day as a smoke haze had obscured the daylight. I was trying to organize a private ceremony with the Navajo medicine men and it was getting late. Russell and Dawson were nowhere to be found. Carter and I loitered for a while at the community centre where the men were once again playing handgames and the women played cards at their table near the door. We had hoped Dawson and Russell would show up but they never did so the two of us went down to look for the village guest cabin near the lake edge where the medicine men were lodging.

It was starting to get dark, where, in Tadoule, 10:00 pm is gloaming twilight. The nighthawks had begun their perfunctory dances upon the evening thermals. The guest cabin was easy to find. It was dark inside. There were no lights on but I could hear voices, white voices, which was odd because the Navajos rarely spoke English and never amongst themselves. I was nervous about disrupting a ceremony that might be taking place inside; I paused briefly then knocked quietly on the door. No answer. I knocked harder. Finally, one of the shamans opened the door about a foot. I could see that the T.V. was on; the film *Robin Hood, Men in Tights* was playing. I thought, okay, they're entitled to white-man technology and entertainment. Laughing to myself, I thought they could have picked a more inspiring movie.

I told them what we wanted, and was invited in. The movie was put on pause. More specifically, I asked if we could have a ceremony for safe passage down the river, for the four of us, including the two who were absent. I handed the healer two pouches of Borkum Riff tobacco and sixty-dollars. Two of the Navajos left the room while the remaining healer instructed us to sit on the floor, cross-legged. In broken English he told us to clear our minds of any thought. He left the room for a few moments and returned carrying a beautiful ornate box full of shaman paraphernalia used in ceremonial work: stones, eagle feathers, beaded ornaments, sprigs of sweet-grass and smudge-sticks of sage and cedar. He sat across from us, placed a Styrofoam cup full of river water on the floor, lit the sweet-grass and fanned the smoke over the water and around us. I closed my eyes like I did during the handgames and inhaled the fragrant smoke. I drifted away. I could see the fire and the sky was red, as if all the heavens were bleeding but the only sound was that of the river and the soft chanting of the Navajo healer, sweet and lovely. When the medicine man stopped singing, he asked us to drink the river water, saving just enough for Dawson and Russell. In order to complete the ceremony, we were to search for the others and make sure they drank from the cup. If we didn't then the blessing meant nothing.

Hodding and I thanked the healers and left with the sancti-fied cup of water, relieved and somewhat intoxicated after the supplication and then spent the next hour trying to track down the others, walking around the village with a coffee cup half-filled with spirit water. By the time we located Dawson he was already high as a kite and he would have drunk his own piss let alone water that had been blessed by a Navajo shaman.

We spent the final night camped near the remainders of the old sweat-lodge. Our surroundings never attained the full gloom of night until well past midnight, and then it was only dark for a very short time. The others went to bed while I stayed up to reorganize the gear and dump out the gallon of 'cellar-cask' wine that Dawson had smuggled along for the trip, then retired to my own tent to write in my exploration journal.

I thought about the environment here, so much different from what I was accustomed to. It was harsh, cruel almost, the biting flies unbearable at times; and the winters, I supposed, would be unbearably long. Tom Ellis had commented about the winter, remarking that the last snowfall of the year was July 8th, and the first, July 9th! It was truly the land that God forgot; a land of extremes and endless vistas. There was nothing to the north of us but a vast wilderness that crossed the open tundra bleakness, across the north pole into deep Siberia.

I contemplated the resignation of the Dene, their peace of mind, and whether or not they were happier now than they were before the European invasion. Certainly, technology had vaulted them, in such a short span of time, from primitive Shield Archaic people to modern Indian. The answer danced uncertainly in my mind. There was no starvation, no need for the tiresome hunt, but yet something was missing from their lives and I knew that social conditions amongst the Dene spawned a sort of apathy.

The suicide rate was high. There were abuse and drug problems.

I tried hard to fall asleep but I was exhausted. I couldn't tell if it was blowing sand hitting the side of the tent or the relentless wave of mosquitoes caught under the rain fly. There were too many questions going through my head; too many thoughts about the Dene Nation, the expedition and Dawson's unpredictable nature. Despite the odds and the circumstances, the Dene are an impressive people: physically athletic, good humoured and generally welcoming. It was interesting to note how the Canadian environment defined them, linguistically and physically; dissimilar from other First Nations in different ways – skin colour, stature, demeanor.

My sleeping bag suddenly seemed claustrophobic. I threw it open and realized that I was sweating, anxious and fully awake. I tried writing in my journal by flashlight but couldn't concentrate; other considerations clouded my train of thought. It was the snoring coming from the other tent, that pervasive irritant that finally forced a fitful sleep.

Chapter Five

Initiation

I slept poorly that last night in Tadoule. There was a nagging angst that even the Navajo ceremony could not delete from the bank of concerns I had about the trip, mostly about whether or not I'd be able to get all the gear properly and safely stowed in the canoes. The fact that Dawson missed the ceremony may have been an omen of bad luck. I tried not to think about it. Instead, I made my mind up to initiate another ceremony of our own later on down the river at the first opportune time.

When morning finally arrived, the dread had washed away and we all busied ourselves by carrying the gear and canoes the short distance to a small beach landing on the lake in front of Allan's house. The resultant heap of packs, camera equipment and wannigans seemed too much for the two canoes. Whether it would all fit into the two boats was the impending fear that had kept me awake for most of the night. Now it was staring me in the face.

Allan watched us pack. I could tell by the look on his face that he held some doubts about this expedition. The wind was building fast and it didn't favour our direction and it was a very large lake. Allan was a sailor and he knew a lot about winds and freeboard. In fact, Allan felt obliged to follow us across Tadoule Lake in his pointer – a customized sailing craft he had shipped to Tadoule for his own pleasure. It was comforting to know that he would be riding the waves with us for the first leg of the trip. Whether Allan was just curious, concerned, or simply enjoyed the company of visiting non-native folk I wasn't entirely sure. Maybe he was a bit envious too and wanted to be a small part of the adventure.

Packing; it's a venerable art and not as easy as one might think, certainly not at all like shoving groceries in a grocery bag or packing a suitcase. Doing it well requires a trained eye in order to maximize the minimum allotment of space available. Weight has to be low and packs flush with the gunwale line so that the spray-skirts can be fastened down neatly. Then the load has to be balanced from bow to stern with a slight rise in the front to break the waves and keep the canoe from ploughing awkwardly through the water and impossible to steer. Russell had at least twenty extra pounds on me so that also had to be taken into consideration. Weight also has to be equal obliquely to avoid leaning to one side. Never in my life on the trail had that art been so taxed as it was that first morning on the shore of Tadoule Lake. When finished, each canoe was maxed out with only about four inches of freeboard – the bare minimum space between deathly cold water and the top of the gunwale. With much stretching and coercing, our nylon spray-covers reluctantly cooperated although Dawson's and Hodding's cover wouldn't stretch over the huge Keewaydin camp wannigan and Dawson's second personal pack. I suggested that they fasten down the one side only and keep the partly open side to the lee of the wind while crossing the lake. Dawson's second pack was foot-jammed into the cavity behind his stern seat. Although our deck was fully secure we were still riding lower in the water than the other canoe because of the weight of the extra camera equipment. We were pushing the limit, something I tried to avoid; wearing wet suits helped ease some of the nervousness about the cold water factor; still, it was a massive lake with expansive crossings to make.

We were about to push off into unknown territory, on a river that was not particularly forgiving, and here was a city-bred and pampered photographer sitting in the bow of my canoe with such a look of despair and worry that anything I could have said could not craft a smile on his face. After all, everything Russell had heard up to this point had been full of proper wilderness rhetoric and "don't do" scenarios. It was little wonder that he was over-conscious of his own abilities, knowing that he had never done anything like this before.

Hodding, though, looked comfortable and eager to get the adventure started while Dawson had that 'not-a-care-in-the-world' posture. I was worried that I was wearing my own misgivings on my sleeve and that Russell was picking up on them. Similarly, I had flown with bush pilots who, upon knowing we were in some sort of predicament, blatantly showed distress on their face, would lean forward and grip the controls a little tighter. I could pick up on this right away; anyone adept at reading non-verbal expressions would see this as well. I may have been doing this with Russell, although I was pretty good at masking my own trepidations; the NO FEAR face in front of clients who always expect the guide to be stalwart and dauntless. Even so, I was still worried, more about the fragile nature of Dawson's personality and whether or not he could be relied on if our canoe was upset, or if either Russell or I needed help or rescue. Dawson's job as assistant guide was somewhat like a co-pilot or first mate on a ship: to assist if the leader was incapacitated. To assist was imperative. I pulled a small wad of tobacco from my day-pack and dropped it into Tadoule Lake, took a deep breath then pushed us out into the waves and wind of the fierce lake.

It was a fifteen kilometer open lake paddle to the mouth of the Seal River in rough water. We paddled south-east across Thaynuaytoway Bay, away from Tadoule village, away from the encroaching fire that spewed smoke into the morning sky, and steered towards a group of islands where we could benefit from shelter against the wind. It took some effort to get there and progress was measured in inches as Tadoule village didn't seem to be getting any further away than when we first started. Reaching the islands, already exhausted, they offered only momentary respite from the turbulent wind; and the waves now began to roll and break. We rested behind the islands, each of us taking a pull from our water bottles. The ice cold water seared my throat. *Shit, that water IS cold*, I thought. Back at my cabin in Temagami, hundreds of kilometres to the south, we would have been swimming already for several weeks.

Dashing from island to island we made slow headway, edging eastward into the open breadth of Tadoule Lake, headed to a distant point where I could see the waves dashing against the boulders along the shore. Sandy Clipping was a resident of Tadoule. He was notable enough to have a point of land bequeathed to his honour, and it was at this ominous jut of rock that the full fury of the wind was unleashed and the full expanse of the lake gave no resistance to the turbulence that held our canoes stationary to that place as if suspended, languishing, while Clipping's ghost probably mocked us from shore. Paddling was almost futile, trying to keep up such a vigil was a losing struggle, but there were no kind places to beach our canoes so we persevered until every muscle fiber cried for rest.

"Short, fast strokes!" I yelled at Russell, "And keep your head low, into the wind and paddle hard; we can ride it through!"

Then, almost as if Moses himself parted the Sea before us, there was a break in the wind and we surged ahead, cruised around the point with the tempest now at our starboard side and out of our faces. There was no time to rest. Paddles remaining in the water for balance, we did manage to ease up on our stroke and hit a more comfortable rhythm, changing paddling sides often to proffer a break for strained muscles - muscles that would surely ache that night.

Tadoule Lake was over twenty-five kilometers from north to south and it was a savings grace that we were now only subject to paddling about a third of that breadth of stormy water as we continued our track east and north towards the outlet. Allan Code followed faithfully in his pointer. He must have been curious and, I think now, that he was somewhat impressed by the seaworthiness of our decked canoes; such small, insignificant crafts for such wild roving yet managing quite respectfully.

Allan had been considering running trips down the Seal River, but he wouldn't outfit with canoes. "Too dangerous," he said scornfully. "I'd use zodiacs with motors or river rafts, like the ones they run on the Colorado River. Boats that are more suited to the big rapids." He was definitely a boat aficionado, perhaps uncomfortable in a canoe. He kept his distance from us, about half a kilometer away as he tacked his boat upwind, back and forth, neatly and expertly driven as the small sail was tailored to catch each breath of wind, and the boat would surge ahead, reach a final point, almost faltering, then he would change direction again and start a new tack.

For us it was rough muscle work, tedious yet exhilarating. Each wave had to be acknowledged, measured for size and how it would funnel into the side of the canoe. The three-foot waves impacted the canoes at a 45 degree angle. This required a roll of the hips with each swell and then a quick rebalance conversely with every upper body ply on the paddle. One wrong movement or break in cognizance of wave pattern could easily swamp the canoe. But Russell did amazingly well for a Brooklyn greenhorn, and he kept his balanced rhythm that beat to the timely music of the waves – a water dance, fluid movements. He had a natural sense for body movements, to allow the hips and lower body to stay aligned with the canoe while the upper torso maintained a vertical pose, keeping up a steady pace, like a metronome guiding the debutant piano player to keep the right tempo. A lot of my concerns about his ability and our general safety had dissolved by the hour as the day slipped by. I had many clients over the years who could never adjust; unfamiliar with their own body movements or simply lacking the upper body strength to wield a paddle comfortably. It was a pleasure to have Russell in the bow of my canoe; whether his balanced efficiency was due to body language or plain fear I didn't care. It was far less work for me in the stern if my partner was comfortable in the canoe. And from the stern I could feel every vibration or misguided impulse that my bow paddler made. The canoe reacts to the paddler's every nuance, whether it was a good move or not, and Russ made very few wrong moves. It was a true blessing.

There was little commentary between Russell and me. No dialogue to interrupt the composition of motion which, in a meditative way, was rapturously dangerous. The human voice could have broken the spell. Russell may have had his own reasons for being quiet. I don't think he had quite reached the blissful state that I was in because he was intent on learning the skills quickly for his own survival. He had yet to feel comfortable with Dawson or me, his guides through this, strangers really, who in a huge way controlled his fate. Russell may have been thinking about what I had conferred with him that morning upon our departure.

"The water is bone-cracking cold from here to the Bay," I said sternly. "If you fall in, or if we swamp we may have only minutes to save ourselves, to get out and get warm." Russell listened as a first-time parachutist listens to his coach before the jump.

"With the wet suits on we have a little more time," I said, "but not much. And if we did reach the shore we may not have the strength or agility to even get a fire going. I know, I've been there." Russell raised his eyebrows. I would have left it off there but he wanted to know what had happened and implored me to go on. "A couple of times," I told him, "years ago when I was foolish and young, I almost died. I do things more carefully now so don't worry." I wouldn't tell him the story, not that day anyway. Not on his first day out, for his sake.

My partner grasped the seriousness of the inherent dangers of extreme paddling in the far north. Allan had added his own anecdotal historical drama by extolling the story of two canoeists who had lost their canoe in the rapids along the Seal River and had to wait over a month to be rescued. That said a lot about how much traffic there was along the river. It is also a well-known and practiced tenet of expedition survival to travel in canoe parties of three canoes; if one canoe is destroyed through miscalculation, the remaining two canoes can be tripled up and the expedition completed, albeit a little heavier and awkward. I've solo paddled many times on challenging rivers but have always calculated my odds of survival carefully.

"Fear," said Edmund Burke, the great British statesman, "is the mother of all safety." And safety was foremost on Russell's mind and on my own, of course, although I was in a comfort zone only because of my experience. I was more prepared than he was for what might lay ahead. Fear *was* an integral component of whitewater canoeing, although at times it is difficult to

85

delineate between it and sheer, ball-breaking bravado, driven by adrenalin, mixed congenially with trepidation and, hopefully, all commandeered by common sense and caution.

The thought and fear of an icy death in frigid arctic bound water, for any of us, did keep the senses alert; enough so that we could transform danger into fun, and fear into controlled and enthusiastic waterplay. I could feel Russell gaining confidence each hour that we paddled. He began to relax into his strokes, the rigid and anxious novice actually enjoying the ride as the canoe rode high on the crests of the waves and surfed through the following troughs.

We paralleled the boulder shore as best we could, for safety and the comfort of knowing that if we did roll we could still get to land in time to save our necks. Dawson though, was oblivious of the potential risk and steered his canoe even farther out into heavy waves. As guide for the expedition it was up to me to set the pace and chart the safest route; Dawson already broke the golden rule by not complying with safe distance procedures and keeping tight together as a unit. This is a critical rule whenever tackling dangerous waters. Later, I made a point of telling him about the danger of separation but he just looked stunned and puzzled as to why I should even bring up the matter. "I know what I'm doing," was all he said.

After four hours of battling the headwind for fourteen kilometers we decided to regale ourselves with a much needed reprieve from the elements and retreated behind a small island for a lunch stop. A bedrock shelf made the perfect picnic table. As we set about slicing up our bread and salami, Allan pulled in with his pointer and gave us an eight-pound lake trout. "For your dinner tonight in Dene land," he said smiling, tossing the fish onto the slab of rock beside us.

We shared our lunch with Allan but he ended up gifting us

with what he had brought with him in the sailboat. I had the feeling that, although impressed with our paddling so far, Allan knew that we still had to contend with what lay ahead, much of which he himself was not that familiar. He had made his way down the river a couple of years before with the Canada Parks crew on a survey mission but they travelled in motorized rafts, not canoes. Canoes are far less stable than rafts and require deft moves to avoid rocks in fast water; zodiacs could easily bounce off or over rocks without undue concern. He wished us good luck and headed back to Tadoule with the wind at his back, where he would have to deal with the impending evacuations, the approaching fires and moving *his* people to Churchill.

The relief of the lake remained unelevated, almost withdrawn. The lichen-encrusted, rocky shoreline to the south, both scabrous and burned-over, remained strangely studded with dejected clumps of spruce struggling to maintain an identity, the vista giving prominence to the supremacy of the lake across which we struggled slowly. Remaining close to the north shore we edged closer to the Seal River mouth, the lake gradually narrowing to less than half a kilometer. Even at such a great distance from the river we began feeling its pull, like gravity drawing us downward, initiating the beginning of the almost one-thousand foot descent to Hudson Bay and the Arctic Ocean.

The Seal, after all, was Manitoba's fourth largest river, absorbing ground-water from an immense boreal sponge 44,300 square kilometers in dimension. Consulting firms, contracted by Manitoba Hydro as early as 1955, had already identified at least nine sites along the river which were suitable for hydro-electric power and dam construction. In 1965 Manitoba Hydro began studying the possibility of diverting the Seal River south into the already stultified Nelson River. Plans were on hold pending future demands for power.

The actual mouth of the river was over 600 meters wide. That immediately upgraded the Seal as an exceptionally potent whitewater river. Hydrology reports had gauged the outflow of the river during spring run as high as 800m/3 second – an incredible discharge comparable to the largest rivers in North America. Almost all of the rivers in the Ontario and Quebec Shield regions that I had been paddling for many years only averaged a late spring flow of between 75 to 100m/3 second flow discharge – considerably smaller than what we found ourselves in now. The lower Shield rivers were typically "pool and drop" type, having short and sometimes abrupt plunges through rapids and chutes that could be portaged around if necessary. I had the feeling that the Seal River was going to be a lot different.

The melt-water flow had just peaked two weeks earlier in June but the water levels indicated that the spillover had only now begun to recede. The high flow had all but drowned out the first rapids. Boulders, polished white by the elements, inches below our canoe flashed by at an alarming speed. Although paddling just slightly faster than the spirals of foam drifting around the canoe, our pace was deceiving, noted by watching either the river bottom rocks or the shoreline which indicated an actual speed of over ten knots. Knots are calculated at nearly 2 kilometers for every knot of speed; we were travelling at a river speed of twenty kilometers per hour!

It is here, at the onset, where the river – *any river* – dips its hat to the landscape and the water takes on a new dance, when you first realize the temperament and character of your host, its power so absolute, its superiority something to humble yourself before. The first rapid, the draw of the current, was more of a warning. Our canoe suddenly felt inordinately small, precariously tippy, sluggish and ultimately vulnerable. The dynamics had changed from surface waves to deep, voluminous undercurrents, boils and crosscurrents. It is usually at the first rapids where overconfident paddlers run into trouble.

The understanding of pushing a craft through moving water transcends the science of hydrology, mathematical compliance to *volume versus gravity* theories, and the presumed logic illustrated in "how-to" books. It requires more than just the basic skills. The technical aspect of running a river delves into the psychology of self-limitation – the parameters we set for ourselves in any life-threatening situation. It is now believed that those people seeking "extreme" adventure and high-risk sport may actually possess a genetically processed *extreme gene* that serves as a constant stimulus and motivational energizer. Many outdoor extremists, including notable wilderness guides, rock climbers or whitewaterists, have perished because of their insatiable need to "one-better" even themselves until the risk is so great, the odds so perilously stacked, that temptation and bravado overrides all sensibilities. It boils down to ego. Elevating oneself above the laws of nature, defying the relativity of gravity or the force and fury of moving water against rocks; a combatant mental affliction that sees nature as an opponent, something to conquer, just doesn't work at all. Chances are then taken and a false sense of complacency opens a devilish window to the winds of fate. It's like driving at a high speed along the busy interstate, then trying to text on your phone while balancing your lunch on your lap.

Knowing when to listen to that little voice of sobriety, the mercurial strands of reason, sometimes eludes even the most adept and humble outdoors person. On an expedition, the wilderness guide typically calls the shots, thinks for everyone when issues arise, and all participants rely on that expertise and diplomacy. Whole parties have perished, miserably, because of the ineptitude of the guide whose ego rubs shoulders with the devil.

A case in point took place when I was a park ranger in

Temagami, Ontario, in the 1970s; decades later, still, the mishap resounds within the canoeing fraternity. I did share this story with our crew, but many days later when we all became more familiar with the character of the river. St. John's School, founded in 1977, believed in pushing their students to limits through ordeal and corporal punishment. On June 11th, 1978, twelve students and one volunteer succumbed to hypothermia while attempting to canoe across the Ottawa River in heavy winds. Inexperience, bad judgement, and overloaded canoes all contributed to multiple capsizing in the middle of a river notorious for taking lives. Because the Ottawa River is such a deep water body, temperatures remain cold throughout the summer. Only a few survived this tragedy. And it was misadventures like these that I experienced at close hand, floating around constantly in the back of my mind that reminded me of my great respect for cold water.

*James Raffan, writes about this in his book *Deep Water, Courage, Character and the Lake Timiskaming [Ottawa River] Canoeing Tragedy*.

Once we hit the river Russell noticed the changes right away and shifted nervously, resting his paddle on the gunwale of the canoe. "Keep your paddle in the water," I instructed and took a few deep breaths as I shifted my own weight lower, spreading my knees on the pads I had glued to the hull bottom. I told Russell to do the same. I took the moment to explain to Russell about the *how-to's* of running heavy current using the paddles as motion "outriggers", which would act as lateral stabilizers. He caught on quickly, moving downstream more relaxed and in tune with the flow of the river.

The middle course of the Seal erupted into larger waves and growing haystacks – the stationary waves that break up and spread at the top like stacks of hay. These were avoided by running close to shore, a practice we would employ for the better part of the river. During high water the bulk of the flow pulls away from the shores and funnels down the center causing much larger waves. The shores being flooded are often unnavigable during low water, studded with rocks, ledges and sweepers (fallen trees) but now can be paddled with apparent ease. I explained to Russell about ferrying, both up and downstream; a rather complex manoeuvre to teach to him at such an early stage just when he was getting comfortable with balance and forward stroke.

Ferrying is the technical procedure applied for moving the canoe laterally in current, used to avoid ledges, boulders or other obstructions that loom ahead, or when you need to get the hell off the river quickly. It's a little unnerving for the paddler in the bow because the execution of a downstream ferry usually points the bow of the canoe in the direction you don't want to go, compensated by a series of strong backwater and drawing strokes. Conversely, for the upstream ferry it is a quick succession of powerful forward thrusts and draws that take you out of harm's way efficiently, most of the time. Angling the canoe so that the downstream current hits the hull, beautifully and almost effortlessly propels the craft in the direction you want to go. A lot of inexperienced paddlers depend on forward speed to get them out of tight situations and ditch the ferry completely, often driving themselves over drop-offs or ramming up on rocks, getting into all sorts of trouble. If there is ever a time to finesse anything, it's on the river, in the rapids.

Russell caught on quickly, not just the skill of the maneuver but to the actual movement of the body, applying just enough weight and effort to be able to command his end of the canoe with almost expert precision. I could visibly see the stiffness and insecurity draining away from his actions and I began to feel more at ease. I could now spend less time overseeing his paddling ability and concentrate on the surroundings, write in my journal, take photographs as we drifted along.

"I think I'm getting it," Russ said excitedly.

"You are Russ, and doing a fine job I might add. I've had a lot of clients who claimed to be good paddlers and they weren't at all; and that makes more work for me trying to correct them all the time when they keep going back to their old habits."

"It feels good, my stroke...I'm more relaxed now, not so nervous," Russell beamed.

"I can tell. When you're relaxed I can relax then too, less work for me." I said.

It had been a rough first day, as first days often are when you have fresh paddlers, a heavy load and harsh conditions. We were all wind-beat and tired. Ferrying over to the east shore we headed where it looked somewhat hospitable enough to set up camp just as it started to rain. Tents were thrown up wherever there was a flat, well-drained site and the 12X12 kitchen fly was suspended directly over a quickly constructed fire-pit. The patter of rain on the tarp and the crackle of friendly fire played harmony to the rush of the river; we sat in primitive comfort, feasting on a chicken stir-fry, chatting about the day and going over the maps, planning how far we would go tomorrow.

"You guys were awesome today," I remarked, wanting to let Hodding and Russ know that they did well on their first day out.

"I think I got the hang of it," Russ kept congratulating himself. "It took a while at first and I was stiff and awkward and I was getting tired."

"Yeah, it's not until you relax into your stroke, time it with your breathing too, then you won't get so tired," I remarked to Russ. Hodding and Dawson were having a smoke by the fire but were listening in.

"I couldn't believe how fast we were moving when we hit the river," Hodding said, cocking his head to face Russ. "It was pretty cool...felt like the paddle didn't do anything and it was the river that picked us up and tossed us along."

Dawson flicked his cigarette butt into the fire, smiled but said nothing.

"I have a feeling the river is going to get a little more challenging," I assumed, and that remark livened up the conversation.

"How so?" Russell asked with a hint of foreboding.

"It was mostly current today and I checked the contour drop on the topo map and the drop wasn't significant," I explained, pulling out my map case to show everyone. Every contour line on a topographic map signifies a drop of fifty feet and we hadn't even crossed a contour yet.

"Shit, you're kidding," Russ whispered, staring hard at the map where the Seal River leaves Tadoule Lake.

"Bigger stuff coming up, for sure, once we start crossing the contours," I added.

"That's fucking great," Hodding beamed. "I can't wait." He was obviously in a different state of mind than Russell. I liked Hodding's zeal for paddling but was worried about his personal level of caution.

"Well, Hod, we're going to get a good dose of heavy rapid running tomorrow by the look of it," I announced, knowing everyone was listening intently, eyes still wide with the days' events. I didn't share my own anxiousness about the river; not at that time, yet, as I didn't know enough about what was ahead. My gut told me that we hadn't seen the full power of the Seal yet; and if most people travelled the river in motorized zodiacs, we had to have our wits about us if we were going to get down without incident.

*   *   *   *   *

The vague twilight of late evening settled over the ravaged boreal plain, burned by recent fires and left barren save for charred
stumps and scorched glacial erratic boulders. It resembled a
post-apocalyptic scene: eerily impotent and final. It had to be a fire
from the year before; there was little in the way of new growth.
Cloudberries should have been plentiful here, just beginning to
grow out of the rich sphagnum hummocks; their raspberry-like
fruit tasting more like the local bake-apples, a generous yield of
fruit that is sometimes collected by the resident Dene children.
Instead, there was a desolate and lifeless landscape made even
drearier by the darkened skies and cold rain. I was tired. We were
all tired and conversation laboured into yawns.

   I slept alone, which was my custom as guide, choosing to
pitch my tent some distance from the others who were grouped
in a large base-camp tent pitched nearer the fire-pit area. I enjoyed the end of the day privacy; my quiet time, sanctuary where
I could write in my journal by candle-light, reflect on the day and
make plans for the next. The first day was gruelling but had gone
off remarkably well. There were no incidents. Dawson seemed
to float along in his own world. Hodding was his captive audience for his incessant ramblings and philosophical rants. Around
the campsite Dawson excelled; he loved to cook and was rather
adept at detailing even simple fare. I thought that he would have
made a far better chef than wilderness guide. Beyond the kitchen
wannigan there was little else to commend him for. Although he
liked to prepare food, he already prodded me to give him more
liberty to change up the prescribed menu and to dip into items
typically saved for later on when they would be more appreciated. I did honestly try to excise any negative feelings I carried,
knowing well that after time they would affect the general mood

of the expedition. I had applauded the newcomers for their growing skills, commendations all around for everyone's hard work and initiated a grand evening toast to coming adventures around the next bend in the river. Our introduction to the Seal River was not yet complete; I knew that Sheth-tie-eye-desay had more in store for us.

*   *   *   *   *

It rained all night; not in torrents, but in gentle, constant waves, like the timed breaking of the sea surf in a protected bay. My dreams were sporadic and sleep did not come easily. Darkness was transient, hovering briefly like a cloud passing by the sun on a windy day. Night was short-lived and the time for dreams temporal. Dawn came way too early.

Back home I was attuned to sunrise and would get up promptly at first light, enough light to at least find my socks and shoes; and that was around 5:30 or 6:00am – a decent hour to get things hustling around the campsite. Here, morning broke at 4:00am and I was obligated out of sheer habit to accept the day on its terms, albeit trying to force a fitful sleep for another hour or so, forced to listen to the mounting drone of mosquitoes outside the tent. I watched them coat the door screen, ready to take a bite out of my hide the moment I stepped outside. They seemed to like the modicum of heat emanating from inside the tent.

Everything was damp from rain. I kindled a quick fire for coffee and perched the pot on the fire irons, hesitating a moment by the heat and flames, warming my hands and shaking off the morning chill. Still too cold for mosquitoes to swarm, but they would be out soon enough. The heat of the fire would act like a beacon.

We had planned to paddle an easy ten kilometers to Sheth-anie Lake, as far as an archaeological campsite indicated in the Canada Parks report. Explorer Samuel Hearne had made a winter stop there in 1769. There was no need to rush breakfast and nobody wanted to extricate themselves from the protected cover of the kitchen fly, just yet anyway. The cold rain was sheathing the landscape in a dreary lacquer. Because of the relatively short distance to paddle, we would be setting up a comfortable basecamp at the Hearne site. But it was windy, and the temperature had dropped considerably through the night to just above freezing. This presented an omnipotent pall around our campsite and reluctance to pack up the gear and move on. Dawson talked incessantly to Russ and Hodding, cigarette in hand, and usually about things other than the trip, which kept attention away from breaking camp.

"Dawson, enough with the chit-chat; get your ass in gear!" I'd yell like a drill sergeant. That always seemed to work.

We kept moving to stay warm and the camp was dismantled quickly, folded wet and heavy, adding more weight to the overloaded canoes.

It doesn't always happen - good weather that is, and its nature's way of letting you know who is in charge. Although it is always nice to start a trip off in pleasant weather with dry gear and warm temperatures, the reality of exploration almost always assigns a variable of sorts; a twist in the scheme of things you hope will unfold in your favour. I've often come across sorry wilderness travelers, soaked to the skin, tents floating in depressions at campsites, wet gear strung out on makeshift clotheslines, simply because they assumed it wouldn't rain during the night. Nature can be the consummate trickster.

We set out into the mad current of the river and in no time saw the opening beyond the riverscape that indicated Negassa

Lake – *Nu-gay-ah-say-tuay,* or "bald island lake", so named by the Dene for its particular crust of rock, barren of growth. There was a noticeable downrush sloping into Negassa but no rapids present until the river current collided head on with the oncoming white-capped waves of the large lake. This created a bizarre cross-chop that I had only once before experienced as this bad: paddling alongside of cliffs on Lake Superior where the waves ricocheted back onto themselves in a rather deadly, fluid ballet. The Seal River current propelled us headlong down the middle channel and out into the lake.

Our canoes were immediately thrust into a dangerous, chaotic maelstrom of breaking waves that pitched our boats at odd, uncontrollable angles. Negassa Lake was shallow, and shallow lakes are notorious for constructing the biggest waves in the most modest of winds. Here, the wind had at least five-kilometers of open expanse to conjure up legions of meter-sized breakers, any one of which could have easily flipped our canoe. Paddling hard, straight into the wind at almost no gain until the point of exhaustion we found it too dangerous to continue. We gave in to the wind and turned the canoes back to the coastline and followed the shore until we located a protected cove and a small beach landing sufficiently large enough to accommodate a workable camp.

One canoe was pulled up, flipped over as an anchor for the lower end of the kitchen tarp, the tarp then was suspended over a rope strung between two spruce trees then secured tightly. Rocks were gathered for a fire-pit, wood was collected and sawed for burning, gear was arranged and stowed under the second overturned canoe and one tent was erected for all of us. We had the feeling that it was going to be a long wait.

It was days like this that guiding prowess was truly put to the litmus test. To be competent in the "off-water" talents were as important as those required for canoeing. Maintaining morale was critical to survival. Historical case in point was the incredible Antarctic expedition, in 1917, by explorer Ernest Shackleton where after months of privation and near-starvation he managed to rescue every single crew member. Shackleton managed to save his men not only through his skill at team-dynamics and survival, but by giving them hope and continually finding ways to boost morale.

Unlike Shackleton's heroic effort, there was no shortage of food or the need to be rescued for us. It was days like this when the world outside the rain tarp was inhospitable and people retreated to where simple creature-comforts were best tended, and it didn't matter if you started to retell the same stories or jokes; everyone laughed and cajoled, regardless.

Here, sit on the wannigan closer to the fire and get warm; pour yourself a cup of hot tea and put plenty of maple syrup in it. The wind tries angrily to break through the makeshift sanctuary and the tarp is snugged down a little tighter on that side. People sit shoulder to shoulder a little tighter, a little warmer, and life in the cold rain and wind is idyllic; the harder the wind blows, the more ridiculous the stories. It was like that. Hardship can encapsulate the most pleasurable haven for story and appetite.

So we ate meat pies baked in the reflector oven. The reflector oven is a piece of historic brilliance – a three-sided, folding metal contraption that is perched close to the fire and has a simple rack that seats a nine-inch square pan comfortably. Along with the store-bought pies we drank copious volumes of bush coffee: java strong enough to float a caribiner. There was no shortage of fuel-wood; the wild fire that had razed more than a thousand acres of timber had bequeathed a surfeit of bone-hard deadwood; simple enough to gather, saw up, split and stack under the rain tarp.

The wind persisted all day. Rain descended in periodic bursts, cold and chilling, but life under the palatial nylon tarp was good, cheerful, relaxing. Dawson made a cream fish-chowder with the lake trout Allan had given us; Hodding shared his Trans-America adventure by motorboat in the footsteps of Lewis and Clark. The Carters were a well-known crusading newspaper family who hailed from Greenville, Mississippi, sticking their necks out to champion civil rights in the 1960s. Hodding's grandfather, known as "the conscience of the South," had published a popular book entitled, *Where Main Street Meets the River* and worked as editor at the liberal *Delta Democrat Times*. Hodding's father, a Democratic Party reformer and major player in American politics ended up in Washington with President Jimmy Carter, later becoming spokesperson for the State Department during the Iran hostage crisis.

In 1804 the Lewis and Clark Expedition, also known as the Corps of Discovery Expedition was commissioned by President Thomas Jefferson and set off from St. Louis Missouri, making its way westward over the continental divide to the Pacific Ocean. The objective was to claim American ownership before the Brits or Spanish did and carried out under the auspices of a scientific expedition. A select party of U.S. Army volunteers under the command of Captain Meriwether Lewis and his cohort, Second Lieutenant William Clark, succeeded as the first colonizers to cross the western half of the United States.

"Tell us about your trip," Dawson asked "That's quite a haul in a canoe."

"Well, it's more like *Animal House* on a nature hike, that sort of thing," Hodding smiled. "My buddy Preston [Maybank] and I figured we'd make the run from St. Louis to the ocean in a motorboat instead." Dawson and I looked at each other, maybe expecting a different answer, even though Hodding was supposed to have had little canoeing experience so it made sense that they made the trip in a motorboat.

"Is that why *Men's Journal* hired you for this expedition?" I asked.

"Not really, maybe; I'm the not-so-famous-son of a somewhat famous politician. Maybe because of my book I had published through Simon and Schuster about the Lewis and Clark trip, but I like to think it's that and not because of my dad."

"What's the book called? I'll look it up when I get home," Dawson inquired.

Westward Whoa: In the Wake of Lewis and Clark, Hodding said proudly; "Mostly by boat, some car, by foot; even by horse, and oh, and by hitchhiking too."

Hodding went on to detail some of the bizarre stuff he did on the expedition, like his infatuation with animal scat, and about his life in general.

"Sounds like a Jack Kerouac escapade *On The Road* sort of adventure," I supposed.

"You got it, right...a little less philosophical perhaps but our way to question authority and the mainstream. We just made the trip up as it unfolded."

Hodding had grown up in Mississippi, graduated from Kenyon College in Ohio then spent time in the Peace Corps in Africa. He became a staff writer for M. Magazine, eventually moving from Boston to Thermond, West Virginia to raise goats, but instead landed a job as a postmaster.

"Okay Russ, it's your turn," I demanded, "tell us a bit about your sordid past."

"Well, not quite as glamorous as Hodding's, I suppose: I really started my studio photography work as a freelance assistant in New York."

I could tell Russ was a bit timid or just humble about his accomplishments. *Men's Journal Magazine* wouldn't have picked him for the job if he didn't have impressive credentials.

"What's a freelance assistant photographer?" Dawson asked.

"I worked with established New York photographers who had made a name for themselves," Russ told us.

"Like who? Maybe we've heard of them," I said.

"Robert Mapplethorpe for one."

"You're kidding? I have heard of him," I blurted with enthusiasm. As a photographer myself, I had certainly been interested in other photographers work. Mapplethorpe was legendary.

"He's dead now isn't he?" I asked.

"Yeah, really sad too, just in his prime. He was forty-two; died of HIV Aids in '89 - five years ago."

"His work was mostly black and white wasn't it?" I queried.

"Mostly. A lot of celebrity portraits, pornography..." Russ was cut off suddenly.

"Shit, pornography?" Dawson asked, perking up.

"You might call it that but it was very edgy, artistic, beautiful really."

"Who else did you work with?" I asked.

"Arnold Newman...he did portraits of artists and politicians; he did JFK's portrait. Oh yeah, there was also Neil Selkirk who often did assignments for *Esquire* and *New York Times*...older guy – like you Hap." Everyone laughed. "There was also Bruce Wolf who was known more for his design talents; Harold Slavin and, oh yeah...I spent two years with the Alan Kaplan Studio assisting on commercial lifestyle and fashion assignments; mostly studio stuff or on location for *Coca Cola, Benson and Hedges, The Limited*... what else...yes, *Spiegel.*"

"What about any outdoor work, like outside the studio?" Dawson pried, "You said you did some photo-work on location."

"Not that much; I've been to a jungle shoot in Ecuador, the

Florida Everglades, and an old-growth forest stint in the Pacific Northwest. Nothing like this."

"You must have won awards for your work," I prodded Russ. There was a moment of silence and I could tell Russell Kaye was a bit modest about his accomplishments.

"A couple, yes. In 1990 I won Best Travel Photography for the Society of American Travel Writers; two years ago I received the Award of Excellence."

None of us said anything. We just sat there with our mouths ajar, wondering what to say.

"Russ, that's quite a work history. This trip is pretty far outside the box for you isn't it?"

I needed to ask that for some reason. It seemed Russ had a lot more experience than he let on; maybe not so much wilderness familiarity, but as a photographer he had already built up quite a reputation.

"Yup," Russ said simply and to the point.

Just listening to Hodding and Russell talk about themselves and their achievements raised an awakening for me. Until now I had accepted the two of them as something much less than who they actually were. That's the thing about trail life – wilderness is a great *equalizer* and it modifies who we are in a pack. I saw them as two American rookies who had little wilderness experience; a studio photographer and a postmaster with no recognizable achievements other than the fact that they had made their way onto this expedition, possibly by arbitrary and last minute selection. And out here, away from personal definitions everyone was an equal. We were all on a group schedule, shared a common goal, ate the same food, slept in a tent, experienced all the same nuances that nature can throw at us.

I felt stupid. Not just stupid, but embarrassed for waiting so long to ask them about their lives and interests. I was still a bit miffed about not covering the expedition by promoting my own photography and writing; I hadn't quite accepted the fact that I was simply the guide. The Seal River exploratory expedition was gifted with two very special and exceptional individuals. Just that raised the bar higher along with the fact that these neophytes had something to teach me about life, tolerance and sensitivity.

So unrolled the long day into the evening waiting for some reprieve from the wind, exchanging tales and life events, eating fried bannock and drinking black coffee. By 11:00 p.m. the sky had cleared and the sun dropped below the far shore horizon, a brilliant crimson that etched an unusual artistry over a forlorn looking and wasted world around us. The wind was ceaseless, still, whipping through the few remnant spruce that clung along the shore without pause, the rain tarp flapping wildly above our heads.

A night wind meant that it would still be blowing valiantly into the next day. It was a mild concern at this point since the rest days were well spread out sufficiently along the expedition route, although it wouldn't be good if we were to use up all of them in one place so early on in the journey. It would mean little rest further along the river, just when we would need it the most. Rest days were often "banked" depending on how far along on the planned route you were. Paddling a couple longer days or doubling your distance quota, taking advantage of decent weather, could "buy" an extra half-day rest. Conversely, getting wind-bound for days on end, which could happen, meant having to make up the distance somewhere else along the route.

I slept well, retreated into forgettable dreams; and by morning, at a time I would have already had the coffee brewed and the breakfast started, I elected to lay in my sleeping bag not really worrying about the hour. I knew the other guys wouldn't get up of their own volition. Outside it was still windy, the rain tarp kept up its monotonous one-note melody, shore trees that had been spared from the ravages of the previous fire creaked around the campsite, and I could hear snoring coming from the other tent. There was little prospect of departure so we slept through the hours of morning.

Waves piled up on the shore. By the time we finally rolled out of our respective tents it looked pretty dismal so we tried to pass the time by taking short hikes through the burned out forest of rickety sticks and black boulders. We didn't stray too far from camp because of the fallen timber that criss-crossed over brittle, dead sphagnum and the difficulty it made for walking. By 3:00 p.m. the lake waves stopped capping, the wind calmed and we were sufficiently stir-crazy enough to get our kit together quickly. We loaded the canoes and shoved off into the wind. Back in Ontario this would be about the time I would be setting up camp for the day. Knowing we still had light until near midnight, the time of day didn't matter much, and we were anxious to get moving.

We set out across Negassa Lake, heading for the long set of rapids that would take us to Shethanei Lake, a distance of less than seven kilometers: yesterday's goal, and several hours of available light left. As we passed the point at which we turned our boats around, the wind picked up once again, and once again we turned heel to follow the shore as best we could, and bucked the wind the two kilometers across the lake to the mouth of the next set of rapids.

The sound of the long stretch of whitewater could be heard from a long way off. Shethanei Lake wasn't that far but there was a thirty-foot drop to get there, guarded by a double channel of furious water. There was a visible drop in the river and the topographical chart showed just one double rapid circling an island – a strenuous one-kilometer grind but it didn't look like a thirty-foot descent. The pitch that now confronted us was not substantial, but the curve in the river and the roar around the bend indicated rougher water that was out of our line of sight. The canoes were steered carefully across the top of the rapids and beached out of the current. We would take the time to scout the run.

It was a Dene campsite and garbage was strewn about the shore and underbrush. There was no portage, just a collection of plastics and discarded tins. It would be the last sign of recent human evidence we would come across for the rest of the expedition. To view the rapids from a good vantage point was not an easy undertaking. I realized quickly that this was not typical Shield-rock country where rapids were portaged easily over long tongues of smooth bedrock, or canoes lined by hopping along flat boulders. We were confronted with knee-deep sphagnum and tundra moss, locked in formidable hummocks by an intertwined mesh of tangled spruce. Walking any distance was pointless. We weren't getting anywhere. I told the others to go back and I continued to push on, trying to get close to the bend in the rapids. An immature bald eagle soared just above the treetops and I envied him his freedom of movement.

I finally reached a point along the rapids where I could read the water-play. The main flow took the center route, tossing up relatively easy standing waves and leaving a less taxing route along either shore that seemed shallow, full of pillow rocks. Pillow rocks are just below the surface of water that can easily snag a canoe. It was a go-ahead. Getting back to the head of the rapids where everyone was waiting for my assessment was just as difficult and I was soaked to the skin from pushing through wet brush. Adrenalin was running high as we lined up for the run. It was the inaugural testing ground for the newcomers and a textbook run for old hands. Everyone kneeled down on their respective knee pads and cinched up the draw cord tight on the spray-skirt. We edged the canoes out into the main downstream "V" of the rapids and followed a straight forward channel through the standing waves.

It wasn't a difficult rapid at all and it seemed the high water had washed out most of the obstacles. The rapid did get progressively more complicated as the gradient dipped around the corner where we still hadn't scouted. A train of boulders changed the course of the run, which required a few excited, broad strokes in order to sideslip around them, eddying the canoe into heavier water where braces and balance saw us through to the calmer current below.

Russell had done well and he was elated by the time we finished the long run.

"That isn't the end of it," I assured him. "There has to be a much bigger drop up ahead somewhere." We had only dropped a couple of meters and that meant that the bulk of the descent to Shethanei was not marked on the topographic map. That didn't surprise me at all. Government maps were often inaccurate, or at least imperfect. I checked the Canada Parks field survey map, but it didn't make any sense at all. I flipped the map over and held it up to the sun and realized that the CP cartographer had printed that section of the river map upside down and backwards. No additional rapids were marked on their cockeyed map either. There was an obvious discrepancy here and I began to think that there must be an error with the elevation figures between Negassa and Shethanei Lakes.

As we floated casually downriver in the current, discussing the maps, we disregarded the fact that we had picked up considerable speed and were now rushing backwards into the maw of a very large rapid. Without the time to discuss options, Dawson and I both stood up to get a better running view of the rapids ahead. There was plenty of water but no place to land or line along the shore because of the heavy willow growth, partly flooded by the high flow. *Shit!* And that was it: we were committed to the run, having already entered the massive "V" of current formed by the narrowing of the river; once in the prescribed "V" we were at the point where there was no option but to run.

The view ahead didn't look good. My stomach balled up in knots when I saw the entire river funnel into several colossal rollers. "Pull up your spray skirt!" I barked at Russell as I wormed my way into my own, drawing the closure cord tight around my chest to keep out water. Russell looked back at me, obviously worried, but I said it was nothing, and the run wasn't difficult and we would do fine so long as he remembered the high brace that I showed him earlier.

Our canoe took the lead position with Dawson and Hodding following about twenty meters behind. Boulders the size of Volkswagen vans deflected the heavy current at odd angles, forming huge white pillows of foam, coursing off in diagonal strides, quickly changing the temperament of the river into angry boils and difficult waves. These we dealt with one at a time on the approach by backwatering and ferrying into position then bracing through and driving hard again with our paddles.

The pitch increased and the whole river plunged dramatically into a series of deep stationary waves that broke backwards, upstream, like miniature tsunamis. The sound was deafening, or maybe it was the sound of my heart beating. "Holy shit," I heard a cry from the bow seat, "Are you sure about this?" Russell pleaded. I reassured as best I could, shouting at the top of my lungs to push hard through the first wave and brace into the second in a voice that didn't sound panic stricken. My stomach lurched as the canoe dipped suddenly downward through a trough of white spray and into a solid wall of water. Russell and the whole front of the canoe disappeared into the roller and I braced myself for a cold plunge.

I never thought of dying, or drowning or anything else except what was happening in the moment. I wasn't afraid - *I was terrified!* I had never in my life done anything like this before. Sure, I had done a lot of whitewater, technical stuff in open canoes, but this was more than I was ready for and certainly too much for Russell. The huge wave rolled over the deck so fast I was punched hard in the chest almost knocking the wind out of me. The water was ice cold! The canoe careened sideways momentarily and I leaned out with a heavy draw and yelled at Russell to keep his balance as we swung around and lined up for the second wave.

"What...the...fuck...am...I...doing...here!" I heard Russell yell, eyes wide and ghostly white, "I'm a Brooklyn studio photographer for Christ sake!"

"Brace godammit!" I yelled back. Russell had pulled his paddle out of the water and was turning to face me as if I could magically take him out of there. I wasn't angry but I knew without his front brace we could be in deep trouble. I did have that *'do as I fucking tell you'* look on my face and that was enough to get Russell recharged for the next volley of waves. And this all happened in a matter of about five seconds before Russell disappeared into the next roller.

This time I leaned forward to fend off the rush of water, took a deep breath, and was immediately swallowed by the river, momentarily losing my bearings as my knees slipped off the pads. I jockeyed for balance and caught the black-water tongue of water that carried us out of trouble and into slower current. Russell was still bracing, solid as a stone statue, almost too scared to relax his paddle. The second canoe came up behind us as we were finishing the run.

"Jeezus," Hodding rejoiced, "What a fucking rush!" Dawson

had a glow on his face but said nothing, as if he was surprised that either of us had actually made it down the rapids at all. We let the canoes drift in the steady current. I commended everyone for their remarkable talents in getting down the run unscathed, letting on that this initiation to the Seal River may be indicative of what we were going to encounter downstream.

My heart was still pounding. *Christ, it was a rush,* I thought to myself. I was impressed with the spray-skirts; it was the first time I had ever used them and I realised that an open canoe would never make it down the rapids, and any rescue of a swamped canoe here would have been tedious, slow work in frigid water or nearly impossible, pushed far downstream with no break in the willow-packed shoreline; no place to get out.

If we could make it safely down that rapid then we could manage anything further on. That was a great comfort to know. And this was all new to me: the landscape, weather, magnificent strength of the river, style of river running and *the damnable bugs!* I took out my journal and scribbled down some river notes and a rough sketch of the two sets of rapids we had come down; the others continued to congratulate themselves and exchanged comments on what they thought might compare with the thrill of the last run. Everyone had the same answer.

The wind continued its head-on posture as the river opened up for forty-kilometers. Shethanei Lake was enormous; the distant shore had all but disappeared over the apparent curve of the earth and our only safe paddling line was to keep close to the south shore line of trees. We struggled against the white caps, inching our way to Hearne's campsite, Dawson and Hodding falling far behind us. We paused to wait. Hodding had dropped his fishing line to troll and was now hauling in a sizeable lake trout; quite a feat while balancing the canoe amongst a relentless barrage of waves.

We had paddled a very short distance that day in terms of averages for river travel but our energy had been taxed by the elements and the initial drama of the rapids. It was our inauguration to the Seal River. Having passed the test - after all we were still afloat - we couldn't help feel that grandiose sense of achievement, the opus of hard work and mere survival. This was exploration in its purest form. We beached our canoes and extricated ourselves from the cocooned spray-skirts, emerging like butterflies, a bit shaky, stretching cramped legs, and then we were immediately swarmed by black flies.

Chapter Six

Shethanei

The recording of history is riddled with lies and half-truths. It's a revelation that I've come to acknowledge simply by reading between the lines, balancing the perspectives, and quite often listening to the impartial voices of Canada's First People. Not unlike a lot of other kids growing up in the 1960s, suffering through indoctrination into a consumerist system, I was deluged with the contrived historical trappings espoused in conservative school textbooks – schools that handed out corporal punishment; where the leather strap held dominion over rebellious youth. I asked questions that always landed me in the principal's office.

Canada does own a bevy of historical figures, many of whom I would not credit with the noble title of hero. The United States had an abundance of colourful champions from Davy Crocket and Daniel Boone, to General George Armstrong Custer. I swallowed all that hype in grade-school, watched movies that boldly illustrated how cowboys were good and Indians bad. But it wasn't until much later in my life that I realized it was pretty unlikely Boone could have killed a rogue black bear when he was only three-years old; and Custer's notoriety as an historical hero plummeted after the American Indigenous Rights Movement of the 1970s brought the battle of Wounded Knee to public scrutiny. As kids growing up in the 1960s we were subject to gross untruths about history.

Canadian history accounts continue to glamorize the despots and zealots of our past: the tyrants either employed by the Hudson's Bay Company, or those ordained by God himself. The occupations of the cloth set to relieve Canada's original inhabitants of their own beliefs.

Samuel Hearne is a fine example. Employed by the HBC it was his job to search and locate the great copper mines that purportedly existed near the Arctic Ocean, referred to as the Northern Ocean by the Europeans. Fort Churchill, later known as Fort Prince of Wales, was constructed in 1717 in order to coerce the Dene and Inuit to do business with the Company. Unfortunately for the burgeoning Empire, the northern Indigenous took little interest in white commerce and for years business around the fort remained sporadic. Stories of huge, open copper quarries passed from Indigenous interpreters to European financiers. The English had a responsibility to turn the stone fort into a viable enterprise, one way or another; therefore, Samuel Hearne was commissioned to make good on the venture and was presented the task in order to secure the copper mines for England. This could have been the greatest hoax of the century. Indians often own a rather inane and peculiar sense of humour and may have actually sent Hearne scrambling off on a wild-goose-chase. It was no secret to the Indians that the Europeans orchestrated their own failures with devoted regularity so they were ripe for a good prank.

In the book *A Journey to the Northern Ocean: the Adventures of Samuel Hearne*, chief guide, *Chawchinahaw*, a Chipewyan, "took every method to dishearten [Hearne] and [his] European companions, and several times hinted his desire of [their] turning back to the factory." It was as if Chawchinahaw knew that the mines did not exist and he didn't stomach being part of the chicanery. Hearne, nevertheless, became obsessed with this challenge, making three attempts at securing this fabled treasure and spending much of his time in hardship and isolation, traipsing across the northern barrens. Meanwhile, back in Fort Prince of Wales, the HBC factor, known for his polygamist lifestyle, surrounded himself with a bevy of Indigenous girls of whom he quickly defrocked of their virginity. This was a common practice amongst factor and oblate priest alike, encouraged, in fact, by the Company hierarchy. Since Indigenous were considered heathens, unchristian and worshippers of pagan gods, even the clergy sanctified this social malpractice claiming that it would 'boost the morale of the lonely men on the frontier.'

It was not unlikely that Hearne kept a florilegium of pretty flowers for himself. The King, Pope and God himself knew that the Canadian winters were long and lonely and it was good business to accommodate even the carnal desires of all Company men in order to carry out the States' business.

*   *   *   *   *

We were about to pitch our tents on the very soil Hearne had visited in 1769, over two-hundred years before. Canada Parks in their report, made a big deal of it, never mentioning the sordid background of the Company heroes. Hearne and I did agree that the campsite was nothing less than spectacular. Hearne writes:

"The situation of our tent at this time was truly pleasant, particularly for a spring residence; being on a small elevated point, which commanded an extensive prospect over a large lake [Shethanei], the shores of which abounded with wood of different kinds, such as pine, larch, birch, and poplar; and in many places was beautifully contrasted with a variety of high hills [eskers], that shewed their snowy [sandy] summits above the tallest woods."

Comparatively, nothing at all had changed in those two-hundred years. As I stood on the beach and surveyed the lake I was a bit overwhelmed by the timelessness of my surroundings, and revelled in the fact that *this* was as pure a wilderness as there ever could be. Few people had actually stood upon this shore no doubt, and no traces of modern garbage, foot prints or camp-site industry to be seen anywhere. We all felt the same way, this novelty of discovery and aloneness, four of us just staring out over the lake.

Shethanei Lake, or *Sheth-tie-eye-tuay*, meaning "hill going into the lake", was once an important camping grounds for the no-madic Dene People. If they weren't off killing caribou along the many nearby eskers, they would be busy setting their fish-ing nets across the fast current where the river enters the lake, from where we had just come. They also built canoes here for use along the river as it was one of the few places where birch bark could be collected in quantity. Canoes eventually replaced the long overland haul across the barrens, along the eskers, and were introduced to the Dene by the Hudson's Bay Company in the 1800s. Still, the Dene were not traditional canoe builders or canoeists and most of the boats were stashed at known caribou crossings along the river. The strong current of the Seal would be a deterrent from any travel by canoe upstream. The river was a one-way street whereas the eskers were easily traced in whatev-er direction they needed to go.

Fresh animal tracks dotted the beach. One set belonged to a black bear that had vanished upon our arrival; paw prints in the sand that were evenly spaced and tracked, then suddenly pushed

deep with claw marks, scuffs and wide strides that ended abruptly as the bear hightailed into the thick spruce. There were gentle
tracks of gulls and plovers, a fox, and the signature of a rather
large wolf, some days old.

About the campsite, I recall it being one of the finest I've
ever visited. Sheltered from the ever-present wind by an offshore island, the temperature lacked the chilled wind-over-icy-
water effect. The camping area was elevated behind the beach, in
amongst an irregular pattern of well-spaced spruce, interspersed
by moss-carpeted openings. It was almost park-like and manicured in appearance, as if we had stumbled upon the arboretum
of the gods. I half expected either white-robed deities to appear
before us, or the incorporeal demigods of the aboriginals, none
too happy with us invading their sacred space.

There was a lagoon or runnel about one-hundred meters
from the tents, forming a levee between the lake and the bog
marsh – obviously a source for the healthy population of mosquitoes. There were well-trodden paths leading away from the
campsite, caribou runs branching off in no particular order,
any of which could get you lost in a labyrinth of intersected
trails heading away from the lake. But the most noteworthy geo-
morphological feature of Hearne's campsite was the prominent
bedrock mound that rose thirty-meters above the tree-tops and
was an easy five-minute walk along one of the caribou paths.

It was a drumlin of sorts; not the type composed of boulder
clay or gravel, but of granite blocks piled helter-skelter, forming
hundreds of cave-like hollows and caverns, perhaps denning
sites for black bears. Some of the rocks were unstable, precariously balanced, requiring some climbing skill in order to reach
the top of the mound. The view was stunning! A scattering of
dwarf birch had commanded a foothold in the soilless environment, testimony to the determination of life forms under such

harsh conditions.

It was a rock-hound's Mecca. Literally hundreds of rock types and minerals lay exposed; biotite schists, sandstones, quartz and conglomerates, both along the beach and throughout the area of the drumlinoid hill. The four of us stood at the top, staring in awe out over the expanse of lake and spruce. Minute specs of mica affixed to the drumlin rocks sparkled iridescently in the early evening sun. The sky had finally cleared itself of the thick, grey strata that had followed us since leaving Tadoule. There was clearly a strong energy here, perhaps of a spiritual nature, convinced that the striking oddity of the drumlin may have been some type of ceremonial gathering place for the early Dene.

A perfect place for our ceremony, I contemplated. Dawson had brought the skull of a caribou with him to the top of the drumlin. He had discovered the full skeleton along one of the trails leading up to the base of the hill.

"Leave it here," I suggested, "And we'll use it for our ceremony later this evening." All agreed. We found a large cleft in the rock where we could all sit out of the wind and the skull was perched on the highest boulder, its spirit overseeing the lake below. We returned to the campsite, sensitized to our new surroundings that compared to nothing any of us had experienced in all our collective memories. Beaming with delight at our discoveries, even the hard struggle against the wind, *and the rapids!* It seemed all too perfect. Even the nastiness of the twilight scourge of mosquitoes seemed trivial. *What more could add to this moment?* I wondered as we sat around the fire at Hearne's hideaway and we laughed heartily about the big rapids and the look on Russell's face after pushing through the first wave.

The strange band of cloudless, clear sky did not move out of the horizon all day, contrasted by the weight of a leaden and bleak sheathe of cloud that framed it in. We had almost forgotten about the fires and wondered whether or not Allan and the other village men, and sweet, old Carolyn who sold me the moccasins had been evacuated. We were deep into conversation about the trending in the outdoor-gear market. "C'mon, look at the quality of rain gear these days compared to just a few years ago," hailed Russ, sporting his brand new North Face jacket.

"True enough," I said, "but gortex is over-rated, gets soaked inside from sweat because it doesn't breathe as well as advertised, especially if you're working hard or paddling."

"I'd rather get rained on than wear a jacket anyway."

"Not in the cold weather, paddling when it's snowing...you need the wind-break at least and warm under-clothing," Hodding pointed out.

"Yeah, like you've paddled when it's snowing Carter," I quipped. Laughs all around.

"The wannigan box," Kaye asked, "I don't get it...it looks like it would be hard to carry on a portage."

"I wouldn't go anywhere without it," Dawson cut in, "it's part of a Canadian custom that goes back to the fur-trade days. Keeps things organized. It's not that hard to portage but you have to make sure the tump-strap is personally gauged to fit your body." Dawson stuck his forearm between the wannigan box, stretching out the tump-line crooked in his thumb so that the leather strap was tight. "Like this. Keeping the tump tight between your thumb and elbow it's the equal distance between your forehead and where the box fits comfortably on your back."

"It's something you have to get used to," I said "The camp makes young kids carry wannigans filled with canned goods, and portage water-logged canvas canoes. Heavy, both of them, and I've passed these kids on portages and they're in tears trying to lug this stuff up steep trails around waterfalls; character builder though, for sure - if it doesn't kill them."

"Okay then, what about..." Hodding was cut off sharply.

"Shit, look at that light for god's sake!" Russ blurted out suddenly, standing up and walking quickly to his tent.

The hue of evening light that spread across the campsite had taken on the most unusual radiance. Dawson and Hodding ran down to the beach to see the setting sun across the lake but Russell and I were already half-way to the drumlinoid hill with our cameras slung over our shoulders.

"Meet us at the top!" I yelled at the other two, "for the ceremony!"

I have witnessed some spectacular evening sunsets over wilderness vistas but never to this day witnessed what I saw looking out over that mound of rocks on Shethanei Lake in northern Manitoba. There are no words that can describe it, no emotion that could equal that photogenic moment. The peculiar thing about nature photography is the incident light that creates an ephemeral, fleeting moment in time; always remarkably soulful. The tops of the spruce trees exploded in brilliant orange light, not just orange but phosphorescence that beguiled description; there was a creeping radiance that seemed to have an eerie purpose as if it were a living thing. We knew that our timing would be critical. The magic light-show intensified as if the world around us had caught fire.

We couldn't climb the scrabble of rock fast enough. Each rock glowed like a hot coal. The ambient light from the sun projected oddly through the haze of smoke over Tadoule. It was emotionally spectral, crimson in design, painted over the stone like flowing lava, crawling stealthily over and through the landscape as the sun descended, mesmerizing and strangely other-worldly. I could see Russell fiddling with his camera as we ran, getting the adjustments just right, hopping from boulder to boulder like a mountain goat in a rush to get to the top.

Hodding and Dawson reached the summit shortly after we did. The four of us stood there, open-mouthed, and we looked out over a chromatic sea of spruce. The world had changed from drab green to fire-red vermillion. Even the lake danced with a blush of ochre. The esker sand ridges across the lake resembled red snakes, uncoiled and peaceful. So taken with the beauty of the moment I had forgotten to take pictures. I was almost afraid to take my eyes away from the spectacle of light draped over the land that taking pictures and watching it through the lens of a camera might strip the magic from it. I waited until the last fleeting glimpse of the sun, just before the supernatural light vanished and I took a couple of photographs.

For less than fifteen-minutes Shethanei was suspended in co-lour animation. The intensity ebbed as the sun dropped behind the horizon shifting the scene again to colourless dusk. It was already midnight. We gathered in the depression located earlier and I placed a wad of tobacco in the skull cavity of the caribou, lit the smudge stick I carried in my own medicine bag and wafted the four of us in a liberal cleansing of sweet sage smoke. "This is for good luck," I said. Appealing to the resident spirits I asked for safe passage down the Seal River. It was time for serious talk.

I took the occasion to impress upon the others the impor-tance of co-operative effort and the need to abandon ego; it was to be a full team endeavor. And as I talked I looked Dawson in the face and he knew that I was directing the homily at him in particular.

"Look, everyone here is a part of a team, and we need to keep that in mind," I told them in a serious tone. Everyone stopped shifting and talking and listened, even Dawson.

"This will only work if we all look out for each other," I said, looking directly at Dawson.

"There may be times, perhaps further downriver, when we

need to help each other out of a jam, maybe an upset and someone needs to be rescued. It happens, sometimes, and time is
important as the water is cold and a rescue needs to happen fast.
We all need to make the effort in case of an emergency."

The first to respond was Dawson.

"For sure, we're a team," he said sounding surprisingly sin-
cere, "you and Russ can count on us because we know we can
count on you."

We were all flushed with the spectral finish to the long day,
finishing the ceremony by placing the caribou skull on top of
the sentinel rock. I pulled out three caribou teeth that I had been
saving from my medicine bag and gave one to each of my compatriots as a good luck token. None of us wanted the moment
to end and the walk back to camp was deliberately slow, pensive
and quiet. For some inane reason I felt that the ceremony might
actually work.

Pouring over the maps, aided by the light of the campfire, it
was decided that we would linger an extra day on Shethanei Lake.
There was an esker formation only three kilometers away where
camping looked favourable and we could do some exploring on
foot. Mosquitoes finally drove us to our tents but not without
noticing that the ghostly carpet of deep moss that pervade the
forest floor still radiated an iridescent, surreal glow almost as if
it had captured some of the earlier radiance and held on to it. I
hesitated momentarily before slipping in to my tent, breathing in
the cool air, savouring the calming beauty of this place. It had
been a long, remarkable day and Hearne's campsite carried an air
of mystery about it; an unusual energy that often resides at such
places. Places haunted by old ghosts.

I wondered about Samuel Hearne and his entourage of
Chipewyans, the young maidens who warmed his sleeping robes.
I missed the enjoyment of such company, the closeness; and I

was suddenly reminded of my own aloneness, an unrequited love and the hardships I had endured over the past several years: a loveless first marriage, the long drawn-out environmental battles, back-to-back guided trips. But on days like this day it is hard not to feel blessed in some way; thinking that the experience of one, single special evening is enough to gratify any superfluous need or erase any prevailing regret of the past.

I sat up late in my small tent, writing in my journal, long past the hour since the other three voices fell silent: wondering, tired, a bit lonely, although I had the company of many mosquitoes hovering about my head just outside the door screen. I had been doing a lot of solo trips over the past few years, difficult journeys, pushing myself to exhaustion, trying to accomplish more than I could possibly endure and paying for it not just physically but psychologically. The environmental crusade, the blockades, battles won and lost, and soured relationships had all taken a toll on my consciousness. Paddling the Seal in new territory, maybe fresh experiences could be the elixir to regain some of that lost faith, I hoped anyway. Too many thoughts were getting in the way of sleep, excitement mostly, anticipation of what was ahead of us.

$$*\qquad*\qquad*\qquad*\qquad*$$

It was a short, brisk paddle to the esker beach. It was now a certainty that the wind was an ever-present condition of the boreal fringe and a force to be reckoned with for the remainder of the expedition. We had passed a German couple camped a short distance away, drying their gear, after obviously having a good soaking the day before on the rapids. They were paddling the most unseaworthy-looking, home-built touring kayak, and by the sight of the bottom hull, it looked as if they had seen a few hard times. Both parties were surprised to see the other, knowing the infrequency of travellers along the Seal River.

Russell and I pulled up on the beach of our new campsite, waiting again for Hodding and Dawson to catch up. Hodding had another lake trout on the line and was taking some time to bring it in, all the while trying valiantly to keep the canoe from being blown back down the lake. It was a good catch, a splendid addition to our pantry.

The beach looked more tropical than boreal, autographed by semi-palmated plovers, lesser yellowlegs and the occasional gull. There were also faint traces of bear and fox leading up and beyond the raised peninsula, trailing off towards the esker that rose slightly behind the open terrace campsite. There was a picturesque kettle-lake at the foot of the esker which, no doubt, was home to a myriad still-water crustaceans, amphibious life and unhatched mosquito larvae.

It was a traditional Dene campsite of long ago as there was no sign of modern garbage. They would come here in great numbers as was evident by the hundreds of stone chips and flakes, crude scrapers and cast-off arrowheads, all being continually exposed as the winter ice disturbed yet another layer of sand along the shoreline. These artifacts may have been thousands of years old. A more recent find of several rolls of birchbark that Hodding had discovered, neatly tucked under the mantle of a thick spruce tree, indicated that this was a major canoe-building location. I did know that the local Dene collected bark here up until the 1940s as it was the only place birch trees grew large enough to harvest. It was somewhat of an anomaly for a birch tree of this dimension to be so far north of its usual habitat and we were only a short distance from the tree-line.

Again, the landscape here was park-like in natural design. Even the grass looked as if was periodically mowed, and I expected trash-bins and public privies and "Do Not Feed The Bears" signs posted. Trees grew in tight, almost segregated tussocks: tamarack, jackpine, trembling aspen and birch trailing back towards a confused maze of low sand ridges, congregating farther yet into the main backbone esker that bore the tracks of wolf, bear, moose, fox, wolverine and caribou.

We set about to make discoveries on foot by following the esker behind our camp. It was easy walking and plain to see how the Dene preferred to follow these glacially formed 'highways' instead of fighting their way against wind and rapids along the river. On the crest of the ridge we could easily see where it dissolved into the big lake and had reappeared on the opposite shore, henceforth the explanation of the lake name. The Dene would build rafts and canoes here so they could cross the lake and continue their trek along the esker. And every esker tells its own story; sometimes with a subtle voice; an old voice; and there were always treasures and epitaphs left upon the golden sands. If you sat there long enough, staring at what remained of several crudely hewn grave markers, the story would unfold. A small picket fence implicating a Catholic influence; the size of the plot belonging to a child, possibly still-born, maybe cholera or pneumonia, even starvation; a shallow grave because of the permafrost but deep enough to keep the wolves from digging up the remains. Sometimes human bones mingled with those of other animals, scattered about a burial site as if thrown to the ground by a mystic or divine prognosticator.

Further along we discovered a sizeable hole excavated in a depression, ringed with a heap of bones and animal parts in various stages of decomposition. It was a wolf den. A busy one at that, indicated by the amount of footwork in and around the three separate holes we discovered. The half-meter diameter holes provided multiple access points to the burrow and all portals were littered with the remains of various prey and mounds of wolf scat.

This esker was one of many hundred in northern Manitoba fashioned by the retreating movement of the glacial ice-sheet, heaved up by an accumulation of melt-water silt. Most tundra-born wildlife continued to use these elevated 'roads' long after human traffic stopped and on its back were bones of every conceivable animal and, of course, those of humans. Although the esker was a linear entity, the bleached bones bore testament of the cyclical dynamic of nature and the dry climate.

It was hard to turn around and go back. Following this theater of existence and death was like reading a mystery novel, the kind that's hard to put down. Some eskers are more than a hundred kilometers in length. This particular one was quite short as it eventually dissolved after about two kilometers into the spruce landscape. The trail ends and we head back to our camp by the lakeside.

Eating fresh baked lake trout we lounged on the campsite meadow. A warm breeze wafted over the lake that kept flies to a tolerable level and we watched the sun slowly descend behind the far shore esker. I almost hated to be leaving this place of comfort and refuge, but we were eating up valuable expedition time. Such is the life of an explorer: forever on the move, the quest for discovery paramount. The thought of a summer camp-out here, perhaps similar to a Dene family of long ago, just wasn't a reality. We had to stick to the schedule. We had a long way to go yet.

From our vantage point upon our semi-barren and parched bone-orchard we took notice of the large, stationary clouds, both upriver from where we had come, and downriver in the direction of our travels. They were beautifully sculpted, like a Jacob van Ruisdael landscape painting; tumultuous thunderheads building in the heat of the day and accentuated by a waning sun, ornamental and entirely pretentious.

"Those are fires," someone remarked. We all looked again. I pulled out my field glasses to get a better look. Sure enough, the upriver cloud appeared in the horizon in the general vicinity of Tadoule. It had grown considerable since we left and it was likely that the entire village had been evacuated. I was more concerned with what lay downstream. I scanned the horizon with my binoculars in the direction we would be travelling and saw that there wasn't just a single cloud, but several of them.

"Christ! I hope they're out before we get there," Russell lamented. Nobody else said anything at all, transfixed on the immensity and seriousness of the distant conflagration. For the time being we didn't have a thing to worry about. I told the others the fires looked to be at least twenty kilometers away and would most likely burn themselves out by the time we got there. I was actually trying to convince myself.

*   *   *   *   *

The dread and anxiety of the first few days and even the weeks leading up to the expedition, of Dawson's moronic stunts and inconsiderate behaviour, all but vanished. *I must be getting old and intolerant*, I mused, laughing to myself and feeling a bit ashamed for being too critical. The ceremony at Hearne's campsite may have liberated the heavy burden on my back and I was thoroughly enjoying the expedition and the company of my comrades.

By the next morning the wind stopped altogether, but with the stillness and the rising temperature also came the biting flies. They descended, merciless and resolute, determined to exact their levy charged for our right to be tourists in their country. And it wasn't just black flies. Every variety of blood-sucking, winged tormentor attacked without hesitation: bull-dogs, blackflies and deer flies, mosquitoes the size of dimes, all demanded their take of blood and seriously strained our ability to maintain some semblance of composure. They followed us far out onto Shethanei Lake. We were so busy packing up camp and fending off flies that we failed to notice that the fire-clouds over the east horizon had not changed at all from the evening before.

There is always something profoundly exhilarating about paddling across such an immense body of water when the surface is mirror-smooth; but at the same time there is a degree of apprehension because the weather and conditions can change rapidly in the north. Common sense usually demands a charted course along and close to shore, especially if the lake is rough and the water temperature hovering just above freezing. There was almost a thirty Celsius degree difference between the air and water temperature. Our wet suits stuck to our skin like flypaper as the sun beat down mercilessly.

I made the decision to island hop down the middle of the lake, thereby avoiding the deep inlets and bays along the erratic south shoreline. Shethanei was forty-kilometers long, but never more than three or four kilometers wide at any point. The safety crutch in doing this was the possibility of simply riding any big waves the relatively short distance to the north shore in lee of a sudden wind.

As it turned out in our favour, the calm persisted and the threat of any change in weather was an unwarranted precaution. We leaned into our paddling strokes, feeling a bit rejuvenated, and being pumped up we averaged six kilometers per hour. Before we knew it we had put twenty kilometers behind us, arriving at *Sheth-than-nee*, the legendary "high hill running into the lake" before lunch. It was also another of Sam Hearne's legendary campsites.

The esker skirted the shore for some distance: impressive

but subject to severe wind and other erosional factors, whole sections being besieged by wave-action were barely held together by a tenacious growth of aspen and birch. The esker swung inland away from the lake but we caught up to it again where the lake narrowed. This was the *"eh-dah"*, or crossing place along the migratory caribou route. The Dene would camp nearby and wait for the animals to enter the water at the sacred *"Ben Kah Dah"*. Hunters would station themselves across the narrows at the *"Chah'l Dah"*, or lookout. Once the caribou plunged into the water they were dispatched easily by hunters casting spears from the crude boats they had constructed just for that purpose. After killing as many caribou as they could, they were hauled ashore where the women did all the 'processing': the butchering, drying and pounding of the meat into jerky or processed into pemmican. The marrow and the bones were boiled down for the fat used to manufacture pemmican, consisting of half rendered suet, half ground dry meat and mixed with a variety of local dried berries.

Evenings in a Dene camp were spent preparing hides for clothing, blankets, sleeping mats and teepee coverings. It took forty caribou hides to make a covering for one teepee. If there was a surplus of meat, the Dene would cache it under a pile of rocks, or freeze it in the snow or blocks of river ice. During difficult times when caribou could not be located, the people would head for the Eh-Dah in hopes of finding an old cache of edible meat. Some preferred the slightly green, rancid taste of the cached meat.

Much like the esker we had previously explored, it was apparent that the Dene had spent much of their time here. Remnants of projectile points were scattered about although we failed to find any gravesites along the summit of the esker. Perhaps they thought it bad luck to bury their dead at such a fine hunting spot.

That didn't mean the dead may not have been interned there. It could have been that the pickets had long disintegrated in to the fine sands, or perhaps even predated European contact altogether. The most recent sign of human activity was a weather-worn trapper's cabin still standing beside a shallow kettle-lake that paralleled the esker. A log kennel built to house sled-dogs stood as a reminder of a way of life which had passed into history.

Years of erosion from wind, rain and snow had abraded a once lofty esker ridge into several flat, bowl-shaped depressions known as "blow-outs." Pioneer lichens, mosses, aspen and dwarf birch continued to fight an endless struggle to stabilize the constantly eroding sand dunes, creating polygonal designs that resembled patchwork quilting. Again, there was no shortage of animal tracks held in the sand. As I found myself straying from the others, each of us following our own nose of interest among the maze of landforms, I was enticed to follow a particular ridge of sculpted sand that rose rather abruptly ahead of me. As I climbed the embankment and stepped out from a thin band of scrub trees and onto a blow-out, I was confronted by a rather large tundra wolf standing less than five-meters away.

For about fifteen seconds – an extraordinary length of time under such conditions - our eyes met and locked, neither of us about to make the first move. It was a magnificent male wolf: steely yellow eyes, grey-black and tawny coat and well-muscled. My first thought was, "Holy shit, a fucking wolf!" I wasn't afraid, just surprised. Wolf encounters certainly weren't new for me. Still, every encounter tends to take your breath away when it happens.

It was a lone wolf, as far as I knew, and would not attempt an attack on a human; me being an animal he may never have seen before. I had a lot of wolf experiences in the past, both while exploring by canoe and during winter camping expeditions and had even been surrounded by wolves on two occasions and only once, felt any sense of peril. That was several years ago.

"Tell us your wolf story," Russ demanded later that day. "You know, the one you mentioned the other day when I asked about wolves and bears, when you trekked into Pukaskwa Park in the winter – that's a great story!" So I told him, the others listened.

"My university friend had been contracted to do the avifauna research for the newly developed Pukaskwa National Park off Lake Superior. I was to trek in by snowshoe and toboggan about sixty-five kilometers from the village of Mopert and meet my friends who were wintering in the interior at a station set up by Canada Parks. The first day out had been a tough trek over wet snow along a seldom used logging track. Because of the slow progress I failed to reach the prescribed halfway cabin by nightfall. Luckily I had located a dilapidated and partly collapsed trapper's shack just off the trail, managed to re-assemble a make-shift wood stove and hung a tarp over the now vacant door. I awoke in the middle of the night when I heard an animal scratching at my partly loaded gear toboggan just meters from the cabin. Then, more animals could be heard padding around outside, so close I could hear their breathing."

"Sheeit, what did you do?" Hodding asked.

"I got up and pushed a few boards against the tarp covering the door, looked outside quickly and saw two wolves standing beside my toboggan. Others were close by. It was a clear night, and just enough moonlight to easily make out any details. It was a pack of timber wolves. Everything seemed fine and I kept a vigil at the door, holding on to my axe but they never came any closer than a few meters away. Then the howling began; a chorus of wilderness voices that could wake the dead. And it lasted for at least an hour."

"Were you afraid...I mean, Christ I would have been terrified," Russell admitted.

"Frightening, yes, you better believe it; made worse after they started to howl and wail. They seemed to be agitated and nervous, circling around the shack for what felt like an eternity."

"Then what happened?" Russ questioned.

"They left. Gone. Quietly too, all of a sudden. But they left tracks all around the cabin and there must have been quite a few of them."

"That's a great story," Hodding said. "Then the wolf today and so close too. I'm sorry I missed seeing it"

The tundra wolf I had confronted that day was considerably larger than any of the timber wolves I had seen. I was hesitant to make even a subtle move for fear that he would bolt before I had the chance to unsling my camera. I barely made a gesture to move when the wolf took flight and leapt out of the blow-out in two giant strides, stopping only briefly about fifty meters away to see if I was in pursuit. Dawson came over the rise and just missed seeing the wolf as it sped off down the esker. We followed its tracks for about a kilometer, getting one more glimpse of the wolf before it finally vanished off the side of the esker world and into thick timber.

The esker snaked its way through the boreal plain for at least ten-kilometers, supported by a generous but sporadic growth of jackpine, black spruce and birch, home to both wild animal and songbird. Thrushes, plovers, arctic terns, gulls and countless warblers vocalized the very spirit of the northern boreal landscape, adding a happy melody that pervaded over a land that so very easily becomes dreary and melancholic.

Had it not been for the intensity of the flies we would have lingered here longer; out on the windless lake it wouldn't be much different. We shoved off under a blazing sun and a temperature that had already reached a scorching thirty degrees adding to our overall discomfort. Black flies were persistent, descending upon us in clouds, loitering around our faces and attacking any open flesh with zeal. They worked their way under the folds of clothing to feast inconspicuously on soft flesh. Hodding and Russell put on their mosquito headnets; Dawson toughed it out, refusing to wear his, preferring to lather himself liberally with *Deet*-laced insect repellent. Even with that, the bull-dogs were getting to him and those particularly vexing flies seem to sense a person's anxiety by attacking the most vulnerable areas. On Dawson these were the bottoms of his uncovered feet. He was paddling beside us, about ten-meters to our starboard side, stamping his feet madly, cursing, swiping at the horse flies with his closed fists, waving his paddle at them. It was comical, ridiculous really because he didn't have to suffer like this. Russell laughed but Hodding said nothing. He seemed to be in his own world.

I wasn't wearing my headnet either. I found it to be too claustrophobic, hot and difficult to see through on sunny days. It was like trying to look at the world through a badly scratched pair of cheap sunglasses. I was lucky that the bugs didn't bother me that much. I either let them bite or warded off the worst of them by smearing Tiger Balm around my ears, neck and wrists. Since biting flies are attracted to carbon-dioxide, breathing harder and getting over-wrought just made things worse. I do have to admit that dealing with biting insects isn't always that easy. The bugs can get so intolerable that it's easy to work yourself into a frenzy. It happens to moose during the hot days of June, when the black flies are at their worst and the animals get so incensed by flies that they charge wildly through the underbrush or dive headlong into streams, sometimes submerging themselves so deep in muskeg that they can't extricate themselves.

We were paddling along sharing stories, cruising the shoreline. "You know, Russ," I began a long narrative about an incident a couple of years back, "I once came across a cow moose hopelessly stuck in deep mud up to her shoulders. It was early season and a bad year for black flies. The animal had died there probably from dehydration but had also suffered from predator attack by animals light enough to be suspended by the mud or it was picked apart by ravens and vultures from above."

"Christ, what a way to die," Russ stated, keeping up a good paddling pace.

"Yes, and predators, mostly ravens probably, would have started tearing at its flesh before it had died," I added. Russell feigned a gag response.

At the end of a day it wasn't unusual to have a hundred bug bites or more and I knew that I had to be careful not to get over-bitten. Black flies inject a kind of mild anti-coagulant that also acts as a pain-killer so it's sometimes hard to really determine how many bites you actually have. I've often had to take antihistamines to counter the effects. In Dawson's case, he should have kept his shoes and shirt on while paddling but for some reason he preferred to swipe madly at his tormentors.

Once past the esker, Shethanei Lake opened up and the recumbent landscape almost disappeared entirely as it gently slipped over a visually deceptive precipice. From our visual height in the canoe, calculated at about a meter and a half, the true horizon and the curvature of the earth would only be about four kilometers away. Since the topographic height of trees across the lake was likely less than twenty-feet, any distance over water more than eight kilometers away would put the far shoreline below our line of sight completely. Shethanei looked like an ocean-scape from our perspective; a bit daunting but still calm and unrippled by wind. While paddling lakes the same size further south in rolling Shield country, the shorelines were always in sight no matter what the distance unless it was a lake the size of Superior. This was a new navigational experience for me and a little more difficult to configure on a two-dimensional map. The only guiding tool you could normally trust would be line-of-sight, three-dimensional landforms. A promontory or jut of land could easily be recognized on a map and the directional course plan plotted accordingly. On Shethanei there was only the one shoreline in sight. Granted, I could use my compass and our relative average speed of five to six kilometers per hour to calculate our position at any given time. Although a bit perplexing, this new revelation was exciting and it kept me glancing at my topographic map more often just to make sure I was on course.

Configuring an easier track, we set a course for a point of land that could be a potential camping spot and headed across the lake again. After a couple of lethargic hours paddling under a blistering sun over a calm, windless lake, we reached the far side; the selected point looking quite promising for tenting. It was a raised bedrock shelf overlooking the vastness of lake we had just crossed over. Behind the point was one of Manitoba's most impressive drumlin fields. Drumlins are smooth, oval-shaped landforms with a blunt and a tapered end, generally comprised of boulder-clay; but in Manitoba, as we already explored at Hearne's campsite, drumlins were quite often composed of large boulders and even solid slabs of rock. They form beneath the outer perimeter of an expanding glacial ice sheet during a major advance, and as a result from the selective deposition of material it is subsequently *streamlined* by the moving ice. Their relative axis lies parallel to the northwest direction of the glacier mass.

This was all fascinating and new to me and probably why Manitoba lends itself so well to exploration, chiefly because of the variety and disparately contrasting land and life forms. Already I had determined that this was the perfect river for the *Men's Journal* piece, but I had yet to see Hodding take out a pen and notepad. Russell on the other hand, was never far from any

133

one of his three cameras, taking hand-held shots on the fly or taking the time to set up his tripod while camping. I later learned that Hodding would take notes of the day by journaling in the group tent while Dawson rambled on about his female exploits, the environmental movement and Keewaydin camp days.

To find respite from the black flies, the others piled into their tent while I hurriedly cooked a one-pot dinner. It wasn't long before I joined them. We ate in relative comfort, free of head-nets or repellent, with enough bites to keep us busy scratching and dousing with salve for the rest of the evening. The cool of day's end couldn't come fast enough, once the sun had retreated, bringing out the mosquitoes. Off in my own tent I realized just how noisy the wilderness was in the high boreal: loons yodelled, nighthawks sailed and swooped on evening thermals, a bittern – also known as a "thunder-bumper" or "pile-driver", let out a booming *oonk-a-chunk, oonk-a-chunk*, from a nearby marshy bay and mosquitoes hummed their own tune while bouncing off the bug-mesh of the tent. Snoring from the other tent topped it off... *this wilderness was anything but quiet!*

Chapter Seven

FIRE!

The interlude of tranquil lake-paddling ended abruptly as the Seal River regained its downward plunge to the Arctic Ocean. We were once again swept along its track through a sub-arctic panorama of temporary taiga; a geomorphilogical monotony with no distinguishable physical relief, hills or outcrops, nothing but an endless barrier of spruce hemming us in tight to our river freeway; water and sky, with a thin band of olive-drab in between.

More rapids; easier runs. Russell had become more adept at reading the waves and flow patterns instead of concentrating on the rocks – a common faux pas of beginners, like skiers who run into the only tree or lift post instead of navigating around. Running whitewater is as much a cerebral sport as it is an adventure skill. I got Russell to stop looking at the fixed obstacles and to keep his eye trained on the moving water around them. Hodding was also catching on, probably taking his cue from Russell. I didn't see a lot of finesse coming from his stern paddler; Dawson, usually preoccupied with the telling of his endless stories, simply ruddered his paddle when required.

Because Russell was doing so well I didn't have to concentrate on his every move. I could now scan the shoreline for wildlife, take pictures, even write in my journal if I propped my steering paddle under my arm, or sometimes we would just drift with the strong current. I could also concentrate more on any changing weather patterns. Since we were back on the river, the horizon lines were tighter, offering a poorer view of distant clouds. I was watching for the smoke cloud that we had seen yesterday, but it had vanished from sight. That was a great relief because I dreaded the thought of having to paddle anywhere near a raging boreal fire.

Nah yah eye Desay, or Wolverine River, flowed into the Seal from the north and terminated there in a long set of boulder rapids. To the north, at Duck Lake Narrows, at the entrance of Nejanilini Lake, the Dene once hunted caribou. It was one of the most important *Ed-ah,* or crossing points crucial to the existence of the people. Sadly, it is now quiet and the caribou no longer cross at this place. The cold water of the Wolverine, however, carries a much different vitality and omnipotence - Arctic Grayling!

Stopping at the base of the rapids long enough to catch our dinner, Russell had unsheathed his fly-rod to try his luck. It was pure pleasure to watch the angling artistry as the golden coil of line arced back and forth above the rapids, the bait landing precisely in an eddy behind a boulder, a moment's pause before the surface broke and a fish was secured. Grayling has to be one of the most striking of all cold-water fish: the odd dorsal fin extending like an oriental paper-fan, and a zest for life that rivals only that of the wily brook trout. A dinner of fresh grayling was guaranteed in no time. I dropped a handful of tobacco in the water before we paddled off – a long time custom of mine to make sure the river spirits were thanked for the bounty proffered.

As we travelled east I detected the acrid odour of smoke. At first I had interpreted it as a shift in the wind carrying the smoke-drift from the fire at Tadoule; the cloud movement above our heads though told a different story: the wind was coming from the direction we were now headed. My stomach rolled. Rounding a wide bend in the river revealed the source of the smoke. Several wild fires were burning downriver! A magnificent and vigorous course of rapids, which we were now in the midst, timed their appearance accordingly; the moment we made eye contact with the flumes of smoke rising in our path we were ushered into the maw of a turbulent stretch of the river. Not wanting to go past the bottom of the rapids I yelled to the others to beach their canoe once we were finished the run. After two-kilometers of enervating shoulder-work we eddied into a small cove at the foot of a level, sheltered terrace that looked to be a perfect place for an overnight camp.

Before us was one of the Seal's most pronounced glacio-fluvial formations. A thirty-meter sand esker and escarpment formed a backdrop to our campsite, plunging steeply into the terminus of the big rapids, continuing on across the river to the south side and trailing off as far as the eye could follow. "This is perfect," I told the others. From the top of the esker I could somehow get a map-fix on the location of the fires. The unrestricted view, hopefully, would allow me to see where and how the fires were moving in relation to the river. I was anxious to know just how serious our situation might prove to be.

First off, we were hungry and it was going to be a lengthy meal preparation so the walk along the esker could wait. A hot fire was quickly kindled. Dinner preparations were as much a ceremonial affair and communal effort as much as it was a diversion away from the impending thought of wildfires downriver. I baked a cornbread in the reflector oven and grilled the grayling over the fire: a feast by any standard. Even with such a fine banquet there was a worrisome pall over the group. While sitting by the fire we watched the heavy grey-black mantle of smoke rising and spreading in the east in an unknown and scrupulous design.

Later, from the vantage point of the esker, standing beside the remnant markers of a lone human grave, I couldn't really determine the extent of the fire, whether it was advancing, retreating or recessing for the night. It looked like several fires were burning, not just one, and there was no pattern to it but it was very extensive, flaring across the entire river valley downstream where the forest was most lush and full. I reassured the others.

"Okay, here's what I think," I said with commitment and a slight hint of honesty. "The fire is only burning on one side of the river," I assumed not knowing for sure. "The south side... and the smoke would be carried away from us by the prevailing northeast wind." At best it was an educated guess, but I had to tell them something.

"What happens if we run into fires tomorrow?" Hodding asked. Both Russ and Dawson perked up, looking at me for a definitive and professional answer. I wanted to say "what the fuck do I know?" like I could pull an answer out of all my fire experiences. "We play it by ear, approach cautiously I guess, and hope the smoke stays clear off the river."

"Then what?" Russ questioned.

"Then we hold up for a while, wait 'till the fires burn themselves out." It was the only answer I could think of. It sounded plausible. I felt nervous about heading further downstream but at the same time there was an alluring quality to the idea of confronting a boreal fire head-on; perhaps similar to standing on the lip of a cliff, edging closer to the edge to get a better view - a totally self-indulgent reflection.

A boreal fire is a wild card that could force a number of different outcomes. Get too close and the positive conclusions all but vanish. None of us thought about the prospect of running into a fire. It's not something you pack for, practice for or even think about until you're faced with it. You can prepare for just about anything, but a fire is as unpredictable as the path of a tornado, and every bit as destructive. All you can do is give it a lot of space; difficult enough on a river whose current draws you ever closer to danger.

The caribou trails along the esker summit looked well-trammelled. It was hard to discern whether or not the pathways might still be used since any scuffing on top of the sensitive moss-mat takes decades to repair itself. Sometimes it never does. Since the allotted growing season is minimal and the boreal duff requires at least thirty years to mature into fodder ripe enough to serve as caribou food, any of the trails could be decades old. Even the scattered bones and antlers may sit on the esker sand for many years, decomposing ever so slowly, gnawed by mice and voles, frozen for nearly nine months of the year.

I had butterflies in my stomach. Actually, they were more like bats. I was thinking about the extent and the magnitude of the rapids on tomorrow's roster, the location of the fires, not to mention what to do if we got ourselves into the thick of it. We had no communication; no way of calling for help, and certainly no prospect of a government helicopter in the vicinity ready to pick up tourists along the river, or even warn us to get out like they do in the provincial parks in the south. The burden of decision weighed heavy in my gut, alongside the undigested fish and cornbread. I realized we would be taking chances – *huge chances* – and there was nothing in the "how-to" manuals that could prepare anyone for this. We just weren't supposed to be there.

This day had been unusually silent. Not the rapids. Not the river. It was the land that was devoid of sound. There was no bird-song at all, as if they had abandoned the world altogether. *Must be the fires,* was my first thought. Why would they stick around?

I walked with Russell and Dawson for a short spell then decided to wander off on my own. I needed some space to think. There was certainly no shortage of space along the esker. The sun was setting, an hour before midnight but there was such an alluring force present anytime I found myself following caribou trails. This esker was formidable, much loftier than the others, and this gave it such a commanding view of the boreal plains. It also kept a uniform shape and direction, unlike the others that seemed to splay out into variegated sub-eskers, blowouts and peat plateaus. I wanted to keep walking north. Follow the waning sun to my left and the dark band of encroaching night to my right.

I came across tracks too large to be a black bear and I no longer felt alone. They had been scuffed fresh. By instinct I scanned the immediate vicinity but saw nothing. I stood out in the open esker suddenly feeling very vulnerable and a little foolish. I was at least three kilometers from camp and had left my gun behind. It was common knowledge that barren-ground grizzly bears had, on occasion, ventured this far east into northern Manitoba. I started back to camp at a brisker than normal pace, looking over my shoulder every so often, feeling even more foolish for worrying so much. I started to laugh so hard I had to stop and catch my breath, taking huge gulps of the warm evening air.

At the grave site above the camp I took a few moments to relax. The wind had vanished and there was no bear stalking me. The mosquitoes though were predatory. At least I wasn't about to be mauled to death by them. I laughed so hard I thought I was going to piss my pants. From my vantage point I could see the others milling about the campfire. Before heading down I took another quick glance in the direction of the fires that had now dissipated in the evening calm. The once bold columns of smoke trailed low to the horizon, outlined by the residual sunlight strung out in non-threatening gestures. I felt relieved, for now.

I descended the steep slope to the camp. The temperature immediately dropped ten degrees. From the apex of the esker where the sun's heat still radiated off the sand in waves, to the low flats where the tents stood was enough of a change in atmosphere to generate a shroud of cold mist and a general discomfort along with the mosquitoes that had everyone crawling into their tents. Gear packs and morning firewood were covered by a tarpaulin and the beached canoes secured to a nearby tree with one of the track lines: a nightly ritual. Stars were beginning to push the day away.

The one candle in my tent was enough to take the night chill from the air and I could sit comfortably on my sleeping bag while writing in my journal. I thought about the fires and hoped that they would have already had time to pass over the Seal and that would be the end of it. If we had to face a gauntlet of raging wildfires in the days to come, I would not have any quick anecdotes to draw upon, no remedies or emergency tactics that had been practiced and honed over the years as a wilderness guide, or something they might have taught you at guide school or weekend clinics. Not the same as rescuing clients from an overturned canoe, applying first aid, extricating the injured, coping with adverse weather conditions, snow, rain, *bugs!* There was no quick-sure technique relevant to surviving an all-consuming bush fire except to get the hell out of its way.

It was the smoke that I was most concerned about; the fire itself was virtually harmless unless you were standing near enough in its path to get fried. Back in my home territory of Temagami, Ontario, I remembered the history of the great homesteading fires that raged across the land at the turn of the last century, not just one fire, but two infernos that killed several hundred people. The only escape for many was to walk into the shallows of Lake Temiskaming, but as the thick smoke descended in dense clouds, even the sanctity of the cold water proved to be no haven.

I stayed up looking over the maps again instead of sleeping. The fires, as I had estimated, were about twelve to fifteen kilometers downstream and burning only on the south side of the river. To get there we had to negotiate a variety of rapids, *big rapids,* having gauged what was ahead by what we had already run. It was forty-four kilometers to the intended Great Island campsite with over half that distance in serious rapid-play and a vertical drop of more than forty meters (132 feet)! Somewhere in between were the fires. With the velocity and power of the current drawing us steadily downstream it would be next to impossible to backtrack if the going got tough. For the next hour I went over every scenario but couldn't clear my mind of such questionable procedure, possible circumstance and imminent danger. My candle burned long into the night, until daylight began creeping over the east horizon and I fell asleep, finally, just before it was time to get up.

*   *   *   *   *

It was a slow morning. That was completely my fault. As the expedition motivator I had difficulty in trying to get *myself* moving. The others were shifting around, getting dressed in their tent and I just lay in my sleeping bag attempting to shed the pall of sleep from my brain. It took me a while to focus on the present. I needed coffee! I crawled out from my cocoon into a cold, damp morning, stretched, farted healthily, pissed gratuitously and shuffled to the firepit. The quick fire felt wonderful on stiff joints.

Coffee was brewed, pancakes fried up in great numbers, doused with real maple syrup, excited garble about the fires, the white-water and how nice it was that it was too cold out even for the mosquitoes.

My head cleared once I had downed three cups of strong coffee, but it was a late start and we had a long way to go to get to Great Island. It was past ten o'clock; at least the extra time allowed us to double and triple-check our gear, to make sure everything was packed well and water-tight. There was a slight morning breeze building, but it hadn't yet had the time to lift the veil of smoke that hung over the east horizon. The defining plumes of smoke were not visible, giving us the impression that the fires had already passed through and would not be a confrontational problem.

Immediately after breaking camp and pushing off into the heavy current, we saw our first harbour seal, more than two-hundred kilometers from Hudson Bay. It was lolling about the boulders in the middle of the river, curious, even swimming by the side of the canoe as we passed by. We were cruising along so fast that Russell and I barely had time to take pictures.

I could feel the sinews of the river current flexing every time I dipped my paddle: powerful, commanding, pulling us along effortlessly, like standing on a horizontal airport escalator being whisked along while exercising no effort at all. Out of our own control actually. It was a good opportunity to take in the scenery before we hit the rapids.

The operative adjective to describe the landscape would have to be "ravaged". A taciturn growing season, limited ground-cover to a bare minimum of shade trees. Those with obstinate and determined characteristics were stunted by the extreme environmental conditions that prevailed, misshapen by wind and winter snow-load. Even these were sporadic at best, burnt-over in some

143

places, the landscape rendered barren except for patches of Alaskan birch, showy fireweed and polygons of ground moss, crowberry clusters and lichen beds. Any surviving jackpine or black spruce was incidental, accidental, alive solely due to the fact that they found safe haven from the ravages of fire by taking root in the lower folds, ravines and bog marshes. I had to keep reminding myself that fire was a completely natural part of the genesis of life in the high boreal.

The river banks sloped steeply to form a rather pronounced spillway or trough, giving the Seal River the definition of a geological sluice that kept the movement of water at a vibrant pace of over 12 k.p.h., calculated by the time elapsed against the distance I plotted on the topographical chart. Morainic detritus — the scrabble of sand, clay and boulders that classified the earthwork along the course of the Seal - was interspersed with massive intrusions of rock. Mother Earth. The Precambrian Shield massif exposed itself regally, every so often, indicating that we were still within the transitional world between highland and lowland, rock and swamp, sub-arctic and arctic, boreal and barrenland; heading through the netherworld at the edge of the solid, old earth where it blends with a newer one that was still flexing its muscles. The eager animation of the river contrasted boldly with the lethargic, three-billion year old girding.

For the next two hours the river ran straight and fast, eastward, directly towards multiple flumes of smoke that now towered skyward, spreading ominously across the upper stratum of space, pressing out the direct sunlight until all that was left was a solemn, filtered pall, as if we were stepping into a dimly-lit funeral parlour where the dirge-like music was actually the sound of the river washing against the boulders on its downward rush. None of us spoke a word. There was a predominant and uneasy hush shared as we plied our paddles, never taking our eyes from the growing barricade of smoke and fire that crept closer at every stroke.

Initially, we were quite preoccupied with plotting a course through the heavy rapids. Throughout the remainder of the morning, the river demanded our full attention. Some of the runs had been quite long, up to three kilometers of constant Class III rapids, others rounded tight bends that completely blocked our view of what lie ahead while the backdrop of smoke drew nearer. We had the impression that we would never reach the fires, and at times the river would arc away from the inferno entirely and head in another direction. But every time, the Seal trajectory returned to face the increasingly menacing conflagration.

The wall of smoke became so immense that it soon occupied the entire horizon. It was only mid-day but it was darker than night. It was then that the binding truth hit us all like a huge slap in the face: sooner or later we were going to come face to face with the wild fires. It was now inevitable. The steady current did not let up at all and we took to drifting rather than paddling just to slow ourselves down. A dense smoke-haze had settled over the river like a morning mist, except that it was pungent and hostile. There was a polite breeze, but not enough to lift all the smoke-drift up and away so it rested along the channel of the river in an eerie, blue malicious miasma.

I had to keep clearing my throat and began coughing so I dipped my bandana in the water and wrapped it around my nose and mouth. Breathing in the moist air through the wet cloth soothed my dry throat and the others soon followed suit. There was nothing we could do to ease the stinging in our eyes, save for the occasional splashing of water on our face or re-wetting the bandana and wiping off the gritty film that settled over and on everything. The heaviest smoke still lay to the south, about half a kilometer away, and we followed the sheer-line of haze by keeping well out from the south shore where the line of spruce appeared to be acting as a "brake" for the settling effluent.

Knots were gathering in my stomach again like an angry rally. I started to second guess myself and wondered whether we had made the right decision. To hold back for a couple of days until we were sure that the fires had cleared never was considered. It was too late for the "what ifs" and the "should haves", and now there was nowhere to camp along the river. The current pulled us closer to the wall of smoke and we drifted slowly, rounding a bend and coming face to face with the fire at its leading perimeter. This was not reassuring at all.

We were still approaching too fast so we began to back-paddle in order to gain a little time and garnish some kind of plan as to what to do next. The fire had not yet crossed the river and was contained along the south shore, just as I had figured the night before. That was a comforting reality, for the time being, but the mass of the fire looked as if it were eating its way downriver and out of our sight. Thankfully, the wind had remained in our favour, from the west, which did a remarkable job at containing the fire and the rush of smoke along the south shore.

Breathing was still difficult without the wet bandanas; even then, after a while the cloth would get so saturated with a noxious grit it was better to leave them off. It was almost as if we were getting acclimatized to the 'thin' air, taking short gulps through pursed lips, slightly claustrophobic. Taking long, deep breaths seemed to work, for the time being. So long as it didn't get any worse everything would be okay.

It was a fire of monstrous proportion, burning with no specific design. Judging by the density of the columns of thick smoke, rising like huge Greek pillars, high into the troposphere, it was probably eating up the ozone in billowing waves. Now I imagined what it must be like standing beside an erupting volcano. Gauging the distance we were drifting, we could see the general panorama of the fire, but that expanse was steadily shrinking as we approached the front line of the burn. The layout was now totally obfuscated by the wall of fire that was presently eating away at the spruce along the near shore with a vigorous appetite. I had never been this close to a bush fire and it was absolutely terrifying; but in an obtuse way, incredibly beautiful too, hellishly powerful and oddly spiritual; frightening but divine and utterly final. Drifting along we all became mesmerized by the magnitude and pageantry of such a pyrotechnic show, like kids at a fireworks display. It was truly fabulous in all its destructive glory; perfectly natural. No words were spoken between us.

Huge explosions of bright orange flame shot skyward as each cluster of dry spruce was consumed, spirals of ash and still-burning soot spinning hundreds of feet into the air. We could feel the heat now, from the middle of the river. We rested our paddles on the gunwales, but still moved downriver while thermal blasts seared the air all around us, penetrating our wet suits as if it weren't hot enough already. We began to melt inside our clothing; suddenly, that clothing didn't seem to offer any protection at all. The only blessing in all of this was the absence of black flies and bull-dogs.

I asked Russell whether he wanted to get a closer look at the fire in order to set up some shots for the magazine.

"Sure, let's do it," he said, hesitating, even though the nervous features on his face painted a different answer. And like curious cats with nine lives we both succumbed to that inherent photographer aspiration – *to get the shot of a lifetime*. Here was one chance in a million to capture some incredible pictures nobody in their right mind would go out of their way to shoot. We were stuck on the river with nowhere else to go so we figured we might as well make the best of it; take the bull by the horns. In

147

this case it was a fire-breathing dragon.

The canoes were beached alongside the south shore after running an easy section of fast water. It appeared to be a safe enough landing away from the outer vanguard of flames. Russ and I scrambled out of the canoe with our cameras.

"Shit, no time for the tripod," Russell yelled, cradling his handy SLR that he kept close at hand in the canoe for quick shots. "And it's fucking hot!"

It *was* hot, like a giant blowtorch blowing at us. I could feel my skin tightening and the heat searing the hair inside my nostrils. The fire was moving around us and up the shore, the safety of the river to our right, Russell and I moved closer over the shore rock for the best vantage spot. *This is too close,* I thought. We were now standing inside the arc of fire, shooting, adjusting apertures and light settings, getting caught up in the moment entirely.

"Christ, feel the heat!" Russ screamed above the din, all the while taking photographs. Hodding and Dawson sat silently in their canoe ready to take flight. We were standing on the shore boulders a few meters from the canoes and only twenty meters from the fire. A copse of dry spruce trees literally exploded beside us in a fiery ball and showered us with burning embers.

"We're too close!" I shouted at Russ. The fire at this point was a living, breathing monster and with each fierce breath another stand of trees detonated. The closest trees to us vaporized instantly, consumed by a steaming, hissing cyclone of swirling fire. Instead of retreating, Russ and I stood there taking pictures. It was crazy. The forest was being eaten up around us in sporadic bursts, strangely selective, jumping here and there in unpredictable eruptions. The noise was deafening, in all ranges of the audio-spectrum; there were sharp cracks as pockets of gas erupted from the dry wood; the whoosh and roar of the spontaneous outbursts, to the crescendo of the fire mass itself. We were pushed off our perch on the rocks by a blast of fire, a spurious ball of orange the size of a house, glowered momentarily like a landed comet, searing our exposed hands and face.

"Shit...shit...*Sheeeeit!*" Russ yelled, brushing wildly at his clothes. Looking through the camera lens neither of us realized that hot sparks and still-burning coals were descending on us in a thick, black rain. It wasn't until I felt the sting of embers on my bare skin that I realized we had stayed too long.

"Alright, let's get the hell out of here!" I yelled at Russell, but he was already half way to the canoe. I bellowed at Dawson and Hodding to push off. Burning spruce needles continued to hail down around us in a widening berth, the heat waves sucking up the oxygen, making it hard to breathe. We shoved the canoe out into the current and paddled hard to the center of the river. Luckily, the spray-covers were soaked from the previous bout of rapids we had just run so the hot coals that landed just fizzled out without burning through the nylon.

"What a fucking rush!" Russell glowed. He knew he had snapped some good shots and so did I. *Was it worth the risk?* I would say yes to that years later, but we had taken a huge chance that day, not really knowing the unpredictable disposition of that fire. We were damned lucky, so far; lucky that the smoke from the fire was blowing off in the other direction – it could have changed in a split-second. We were also lucky that the river was as wide as it was and we managed to stay just outside the rim of residual smoke-haze that clung to the south shore.

The fire followed us for the next thirty-kilometers, progressively intensifying as we paddled east. Every so often there would be a violent flare-up and a section of the spruce shoreline would disappear in a matter of seconds. It was amazing how quickly the forest burned and how fast the fire could travel. It was as if we were racing it, competing with it and whenever we felt that we had taken the lead, the fire would pop-out suddenly in a show of force, almost mocking us as we paddled even harder to gain some distance. Nobody talked. All of us were too occupied with the fire show. The only time we exchanged words was on shore when we pulled in to scout rapids, and even then it was usually just me that spoke, outlining where we were to run the canoes down.

"We'll take the right line, through the tongue along the shore, watch the diagonal waves, brace through and pull left at the end to avoid the bottom boulders," I'd say with authority as the others stood beside me. Everyone listened, except Dawson who always seemed to have a better way to tackle a hard run. That contrariness was actually helpful because I'd have to explain why the running line I chose was a better choice. Dawson always wanted to take the big water down the middle but I was attempting to teach our newcomers the art of finessing rapids, to learn how to stay in control, practice ferrying.

We had to run several large rapids. Some of the runs were now textbook: a quick scout from shore (sometimes with the fire too close for comfort), a plan of execution with a plan "B" if things went awry, hop in the canoes and single-file down the run. It was lucky for us that most of these runs were short, heavy volume waves constricted to the center channel and we always managed to find an easier path not far out from shore; lucky that the water was high enough to submerge the boulder gardens that rim the edges of the river. I would explain each run as we stood on a prominent rock looking out over the rapids, what to avoid, an eddy out if we needed to re-position on the run. Russell was a pleasure to work the rapids with. Dawson had trouble lining up or understanding the finer moves and relied on us to initiate the run, followed us reluctantly, and often missed the easier channel.

All in all, we managed to work our way down river without incident and eventually past the fires. So we thought.

We reached Great Island where the Seal River splits into two channels. There was a good beach with a raised moss and grass clearing that would be perfect for setting up the tents. The first thing we did when we landed was remove, or rather *peel-off* our wetsuits which had stuck to our skin like shrink-wrap. Thinking we had 'beat' the fire was a gross mistake. It had caught up to us and was now burning rigorously along the far side of the rapids, across the river. From where we stationed ourselves, directly across the narrowest part of the river and in the path of a virtual firestorm, was a set of lively rapids, two-hundred meters wide. It barely separated us from the incoming blaze. That's a relatively short distance for a fire of this magnitude to 'jump' should the wind come up suddenly.

During a wildfire in Ontario, while I was a park ranger in Temagami, I had been out with my crew doing portage work when we witnessed one of the largest fires in local history. A spot fire was neatly handled and contained and the fire crew pulled to fight another blaze that consumed half the town of Cobalt in 1978. The spot fire, tended by a skeleton crew, got out of hand when strong winds out of the southwest fanned the almost extinguished fire into an uncontrollable inferno. Fed by a thousand acres of timber slash it burned with such a force that it created a fireball that jumped a five-kilometer open expanse of lake. This is a common trait of a fire that suddenly runs out of available oxygen. A huge fire will create its own destructive temperament based on the environment around it.

We stood on the beach for several minutes pondering our situation. *Should we keep going, or wait and see what happens,* I wondered before speaking out. "Leave the canoes loaded," I instructed, "We'll see what the fire is going to do."

151

I was reluctant to have everybody set up camp right away. We were all a bit dumbfounded by the flame-show, not really sure of our next move, tired from paddling, exhausted from worrying. Should the fire jump the river we could still shove off and escape; if we had to break down our camp we would lose precious time. So we did nothing. The fire was picking up momentum as it ate away at the far shore of spruce, sending volumes of flame, soot and smoke high into the sky, enough to blot out the afternoon sun. It was nothing short of spectacular.

The canoes were unloaded but we left all the packs piled on the beach and sat on the sand watching the inferno unfolding a short distance away. The fire now had reached an impressive zenith by creating a massive wall of flame several hundred feet high.

"Let's get some more shots," I said to Russell "We might as well do something productive."

"Brilliant idea. What do you have in mind?" Russell wrestled his tripod and camera out of his dry bag.

"Let's get Hodding and Dawson on the river to run the rapids with the fire in the background," I suggested.

"Awesome!" Russ chimed with an almost child-like giddiness.

Dawson and Hodding agreed to participate and the photo-shots were set up and executed, all the while with such a fiery landscape adding an unspeakable drama to the scene. Russ and I looked at each other beaming, knowing we had captured the essence of the fire on film. "Maybe our last moments," Russ queried, more as a question than a statement.

I had wondered how much adrenalin the body could produce in any one day, over a period of several hours when things were so ridiculously tense and unpredictable. We were all on edge, as if we'd had way too much coffee; excited, agitated, wide-eyed and tired beyond belief. And suddenly, as if it had run out of breath, the fire relaxed and broke off into several splinter sub-burns, edging their way downriver as if the work day was over and it was time to go home.

It was now safe enough to pitch camp on the raised blow-out where the bunch-moss provided exceptional tenting. Scattered stands of black spruce grew out of the depressions that provided scant shade from the intense heat of the late afternoon. I'm sure the massive fire contributed to the extreme temperature. I was still concerned that the fire may be working its way along the opposite shore and possibly jump the river. That would put the fire behind our camp and a slight change in wind direction could mean trouble for us. Trying to figure out the next move was like formulating a battle plan, wondering if the enemy was sneaking up behind us.

Across the river, the fire continued to feast upon every bit of dry tinder, right down to the last sprig of sedge. The air remained clear, thanks to a slight breeze that valiantly protected our ranks but about an hour after setting up the tents, the fire jumped the river only a kilometer downstream and began to burn slowly along our side of the Seal. The evening calmed the fires and the warm summer zephyr pushed the smoke comfortably to the south.

It looked like a hundred campfires burning across the river. We could now hear the rapids over the bellow of the forest fire, which was almost silent. A thick, grey fog of smoke rose from the shattered and frayed boreal shoreline, the abated fire sizzled and crackled, like teeth gnashing. Every once in a while a black spruce tree would ignite in a sphere of bright orange flame, sending out a volley of snaps and retorts like the sound of gunshot and crumpled tissue paper; evening stillness broken.

I walked down to the beach and surveyed the ravaged land-scape while the others traded stories around the campfire. The sun was down and the evening wind helped keep the bugs down to a tolerable nuisance. My mouth was dry and raspy from breathing in the smoke earlier that day but the air was clear on Great Island for the time being and I took long gulps of it as if it were an elixir for a sore throat. I walked back to the campfire, put an extra shot of whiskey in my hot chocolate (we all did), and claimed tomorrow to be a rest day. Nobody argued. Everyone relaxed to the idea of allowing the fires to clear out of our path ahead.

Amazing how a good belt of Canadian whiskey can work its wonder on a troubled mind, calming frayed nerves, dissolving angst, make you happy in the face of adversity. We laughed, we parleyed jokes, told each other what we would do for our rest day. Sleeping in was a unanimous decision and first on the roster, seconded by doctoring sores and bug bites, aches and pains, blisters and so on. But the days were long.

"What are you going to do tomorrow Russ?" I asked.

"I'd really like to fly-fish, maybe across the river where the boulders are creating some good eddies," Russell explained.

"What about you two?" I inquired, looking at Dawson and Hodding. They looked at each other as if they had already decided what they were going to do.

"Play in the rapids, probably, if we ever get out of bed," Hodding said, Dawson nodded.

"Okay, that's fine," I said, "but you'll need a spotter in case you dump. Just let me know when you go out and I'll watch from shore."

"Sure, whatever," Dawson replied, looking away. Russell asked how I was going to spend the day.

"I'll keep an eye on the fires; but I also want to bake several bannocks to last the next several days. Later we can all head over to the big esker by the north channel." Everyone nodded.

I was finally relaxing into the expedition. Dawson no longer posed a threat, or so I thought at the time, and he was hitting it off superbly with Hodding. Both were gregarious and peculiar in their own way. Hodding was good company, and so was Dawson when he wasn't busy being an asshole half of the time. Russell was having a hell of a time with the black flies and several times I had caught him wearing his headnet without securing the collar of his shirt. This left his neck wide open for bug attack and black flies typically bee-line for the soft spots, anywhere the blood flows close to the skin; consequently, Russell's neck, ears and scalp were so badly bitten that the wounds bled freely and he complained of feeling nauseous. Black Fly Fever is a common affliction of the north woods, and he had a good dose of it too. Along with a couple of antihistamines I gave him the ultimatum of either cleaning up his bites and keeping covered, or staying behind as an offering to the bug gods. He laughed. "Okay dad, what-ever."

Hodding was bearing up to the bites and religious about not exposing bare flesh to the hungry hordes. He never complained. Dawson kept sloshing *Deet* onto his bare skin until he had fatigued his own supply then simply started to borrow everyone else's bug dope. He continued to wear as little clothing as he could get away with, keeping the bugs off by literally soaking his exposed skin with *Deep Woods Off.* I tried not to let him get under my own skin. I knew he was trying to impress the *Men's Journal* crew with his wilderness prowess and stalwartness; however, he seemed to be losing all that, bug-dope or not, by swinging ridiculously at the horse flies. He certainly did have a better tan than the rest of us and it really was part of the character he wanted to portray.

I had also wondered what it was that he had stuffed in his second personal pack that he insisted on lugging along. While the others went for a hike down the beach, I lifted the flap on Dawson's pack and, as it turned out, he had a new wardrobe from Roots and a stack of books. Books! It was a known fact that Dawson loved books: classic literature, scholarly texts, trendy novels. His brother had told me that Dawson seldom read them. Lacking the concentration to read a book from cover to cover he would capture a few phrases and categorize them for later recall. If chance led to a witty quote or reference, Dawson was not only dashing, but exceedingly scholastic, current and well read.

I could only speculate that the unsoiled Roots outfit was being saved for the trip back on the train once we got to Churchill; but hauling along all the books was a bit puzzling. The books added a lot of weight to his pack. Considering most people tuck a dime-store paperback into their kit for rest day pleasure, Dawson had a half-dozen hardcovers. *Hardcovers!* Nonetheless, I shrugged it off, even laughed about it. If my assistant guide wanted to be the 'show-man' I didn't really care, so long as it didn't interfere with the expedition.

The black flies took a grand liking to my hide and I'd suffer quietly until I was forced to retreat to my tent, naked and wiping myself down with a cold, wet bandana. Often I would be so busy with chores and instruction that I would forget about the flies, until later when I would feel faint and weak, and then I knew that I was badly bitten. Tiger Balm only worked for a short while; antihistamines worked to settle down the effects of the venom.

Of all the biting bloodsuckers, black flies were the most persistent, from sun-up to dusk, unbearable at times, sticking to the top of the uncooked bannock as it rested over the grill on the fire, I'd beg for a swallow of coffee without having to skim off a dozen flies first. Mosquitoes and midges in the evening and early morning were irksome but at least didn't crawl up your pant legs or inside your shirt sleeves like the black flies did. Deer flies loved the apex of your bare head, or your feet, or if you peeled down the top of your wetsuit they would find a place to bite between the shoulder blades at an exact spot you couldn't reach. Bull dogs, or horse flies, were the least bothersome to everyone but Dawson.

Dene kids back in Tadoule had showed me a trick with horse flies that I found quite fascinating. I watched as a young lad caught a sizeable bull dog then gently pulled out its wings; he then squeezed the thorax or meaty part of the fly between his two thumbs and out popped a bubble of pure nectar. The kid smiled at me "Watch this mister," he smiled and scooped up the bubble with the tip of his tongue. "Try it." I was told. So I did. I caught a bull dog (there was never a shortage of them), yanked its wings off, squeezed its body until it bled nectar, licked it off and it tasted a little like maple syrup; unusually sweet but as natural as you can get; perhaps a little unusual but I could tuck this bit of trivia away in my compendium of 'guide-stories' that mildly shock people.

I told Dawson that he should start collecting them so we can have bull dog nectar when we run out of maple syrup. He didn't think it was very funny and he didn't like being teased. I had the impression that he was starting to realize that his habit of being half naked all the time and swearing and flailing at the flies didn't do much to electrify the *Men's Journal* lads.

Biting flies were just another facet of exploration and the need to adjust to its nuances. Dawson was battling the bugs and losing. It's not about winning or losing, pitting yourself against nature as if it were an opponent. You simply make the best out of a situation and bow humbly to the greater power. Dawson hadn't learned that yet or was incapable of giving in. His antics did lend itself to comical relief every so often.

*   *   *   *   *

I knew I had slept in; the sun was up and had transformed my tent into an oven. I rolled out of my sleeping bag and poked my head outside the tent, coughed to clear yesterdays smoke from my lungs and breathed in fresh, warm air. My chest hurt. Probably too much smoke inhaled the day before. The new day was clear, at least on this side of the river. I walked to the beach to see what was happening with the fire and discovered but a fragment of the drama that had played out yesterday evening. There was nothing but a smoldering heap of charred taiga landscape with fires burning in isolated pockets. The heart of the fire had pushed through during the night and was now burning on our side of the river some distance downstream. The extra day would be ample time for it to clear the river completely. I hoped. For the time being I put my concerns on hold, after all, this was a rest day.

The others slept late while I fried up several heavy bannocks for the trail ahead, washed my clothes, and set up a tether-ball post in the middle of a sand blow-out. I thought the competitive fun might diffuse any tension about the fire, the upcoming rapids, or anything else that may confront us in the days to come. It was close to noon when my comrades crawled out of their own tents; stretching, rubbing, scratching, yawning, farting awake as they made their respective dog-walk over to the fire and the coffee pot. Russell looked terrible. The black fly bites had started to infect. I warned him again about keeping his skin covered, socks pulled over his pant legs, shirt tucked in and his headnet secured. Since I was everyone's senior by almost twenty years I started to feel like a father figure. Sometimes it felt like I was looking after three kids that couldn't look after themselves.

The sun beat down on the sand flats and the only place to

get out of the heat was under the kitchen fly where there was shade. Hodding, Russell and Dawson had disappeared for quite some time and I had paid little attention until I saw that one of the canoes was missing on the beach. After a good hour, Dawson and Hodding appeared paddling back up the shore from the rapids, the spray-cover was attached sloppily and the canoe was partly filled with water. This didn't look good at all.

"What the hell happened?"

"We dumped," Hodding replied rather sheepishly, not bothering to look up.

"Where's Russell?" I asked Dawson but he wouldn't look at me either.

"What do you mean you dumped? And where the hell's Russell?" raising my voice another level. Dawson now looked up, both in defiance and in defence.

"He's okay. He's out in the river fishing," Dawson said matter of factly. I wanted to know more. He explained that Russell had wanted to go fly-fishing in the rapids, so they paddled him out to a large boulder on the far side of the river where a large eddy washed around the rock. Dawson being the showman wanted to run the rapids and then eddy out behind the boulder and then drop Russell off at the rock.

"You can't do that move with an empty canoe and a third passenger Dawson," I reminded him. "What the hell were you thinking?" He gave me one of his *what's your problem?* looks. Hodding said nothing. After all, he was a client and it wasn't his responsibility, so he stayed out of the argument. But Dawson countered with a "We made it out alright," comment.

I was angry and I told Dawson he should have let me know what he was doing and that the rapids and current were strong enough to carry them several miles downriver in cold water with no chance of rescue. He walked away with Hodding and they dumped the water out of the canoe, climbed back in and headed across the river to pick up Russell. When they returned I could tell Russell was pissed with my assistant. There was obviously more to the story than just a simple dumping.

Russell wasn't convinced that it was a safe maneuver either. He had gained enough river savvy over the last few days to know when a canoe was stable and when it wasn't. Dawson claimed that it was an easy stunt and it was the only obvious way to get over to the best fishing spot at the boulder. He was overadorning over the details and convinced both Russell and Hodding that he knew what he was doing. I watched Dawson paddle over to pick up Russell from the rock and he tried to execute the same technical run, this time without the added weight of a third passenger. Still, I held my breath as the canoe careened sideways to the rush of current, floundered and by some miracle, swung into the eddy by sheer chance. I realized at this moment that Dawson was not a proficient whitewater paddler. He was fine in the straight runs where there was a lot of current over the rocks, but as far as any technical prowess, it was obvious that he had little experience at all. I could see why they dumped. The river was still running extremely high and the eddy was protected by an incredibly bold sheer-line – where the downstream rush meets the backwards flowing water in the eddy. The difference between moving and calm water was significant; enough to mandate a finely executed maneuver that even a pro-paddler would have found difficult. They were lucky to get out at all.

In the dumping, the river had claimed Dawson's fishing rod and one of Russell's smaller, expensive cameras. Of course Russell was angry. Later, Russ confided in me that he was glad he was paddling in my canoe where it was safe. Hodding never thought much about the dumping at the time. He seemed to think that Dawson possessed an impetuous outdoor spirit – one that transforms uneven odds into dangerous fun. Neither Russ nor Hodding knew anything about Dawson's past, prior to the expedition. I felt it wasn't my place to cast aspersions on my partner, not just yet anyway.

I felt that I was being tested again by Dawson. That dreaded angst was creeping back into my belly again. It was a leadership issue. Dawson just wanted control, if not by actual physical authority, then by usurping psychological dictatorship. He knew that he should have had a safety spotter in place during his stunt. By not telling me what he was about to do he defied my authority as guide and expedition leader. He defied common sense. Dawson was a liability. If he didn't kill himself and Hodding on the river, he sure as hell wouldn't be able to help Russell or me if we got into trouble. The most difficult, technical rapids were still ahead of us, not to mention the probability of running into more fires, polar bears along the coast, and the paddle to Churchill across Hudson Bay, if we chose to do so instead of taking the barge. The expedition appeared to be fraying a bit at the edges.

I wanted to put Dawson in his place and all I could think of was to challenge him to a tether-ball match. He accepted. I was almost tempted to put the leadership on the line pending who won the game. That was a bit drastic because if I lost I could never allow him to take control of the expedition. He was in good shape and despite the drugs, alcohol, periods of lethargy, drifting from job to job, he somehow managed to maintain a Spartan invincibility. Being half my age should have given him a strong advantage but he lacked stamina.

For fun on rest days, I would always carry along a Frisbee or a stuff-bag that could be packed tight with socks for beach volleyball. Tether-ball is a great competitive kids' game, but in this instance, that softball-size ball shoved in a sock, tied to an eight-foot cord, fastened to the apex of a spruce post, would decide who had the upper hand. Dawson disliked his designation as assistant guide. Tripping for Camp Keewaydin, in charge of young kids, he had absolute power – a monarch to his minions. He could sit on his wannigan and bark orders to the kids who would frantically set up camp, cook dinner and wash dishes, all to his bidding. By winning this match he could at least revel in the glory of victory over his opponent, crushing the authority figure. This would effectively render my position as leader "symbolic" only. The whole affair was silly but strategically important – for both of us.

While employed as a wilderness park ranger in Temagami, I was entrusted with the lives of some of the more "difficult" Junior Rangers – seventeen year-old boys, mostly inner-city kids with a bone to pick with society, authority figures, parents. Many of these adolescent youths had criminal records. My supervisors claimed that the wilderness life and hard work clearing portages would be *"good to curb their iniquitous behaviour."* As it turned out, it was just an excuse to get them out of their own hair and responsibility. Needless to say, I was constantly challenged, psychologically and physically. Testosterone flowed stronger and deeper than any wild river in spring flood. So, up went the tether-ball pole, every day, behind each campsite, and if the days on the trail weren't tough enough, I had to literally "duke it out" with a defiant mob of street kids. I never lost a game, luckily, or I don't know how the situation may have worked out. But that was more than fifteen years ago! The tough kids were the hardest working and most loyal employees once they gained back some of their self-esteem they lost under the feckless government bureaucracy and Junior Ranger foremen who ran the camps like prisons.

Deep down I wished it were boxing gloves we were putting on instead of beating a stupid ball around a post. "You're finished Dawson," I jabbed, playing his game, gaining a psychological edge and putting him off-guard. He called me an old man. Fair enough. We stripped down to our shorts and bare feet. The sun by now was piercing hot and I could feel it searing the flesh on my shoulders and back, the sand feeling like hot coals under my feet. Russell and Hodding sat watching; I'm not sure who they were betting on.

It was to be best three out of five wins. The object was to whack the ball around the post clockwise until the cord completely wound the ball up tight to the upper pole. Sometimes a round would last as long as a good volley in a tennis match. Having a background in martial arts was a definite advantage for me but Dawson gave a good performance of his own. It was a two game-a-piece draw and Dawson was visibly weathering to the heat of the sport. I was just getting my second wind, warming up.

"This is it amigo, you're finished." Taking less than half a minute to punish him brutally, left him spread-eagle on the sand, face down, panting, defeated. He declined a re-match, limping off in the direction of his tent where he slept for the rest of the afternoon. But instead of feeling the elation of victory, I was ashamed and angry. I hated to resort to such macho-interfacing.

I simply wanted to do my job, enjoy the tundra environment, the exploration, my compatriots, and have good things to remember when the trip was just a memory. I had hoped that this little incident would sort things out between Dawson and me, at least for the time being. I pulled down the tether-ball post and tucked the ball deep into my pack.

The German couple pulled in to our beach later that day and asked if they could share our campsite. We complied, even though we both knew there were several other camping areas along the west side of Great Island. But unlike our first meeting, the couple was desperate for company. The trip had proved to be more than they could handle; constantly dumping in the rapids and tired of self-rescue in the cold water, they began the tedious job of "lining" their kayak along the rough shore or portaging it around turbulent water. They looked as beat up as their boat. Their biggest issue was reaching Hudson Bay without a firearm. The prospect of being attacked and killed by polar bears was a huge concern for them. The Canadian government wouldn't allow them to bring a gun into the country "in case they were terrorists" the Germans claimed. Glances at our Mossberg 12-gauge leaning against the wannigan made me feel uneasy. They asked if we minded their company once we hit the coast, but I had to explain that our schedule didn't coincide with theirs. "Sure," I said, "If we're still camped at the coast, you're welcome to join us, but we may already be heading down the coast to Churchill."

They had scheduled a barge pick-up and we still weren't decided on whether we were getting picked up or taking our chances along the coast. For the rest of the day the couple kept to themselves, mostly adding repairs to their repairs on the bottom of their boat. It was the last time we would ever see them.

*   *   *   *   *

Great Island, or *Nu Cho*, was spiritually important to the Sayisi Dene. According to their legends, a musk-ox was once wounded here. Before the hunters could get to it, the animal leapt off a cliff leaving a trail of blood behind. The blood turned to red ochre – a mineral that the Dene used for medicinal purposes and for the manufacturing of a colourful dye. Even the rocks at Nu Cho were sacred. The Dene would collect certain rocks for ceremonial purposes and for healing the sick. The *porte de l'enfer*, or "Hell's Gate", found mid-way along the historic Matta-wa River in Ontario, is one such similar place where the Nipissing Indians collected red ochre. Passing voyageurs were superstitious about the cliff-side cave opening to the ochre mine claiming it was home to the devil. I had passed this site more than a dozen times while paddling the river, always looking up into the dark opening in the rock slope expecting to see some manifestation of the devil peering out at me.

It was easy to understand why the Dene held reverence for Great Island. Physically, it was one of the most beautiful camp-sites along the Seal River, offering an unobstructed view of the setting sun, unlimited tenting space, the best grayling fishing, picturesque rapids, with sounds that padded a tired mind with zen-like music. The ledges and boulders that traversed the river created a milieu of cauldrons, boils, eddies and commanding wave action. In low water conditions the rapids were tame in comparison.

The Island rises dramatically from the surrounding level plain, almost one-hundred meters above the Seal River. At the head of the island, the river breaks away into two distinct chan-nels – the south or main branch, and the Lavalee Channel to the north. We would take the south channel as it looked to have the greater volume flow as indicated by the topographic chart.

Along the west flank of the Lavalee Channel rose a most remarkable esker formation, toward which we were now headed. The four of us paddled the short distance and beached our ca-noes for an evening hike. I was astonished at all the varieties of artifacts that lay glistening in the sun, as if scattered there prior to our arrival. A short distance up from shore was a recently constructed stone memorial to the late Bill Mason. It was con-structed in 1989 by a group of canoeists claiming that the great film-maker and canoeing icon was to make a Seal River trip with them but Bill had cancelled after learning he had stomach cancer. I had known Bill and we had discussed the loss of Canadian wilderness. He was, in fact, scheduled to trip with me in Temagami where old-growth forest clear-cutting was held in disputation by local Ojibwe and city environmentalists against the local bureaucracy and logging companies. It had gained a reputation as an international concern after Temagami was listed on the International Union of the Conservation of Nature (IUCN) list of endangered spaces. Mason wanted to become more involved in the battle so we had planned a trip for the upcoming summer only to learn later that he was diagnosed with cancer. He did make a final voyage down a river he was fond of, and that was the Nahanni River in the Northwest Territories.

I don't think Bill would have approved of the man-made cairn on such a lovely esker on the Seal River. He was the most humble and self-effacing man I knew, and he cared passionately about wilderness and the importance of leaving it alone. The plaque and rock-pile was an honourable gesture, but terribly out of place, especially since Bill had never even been to the Seal.

Modern paddlers would often take to constructing inuksuks on numerous Canadian Rivers; something that was frowned upon by the Dene First Nations. In 1994 only one other group went down the Seal River and they built several stone inuksuks. The Dene were outraged, at first blaming us, but later found out that it was a Sobek expedition. Inuksuks were commonly constructed by the Inuit to aid in hunting and not something you would find in Dene country. The Inuit were also traditional enemies of the Dene so it was understandable they would be incensed by the erection of inuksuks on their river.

Wolf and fox tracks skirted Bill's epitaph and it was obvious by the latent smell that it had become a scent post for passing animals. The plaque read, *"The River, The Canoe, The Paddle, The*

Man. Bill Mason. Seal River Trip 1989. "It was as though the builders had memorialized their own trip down the river and used Bill
as an excuse to leave a sign. I was particularly disturbed because
we were standing on Dene land and the whites had no authority
to alter the landscape, move rocks, disturb the history of the
ancient campsite. I apologized to Bill for the paddlers' lack of
conscience and respect.

Having worked as a park ranger for eight years, wherever I
travelled in the back country where the nouveau-canoeist plied
their paddles, I was confronted with "signs" left behind: garbage and human waste at campsites, names scratched into the
lichen on shore rocks, trip testimonials chiselled into granite, stone inuksuks, and the occasional graffiti blazoned across
Native pictographs. It was disconcerting. The fact that we tend
to "love things to death" did nothing for the general push towards sustaining the adventure-trade market as an alternative to
unsustainable resource extraction.

The four of us trailed off on our own discoveries and
walked for about four kilometers to where the esker finally terminated above the Lavalee arm of the river. Much of the surface
of the esker and surrounding environs had been burned over
some years ago. The gnarled jackpine, devoid of bark, grey and
hardened by fire and wind stood like sentinels to the setting sun.
We gathered together and looked back upon the fire as it slowly edged its way along the river, stultified by the lack of fresh
tinder to burn, calmed by the cool, windless evening. From the
height of the esker we were at the top of the world, with such a
commanding view it literally left us breathless. One of the things
I discovered about the sub-arctic and its propensity to be flat
and unexciting, was the enjoyment of climbing even the slightest
of rise in elevation. In the hilly southern landscapes once you
climbed a high hill, all you could see were other hills. Here, the

vistas were far-reaching and dramatic.

The permanency of the land and its many features contrasted with the nervous energy of the river, as if life remained in stasis here, unchanged for millennia, altered ever so slightly by natural fire. Rich peat-bogs and kettle lakes bordered the esker, interspersed with occasional drumlinoids and boulder riffs. Hodding spotted a huge bull moose in the lower vale. The mammoth animal watched us momentarily, sniffed the air with head raised, then decided to make a hasty exit to heavier forest cover. We watched him from our perch atop the esker as he glided easily across the tundra as if held aloft on a cushion of air; fluid movement, like water.

The sunset lingered. It was almost midnight but light enough to walk back to our canoes and make the short paddle back to the campsite. Numerous spot-fires still burned across the river, certainly not as pretentious as the night before, expended but persistent. The thick moss mat could smoulder on for weeks. Loons called. Perhaps a signal of good luck and an indication that birds were moving back into the river valley.

Chapter Eight

Nine Bar Rapids

The river gods favoured us with calm water on Shethanei, brilliant sunsets, the terrible beauty of a raging wildfire – *up close* – and not having to portage our heavy gear around any of the rapids so far was a good omen. The day we left the comfortable confines of our Great Island campsite it looked as if nothing could go wrong. The fire had crossed the Seal and was nowhere to be seen, at least from our vantage point sitting in our respective canoes. At this point I figured we had seen the end of the fires, presuming that the extra day of leisure put the blaze well ahead of us, or it had burned itself out completely.

It would take two days to traverse the south channel around the island, stopping for an afternoon to explore the Dene sacred site of Bastion Rock. This would increase the berth between us and the fire, wherever it was, if it was still burning at all. The two channels conjoined again, thirty-kilometers downstream with an impressive vertical drop of fifty-meters. That meant some pretty heavy-duty rapid-play up ahead of us, including the infamous 9-Bar Rapids, so named because of the nine bars etched across the river on the topographical map. Up to Bastion Rock it would be easy rapids and clean fun.

Planet Earth thrusts its stony foundation to the sky at regular locations along the Seal, more noticeable where the vertical slump creates endless cataracts and chutes. The river was in full charge here, where a tremendous gorge had formed, pinched tight by an esker on one side and sheer cliffs on the other. Shale and sedimentary rocks had fractured into hundreds of blocks of skeletal-like fingers, standing as monuments or fallen like dead soldiers lined up along the shore. In some places it looked as if the stone ramparts were man-made.

We moved along quickly, hardly moving our paddles at all, making easy and casual corrections, taking in the sights. There was no slowing down even if we tried; riding the back of a water serpent, winding and undulating to the rhythm of the earth and all we could do was steer and balance in the heavy waves, long rapids, neither difficult nor technical, just sheer volume compressed in a sluiceway, wave after wave after wave and it went on forever. The speed at which the river carried us along that morning brought us to our destination in no time at all. We had ample time to explore the Rock and find a decent place to camp.

The Seal had made an abrupt right-hand turn, piling up against a monolithic vault of rock; an island standing firm and impervious to the onslaught of moving water, splitting the river again into two channels. One main channel was alive with a force of water to make one think Poseidon was thrashing his huge tail, creating the rapids and boils, while the secondary channel took a timid course around the backside of the huge rock. A campsite of sorts was located overlooking the big rapids giving us a superior view of the riverscape. Russ and I carried some of the gear up to the site along with our camera equipment while Hodding and Dawson ran the two canoes down the rapids. The light was favourable and Russell had been complaining about not having any good whitewater action shots for the magazine article. I had managed to get a few on-the-fly photographs while we were both running but Russ needed to set up his shots with the tripod in order to get steady, studio-quality pictures. Bastion Rock rapids gave him what he wanted. It was more or less a straight-down-the-middle-run for them to navigate but I kept the other canoe at the ready just in case of an upset. A self-rescue here wouldn't be possible – they would both be deathly hypothermic before getting to shore on their own, if at all. The rapids pushed out into a large bowl-shaped curve of the river with the main current coursing down the middle and far away from either shore. A dump here would mean a very long, cold swim.

The fire had completely gutted Bastion Rock the day before. The thirty-meter vault of rock, sacred to the Dene, stood smouldering in the afternoon heat, a manged and charred landscape, bare and forlorn, topped the monument with utter devastation. Where we stood, on the mainland opposite the rock. The fire had swept through, wild and ambitious, destroying everything in its path. The few trees still left standing were reduced to blackened, pitted sticks, with roots exposed, barely able to support any weight at all. Many of the trees fell as we stood there examining the aftermath of the firestorm.

What was left of the ground-mat puffed up in billows of dust and smoke, still burning underneath in some places. Finding a spot to set up the tents without burning a hole in the bottom was not easy. Choosing to pitch on top of the scorched bedrock, I did find a location just big enough for my small tent. The base-camp tent was another story and it took time to get it set up on another flat of rock, still pulsing hot from the fire. Everywhere I walked I could feel the heat rising up through my boots. There was a pile of animal bones behind my tent; possibly a rabbit, curled up against a rock ledge as if trying to escape the inferno.

I wondered how many other animals had been killed in such a blaze and if any had escaped to safety.

From our perch above the river we could see the fires to the west, from where we had just paddled. I was surprised and dismayed that they were still burning vigorously but in a new direction, inland from the Seal, its effluent smoke creating a shield from the hot sun, transforming the ravaged riverscape around us into a surreal, melancholic fantasy-land. To the northeast we could make out the front line of the main fire, fierce and determined, eating up such a boreal swath that beguiled the imagination. Its path was well back from the river and at a safe distance for us not to have any concerns. The fire was now history and we would need our full attention on the rapids tomorrow, and Nine-Bar had a reputation for being nasty, according to Allan Code.

Hundreds of swallows nested along the cliffs here, one of the oddities that proclaimed a special placement of Bastion Rock in the annals of Dene mythology. Small box canyons excised the topography making it difficult to walk inland any distance from our camp so we pinioned ourselves to the armchair of a rock precipice where our tents stood with a grand view of Bastion Rock, the rapids, the fire, drinking hot chocolate laced with Canadian whiskey.

*   *   *   *   *

I was up early; always the first to rise which was my choice and my time to ruminate about the day, sip my coffee, collect my thoughts, putter around the fire preparing breakfast. I enjoyed the solitude. It was truly the only time I had to relax a bit from the pace of the trip; not that we were travelling inordinately fast downriver. It was the unpredictability and the constant tension that seemed to draw on the nerves. Dawson, the fires, the incredible whitewater, all contributed to a wave of anxiety that ebbed and flowed each hour.

This was a world that I had few resources of my own to siphon off with any experience and nothing I could really do to make things happen any differently. The rapids I could deal with. Up to this point on the river, the rapids had been reasonable. There had been plainly visible chartable courses, and with the added dimension of the spray-covers we could negotiate safe passage through the bigger rapids. And the word "negotiate" implies that we were parleying with some river god. I hated the unknowns.

I poured another coffee. The second jolt of caffeine cleared the residue of sleep from my brain. I roused the others to get up. From here I knew that I would have to keep a vigilant eye on my assistant. I had a premonition that we hadn't even seen the true nature of this river yet, or of Dawson. The Seal appeared to be growing in strength, the rapids becoming more demonstrative and the landscape bleak and almost hostile. Dawson's character also mirrored this as the river became more difficult. His moods also grew more capricious.

Breakfast was simple: half an orange each, a bowl of granola, and as much coffee as one could safely ingest. There was an air of excitement amongst us as we discussed Nine-Bar. The question as to whether or not we would be making our first portage took on a presumptuous tone and a *let's-go-for-it-whatever*, axiom. I assured the others that I didn't particularly want to portage if there was any way at all to run Nine-Bar, but I also explained the dangers of long runs and the difficulty in planning a safe course without having any prior knowledge of what lay ahead. In the past, while mapping out rivers for guidebooks, I spent a lot of time at each rapid and devised ways of eliminating all or at least part of a portage when the canoe could be run in sections

173

or maybe lined down easily. Creative rapid play often avoided lengthy portages. This would not be the case here; the shoreline was flooded into the shore willow making lining impossible and portaging extremely complicated. We were practically forced to confine ourselves to the river no matter what.

"We'll figure it out when we get there," I told them. Hodding and Russell nodded politely, listening intently to every word I spoke while Dawson sat on his wannigan smoking a cigarette, waving at the first assault of black flies. Almost all of the rapids, except for the unexpected drop into Shethanei Lake that wasn't marked on the map, were easy enough to read. And there are a few ways to read a rapid: if you can see the bottom of the run and there are no visible problems that you know you can navigate through without a problem or eddy off to the side; then you simply stand up in the canoe while feathering your paddle for stability, then scan what's ahead, look for the downstream "V" that earmarks the entrance to a run, take the running position and go for it. If this isn't an option and the rapid is complex then you beach at the top of the run and get a look from shore. Shore scouting is tough sometimes on difficult or longer rapids because it all looks different once you climb back into your canoe and try to remember what your plan was when you looked at it from up on shore. Rapids always look smaller looking down on them from vantage points. Once on the run and committed, the haystacks are bigger, troughs deeper and ledge drops steeper. Reading rapids always demands a workable plan "B", sometimes a plan "C" if things don't work according to plan "A" or plan "B". Sometimes there is no plan at all.

Most rapids to this point were Class IIs and easy Class IIIs on the international scale of six. Class III is the maximum grade in an open canoe if the run wasn't very long and cold water wasn't a factor. Because of the isolation factor and the frigid water temperature, classifications are often bumped up a grade. Little maneuvering had been required so far and those short, steep drops – the bigger Class IIIs – could be scouted from shore and usually navigated on one side or the other. The middle channels were crazy maelstroms of turbulence. Nine-Bar could present some unforeseen drama that was not diagnostic of the water-play to this point in our trip. The fires didn't seem to be a factor any longer, yet things could change quickly.

Food packs were getting lighter. It was truly amazing how much food four men could consume. We were probably running a good one-hundred pounds lighter which meant each canoe had a little more freeboard than when we started. That could also be translated into safer runs, tighter eddy-turns, easier maneuvers and cross-ferries. We could use a little extra luck at this point.

After running a couple of "typical" rapids, and enjoying *not* having to portage the canoes and gear, we were basking in an illusory sense of security, a smugness perhaps. There was a prevailing hubris after having good luck on all the rapids, except for Dawson's dunking at Great Island, that I thought might get in the way of good judgement. The river widened to half a kilometer – not a good sign because that meant the rapids would be shallow and strewn with boulders. Rounding a soft bend in the river we came face to face with Nine-Bar and immediately headed for shore. *Shit*, I cursed to myself. If ever there was an intimidating, life-threatening rapid, it was now staring us in the face.

Noon. We were hungry and a quick rest would get us primed for the run. We pulled over to the north side of the river and moored the canoes to a plate of granite that extended several meters offshore. From there we had a reasonably good view of Nine-Bar – at least the first two-hundred meters or so before the river tipped off over the curve of the earth and spiralled down a vortex of fuming waves. Approaching it from upstream, as we were, and seeing its dissuasive personality tip off the visual screen was enough to scare us to shore and solid ground, like we were avoiding contact with a rabid dog.

Anybody who knew anything about the Seal River had warned us about Nine-Bar Rapids. They made it quite clear that we should *portage the three kilometers because the ledges will kill you!* Aside from the rock we were perched on, any thought of hiking along shore through a tangle of thick willow that formed a wall of vegetation at the edge of our picnic spot, was out of the question. So we huddled on the rock eating salami and bannock bread, too excited, too nervous, too full of morning caffeine to sit still long enough to enjoy our lunch.

All morning we had paddled alongside a smoking, devastated north shore. It was almost as if we were catching up to the fire. This thought also did not sit well with the salami and cheese, churning around with a surfeit of anxiety in my gut. We stood along the edge of the river and brooded over our situation. On our side of the river there was a fire, as yet unseen, the smoke drift indicating a close proximity to it and just beyond our lunch site. The opposite side sported one of the most vicious flumes of wild water imaginable. The only place to go was *down!*

At five-hundred meters wide, every inch of that space was lined with angry rollers washing against an infestation of boulders and jagged rocks. There was no way to plan it out from our position on the shore. Canada Parks rated Nine-Bar Rapids as a Class V rapid; "Rubber rafts fare better," the report professed, "however, the rapids are quite tricky and demanding even with the added safety a raft provides." The background study didn't mention any fires. Smoke was settling over our lunch rock so I initiated a move to the canoes.

"We'll run the quieter current on the left, our side of the river, as far as we can, then we'll pull over in an eddy to scout ahead," I instructed the others, not knowing how far or where we would pull over at any given time. "Stay out of the middle!" If we maneuvered into the middle channel then there was no way we could get close enough to shore to eddy out, rest or scout. Once there, we would be committed to the entire run. If we played the left shore, dodging boulders, find a decent eddy, we could beach the canoes and see if there was a better line downstream, look for ledges ahead or any formidable drop that might pose a threat. In that case we would be forced to line the canoes along the shore which presented a fearsome barrier of leatherleaf, willow and a sorry confusion of broken slab-rock; almost an impossible option.

"Quieter current?" asked Russell. It was hard to tell. It all looked the same from where we stood.

"Yeah, it's a little less white on the left," Hodding replied jokingly.

"Dawson and Hodding, you guys are to follow our lead," I yelled above the din of the rapids, "not too far back either in case we get into trouble...leave enough room to maneuver to shore if you have to."

"Russell and I will pick the running lines on a spot basis, as they come up, and then pull over to shore to scout when it looks favourable," I added, "...and...Dawson, keep to the plan. Stay together!"

A rapid never looks the same when you're actually running it. The view from shore, from above, tends to play down the intensity of the drops. The good channel you thought you saw from terra firma quickly gets scrambled in the frenzy of thrashing waves, unseen rocks and surprise ledges. Nine-Bar was over three-kilometers long with a vertical drop of fifty-feet. That's a long way to fall; like pitching your canoe off the top of a six-storey building.

The top of the rapid looked gnarly, from what we could see of it, but better judgement and experience told me that Nine-Bar could only get worse near the bottom where the rocks and boulders had a tendency to gather during glacial outwash. But there was something else that added to the angst of pre-run that got the heart beating; a sense of anxiousness that was prodding us to get going. I threw some tobacco into the water and watched the current swallow it. I could feel my bowels loosening but there was nowhere to take a shit. And I hadn't had a solid bowel movement for weeks it seemed.

The others were waiting for me to motion them towards the canoes. *"Let's do it!"* We climbed into our boats and pulled the spray-skirts up tight under our armpits. We shoved off out of the shore eddy and the river immediately grabbed at the hull and pulled with such a force that any paddle-stroke seemed inconsequential. I took a deep breath and steered us out into the rush of frothing water.

This is the moment I could actually taste the adrenalin surging through every fibre in my body. I could see clearer, hear everything; even the pounding of my heart vibrated along the paddle shaft into my finger-tips. I got the sense that I could smell with the efficacy of a canine. My mind was sharp and the will to survive omnipotent. I felt strong. The aches and pains I had earlier have vanished. It's all about the moment, the fraction of a second, the now.

The moment I would enter the grasp and soul of the rapid nothing else would matter. I wouldn't think of death. The thought of capsizing was expunged from possibilities and I trusted entirely on my ability as a paddler to make all the right moves, and stick with the plan. But at river level, looking down into the maw of the worst stretch of river imaginable, I could sense that there was no plan at all.

Huge boulders reared up out of the seething rollers, sending curling waves off at strange angles, any one of which could have easily overturned our canoe if we struck it at the wrong approach. Rocks flashed by, almost brushing against our elbows, reflecting the cacophony of the rapids into our ears, deafening as if we were sitting too close to the speakers at a rock concert. There was no use calling the moves to Russell, hoping he had the sense to draw or pry with his paddle at the right time. My voice would be swallowed up and any distraction might instigate a wrong move by Russ and that would be it.

We dropped through each chute, hearts in our mouths; quick, deft strokes catching the next tongue of rock-free water, line up for the next passage between boulders and drop through again, and again...and again. There was no time to look over my shoulder at the other canoe, hoping they were still there. I felt our canoe being pulled closer to the middle of the river where the heavier breaking waves were. This easily happens when you play the rapid boulder-by-boulder, getting lured out to deeper water, looking for cleaner runs.

The river got worse up ahead, tipped out of sight, and I started to work our canoe over to the north shore looking for an eddy. I found one with enough room for two canoes, where the shore broke into a dull point with a slight rise behind. Both canoes made it without incident. We rested on our paddles while the canoes ambled in the calm water. Shakily, I pulled myself out from the spray-skirt and climbed up the rise to look downriver to see what was up ahead. I stood there for a long time, studying the rapids and tried to catch my breath. I couldn't breathe, couldn't find any air. I was choking, the smell of smoke clogged up my nose and throat. The haze over the river made it difficult to read. The rapids had splayed out, wider, shallower but heaving up bigger waves with no discernible route through, too shallow by the shore. *Is that the ledge about a kilometer downriver?* I couldn't tell. The smoke was thicker there, obscuring my view.

"We'll get a closer look at it on the run!" I shouted at the others, "Hope for a channel through. Keep together!" Not much of a rallying cry of encouragement. *HOPE for a channel through?* That wasn't going to instill much trust in the guide, I thought. Russell looked at me, waiting for me to say something else that might put him at ease. I said nothing. We pushed off again and worked our way to the middle of the river where there were fewer rocks but bigger haystacks. I knew that once we were in the thick of it we would lose sight of any ledge up ahead. That worried me. Had the shoreline been more hospitable and not flooded, I would have contemplated lining the canoes down the rest of the way but we still had over two-kilometers to go and the only path to take was down the middle. Each drop was girded by a vault of stone, a narrow path through followed by breaking haystacks and more rocks. I could only see the steep pitch of the rapids, like looking down a moving escalator; the smoke hung tight to the river making it hard to see any detail ahead.

Then I saw it. "Ledge!" I yelled and pointed my paddle to the right hoping the other canoe could see the better running channel. Dawson's canoe had the room to power to the right to line up with the only narrow sluice of water that washed over a ledge that traversed the entire river. Russ and I were too far to the left and I knew we weren't going to make the channel. Plan "B". We swung the canoe around and pointed the bow upstream and began a hard ferry to the left, towards the safe chute but the current was too strong, pulling us dangerously close to the edge of the drop. I yelled at Russell to help turn the canoe back downstream because we weren't going to make it and I didn't want to go over the ledge backwards.

"When we go over, power through, and paddle hard!" I

screamed at Russell. "Don't look back!" It was a good two-meter drop, almost vertical, with a recoiling aerated boil sitting below. It was clearly a hydraulic souse-hole known as a *keeper*, where the water pitches down and turns back against the ledge in a continuous cycle. Anything unlucky enough to fall into it would have a tough time getting back out. I was banking on our speed and forward momentum to get us out of it. Unfortunately for us, the aerated water would have almost no buoyancy, and once we plunged into it there would be nothing to dig your paddle into except air.

Sometimes by sheer luck and a hard dose of forward momentum you could drive a canoe through a souse-hole. We had only missed the good channel by a few meters and lined up to tip over the right side of the ledge where the drop was not quite vertical. It was our only chance.

Russell became airborne, his paddle waving madly in thin air while we were held in stasis momentarily while the ledge was thinking what to do with us. Then we dropped, nose first into the white foam and I thought we weren't going to come back up. Russ went under then bobbed up powering forward like a sled-dog on a harness. The stern pitched and heaved and I went under but the canoe remained upright and steady. For the next few moments nothing seemed to be happening. The river was tumbling downstream on both sides of us yet we were being drawn back upstream towards the ledge. *We were stuck in the hydraulic!*

"Power forward, harder!" I yelled at Russell but he was already paddling as hard as he possibly could, so was I but we weren't getting anywhere. We remained stationary for the longest time. The canoe floundered. We could only keep up this pace for a few seconds longer. I began edging the canoe carefully to the one side and managed to catch some of the downstream black-water; the canoe literally jumped out of the souse-hole and we were free. We were damned lucky.

We were now about two-hundred meters behind Dawson's canoe. The temper of the rapids calmed somewhat after the ledge drop; more of a *thread-the-needle* through the boulders but we were bone-tired after the beating we took in the souse-hole and didn't have much more to give if anything difficult came up. Hodding and Dawson had pulled over along the right shore at the bottom of the rapids. I could see Dawson scramble out of his canoe to chase a couple of Canada geese as we approached. "He wants a goose for dinner," Hodding told us, "And I don't think this is a good idea right now." The geese were moulting and couldn't fly so Dawson figured it would be an easy kill simply by bludgeoning them with a stick. Russ and I eddied by the shore waiting. That's when all hell broke loose.

All of us were facing downriver when we heard the roar, then felt the heat. Blistering heat. The sound welled up from the ground, through our feet, shaking the earth and everything exploded into a virtual nightmare.

"Holy sheeit, let's get the hell out of here!" Hodding screamed at Dawson to get back in the canoe. He returned without a goose and at first wondered what was going on, completely oblivious. "Oh fuck..." he said quietly, looked up at the fire, "Oh fuck!" Then jumped in the canoe.

The entire opposite shore was engulfed in such a conflagration that we weren't quite sure what to do. At first we just sat in our canoes, dumbfounded, eyes wide and mouths agape and watched as the fire moved towards us at railway speed. It was travelling faster than we could paddle. There was a mile-long wall of bright orange flame rising several hundred meters above us. We all felt like hot dogs on a barbecue. A towering, curling, descending black mountain of smoke billowed towards us like an airborne tsunami. The sun was blotted out and the day became night. Had we not had the expanse of river between us we would have already been incinerated.

I'd never paddled so hard for my life as I did then - we all did. If we stopped, we would die, engulfed in a choking blanket of soot and smoke. My ears were ringing it was so loud. It was like I was standing on the side of a railway track as a freight train went by. The wave of smoke crept behind us like a giant rolling pin. I glanced over my shoulder every so often, instructing Russ and the others to keep paddling hard. "Paddle harder!" I yelled every few moments. Nobody talked. There was no casual conversation, just terrified looks on all of our faces.

We passed the mouth of the Lavalee Channel where it re-enters the Seal – a shallow, cascading rapids much like the last section we ran after the souse-hole incident. Together, both channels pushed the Seal wider and shallower and I could feel my paddle striking rocks every so often, the canoe sluggish, arms weakening. We had only separated ourselves from the smoke wave by about one-hundred metres.

We had to stop, just for a few moments. The canoe was turned back towards the fire. There was a wave of darkness spilling down the river valley consuming everything that lay before it. Where we had paused at the end of Nine-Bar, only moments ago, was now completely veiled behind a mask of black smoke and ash. Russell and I took a couple of photographs thinking that nobody would ever believe this if we didn't capture some of it on film.

There was no time to loiter. We pressed on our paddles, *hard*, keeping the smoke-wall a couple hundred meters behind us as it heaved and bellowed down the river trying to catch us. Black ash settled over the canoes, over the water around us – a greasy patina that smelled of singed spruce needles. Black Rain! I felt as if we were running down the tracks with a train on our heels;

one of those bad dreams where you try to run from danger but your body remains torpid, impending death over your shoulder.

After paddling three kilometers we paused again to look back. Russell and I pulled out our cameras again but we had missed the best pictures because we had to concentrate on getting the hell out of the path of the fire, thankful that we hadn't loitered any longer than we did, overstayed our lunch at the top of the run, dumped in the souse-hole, or had to track down Dawson who was off chasing geese. Any one of these scenarios could have put us in the middle of the fire and we would have perished. We could easily have been stuck indefinitely in the hydraulic in the middle of the river. I realised that had we not made it through the hole, there was no way to be rescued anyway, no matter what. All these facts began to sink in; that tingling sensation of having just survived something that could have been fatal. An elastic band just snapped against my soul. I think we all felt that way. Had we been one minute later, the outcome would have unfolded differently.

The federal government water-monitoring station was located where we paused to look at the fire, tucked back in from the shore on the north side – the side of the fire upriver. We pulled in and took a look around the cabin, stretched our cramped legs. I knew the cabin wouldn't survive the fire, the way it was moving, the direction and the speed it travelled. It was a good place to get out of the flies and get a quick rest. I was disappointed that we missed the opportunity to paddle up the Lavalee Channel, where it joined Nine-Bar rapids. There was a 1950s mining camp I wanted to check out, just up from the confluence of the two channels. It was operated by the Great Seal Prospecting Syndicate in 1953. They turned up samples with only 35% metallic iron content which negated any prospect of development as a productive mine. The camp was abandoned and left virtually intact. Clothing, bedding, food tins, pots and pans and personal items had been left behind, along with dog sleds, freighter canoes, core samples, saws and a storage shed full of dynamite. The fire had cut off any chance of us exploring the old camp.

On the table in the cabin were two journals that had been left there over the last ten years, signed by prospectors, water-monitoring crews from Thompson, and a handful of canoeists who had descended the river. "We'll take these along with us," I informed the others; all agreed that the cabin would be smouldering ruins in a matter of hours.

"It's the only thing of value here," as I looked around the inside of the shack, past the old magazines, tubs of dishes and food, boat motors and tools. I would mail the journals to the Manitoba Water Monitoring people once we got out. Then we heard the explosions, several of them, more than a couple dozen. Immediately we thought of the dynamite storage shed at the old mining camp. The fire must have razed everything there. We ran outside, down to the shore and noticed that the deadly wave of smoke was still rolling downriver, toward us...and moving very fast!

It was time to go. Although we were all thoroughly exhausted, we had no choice but to keep going, shove off downriver and keep up the paddling pace, find a safe place to camp. We paddled another fifteen kilometers before we felt it safe enough to stop. After what seemed an interminably long time paddling, we paused in the middle of the river and rafted the canoes, holding on to each others' gunwales, and drifted with the current. None of us said much. We were far too tired. I found myself shaking uncontrollably when we stopped. I wasn't cold. It was a lot to take in for one day and my body was reacting to the continued stress. I tried to shake it off. I could see the others trying to cope as well. Heads bowed, paddles across the gunnels of the canoe, breathing hard.

The river paused with us, taking a break from its pell-mell rush to the ocean. It also changed its visual appearance and character. We were now beyond the boreal tract. The once endless vista of black spruce gave way to open tundra heath with the occasional tuft of weatherworn tamarack and scattered spruce. I had to laugh to myself when I realized the fire had virtually eaten itself to the edge of the tree-line. There was nothing else to feed on. And it's not that the actual tree-line is a well scribed transition, it was clearly marked by a change in the scope of growth, from a contiguous belt of green, to a melange of incident tree groupings, boulder trains and open heath. We were safe! We had made it through the wild gauntlet of rock infested rapids, and looked death in the eye of a monster boreal fire. Then came the adrenalin aftershock; a brief period of the shakes and a determination not to cry, or shout out a hearty English "hurrah!" I think we all felt that way, even Dawson.

Chapter Nine

Tundra

People generally have the impression that the Canadian tundra is a flat wasteland. It isn't. The day before, we had paddled almost thirty-five kilometers and Nine-Bar had exploded into fire. That drop was measured in wild whitewater plunges off the edge of the Canadian Shield – at least the Shield that I knew by heart. One should get the impression the drift to Hudson Bay would be melodramatic once the arctic tundra was reached. It isn't.

We had discovered a pleasant campsite on a large island, along a sand beach with raised peat hummocks where we pitched our tents. Harbour seals drifted by, curious and dark-eyed, probably wondering what kind of creatures we were. They perched on a fallen log, staring into a smoky fire, skins of bright colours so incongruous with the earthen tincture of the tundra.

That night marked the two-week point in the expedition. I began to wonder whether the body ever ran out of adrenalin because I was convinced we all produced gallons of it. The adrenal glands were getting a good workout and metabolism accelerated a hearty appetite. Eating always appeased nervous tension, as did the reserve of whiskey, which had taken a beating over the last two evenings. The dearth of supply sparked an urgent need to conserve, just in case events got worse in the days ahead (although I really didn't know how they possibly could).

I didn't sleep well that night; even the tent walls seemed to move around me. It was a sensation privy to those who spend the day in kinetic unbalance; a type of whitewater vertigo, lying motionless in your sleeping bag with the world still moving around you in dark waves. I would close my eyes and see nothing but rapids, moving water around rocks, shoreline blurred by motion. The night was still but the roar in my ears was deafening; the pungent smell of burnt spruce lined my nostrils. Even though the night air was damp and cool, I couldn't stand my sleeping bag pulled up around my head as if I would suffocate from lack of oxygen. I couldn't stop thinking about the fires. I thought I'd wake up suddenly and everything around us would be engulfed in flames.

The wild fires had been a part of the expedition since Tadoule. We were now perched on the terminus of the treed world, the barrenlands - the place God supposedly forgot about. We may have been the only people around for two-hundred kilometers, except for the German couple if they were still alive. I felt the ephemeral nature of my own existence, the thin balance of life and death in such an austere place that could only be measured by one's capacity and will to survive, or how well one adapts to the vagaries of the natural world. Isolation. Disconnection. Fire. We could have panicked, sat dumbfounded on the shore at the foot of Nine-Bar rapids and allowed the fire to consume us. Give up. We were hypnotized by the immensity and strange beauty of it, at first, then we took flight, just in time.

Dawson, always isolated in thought and action, almost betrayed us, again, putting us in serious risk by stopping suddenly to chase geese when the first thing he should have done was to check on the other canoe – *our canoe*, to see if we made it through safely. It was obvious he couldn't prioritize rational thought: life-threatening events from simple play. I was surprised Dawson had made it this far in life. Although his franchise on immortality had to be gauged by some otherworldly being, it was the misfortune of those around him that concerned me most. Strangely enough, Dawson always managed to triumph in the face of adversity. The goose-chasing incident pissed me off, as did his lack of concern for Russ and I; and I honestly think he would have been just as happy to finish off the expedition alone with Hodding. Having pulled out of the fires unscathed was a blessing and I attempted to assuage any bad feelings with gratefulness. We were alive and that's all that mattered, really.

Morning. We were on the tundra now. There were no trees to burn. One less thing to worry about. Still more than a hundred kilometers from the coast and the topographical maps indicated an elevation drop of four-hundred feet. That was a substantial drop. The maps also showed a lot of rapid-play ahead but I had learned not to trust the topo-charts for such information. It was beautiful here, barren only for the lack of familiar trees, the heath ablaze with colourful flowers, wild berries and mosses, thick brown peat, layered, compressed by time, all fragrant and welcoming; such a contrast from the days past. I stirred the coals in the morning fire and slid the coffee pot along the fire irons where it would stay hot. The others were still in their tent, and until I played reveille on my mouth organ, a morning ritual, they would likely sleep until noon.

We were still ahead of schedule, distance-wise, so I let them sleep and I could enjoy the morning peace, watch the seals cruise by like miniature Loch-Ness creatures, terns circling above the camp. No roaring rapids or thunderous wild blaze, just the comforting crackle of the campfire and the gentle buzz of a thousand mosquitoes. It was blissful.

There was a north wind blowing. That meant fresh, tundra-born, smokeless air to breathe; a god-send to be sure. To the west we could still see the smoke-haze of the Great Island conflagration. But today there would be no stinging eyes, raining ash or laboured breathing. The downriver course of the Seal that lay ahead would demand our full attention and that became a reality soon after we broke camp, not just because of the expected rapids but because Dawson was acting strange. He looked and acted as if he were slowly coming apart at the seams. It was disconcerting. And I didn't know why or what was going on inside his head.

For the first twenty kilometers we simply cruised along with the current, took a couple of back-channels behind islands and marvelled at the changing landscape, took pictures. I wrote in my journal as we drifted, slightly euphoric; Dawson's nearby monotonous and incessant ramblings, an undertone of conversation that Hodding politely absorbed unflinchingly. Although the tamarack and spruce followed the hem of the Seal River, we could see the tundra heath backdrop more regularly. As of yet, we hadn't the opportunity to explore the open barrenland. Whereas the park-like manifestation found throughout the spruce-lands afforded such a confusing picture of growth and a restricted view of the environment beyond the shoreline, the open heath would offer a true image of the barrenland persona. The actual phantom tree-line took two days and almost one-hundred kilometers to traverse. We were now, officially, within the arctic tundra.

There was a three kilometer section of easy rapids through a mini-canyon of exposed bedrock, slanted back to the open ground behind, followed by another rather violently pitched rapid, the limit we could possibly run safely. We had to get out to take a look at before running and it gave us quite a wild ride through meter and a half breaking waves. It was a good primer for what we were about to see around a tight corner where the Seal River took a dog-leg bend around a bedrock wall.

Visibility restricted our view ahead and we were committed to an easy run through the cleft of bedrock, a portal of sorts into another world. We were cruising along, running in the middle channel. What we were to see next took me by surprise. My jaw dropped. Up ahead was a steeply-pitched wild rapid that looked like a down escalator, only steps were endless, breaking waves and it went on forever, four kilometers to be exact and the drop was more than fifty feet. It was the same feeling you had looking down a tobogganing slope. The pitch was noticeable and the obvious cause of such violent water-play. We began back-watering to slow down, but it was no use. I stood up in the canoe, Dawson following suit, trying to get a better look to see if there were any ledges to be wary of. It looked runnable but it was hard to tell. The light was good with the sun at high noon so I gave the signal to run. We came to rely heavily on the advantages of the spray-covers to get us through the heavy rollers and we certainly needed them for this wild run. There were boulders to avoid, but you couldn't really make them out until you were right on top of them. About two thirds of the way down, crashing through and over a washboard roller-coaster of meter-high waves and dodging rocks, Russell suddenly lifted his paddle out of the water and turned around to face me. His complexion was pale.

"Christ, I'm going to throw up!" Russ mumbled. I yelled at him to retch over the side of the gunwale on his paddling side so I could brace through it while we kept on track. He never did clear his stomach overboard into the rapids, but it came close. I told him to lean back and that I'd take the canoe down the rest of the run which had now panned out into an easier Class II. By the time we got to the bottom Russ had composed himself and started laughing. We both broke out into hysterical laughter at the thought of getting sea-sick on a set of rapids. And I think we laughed because we both knew that if we dumped near the top we would probably be dead by the time we reached the bottom; banged up, half-drowned and hypothermic.

We coasted up to an odd-looking island at the foot of the last rapids. It was mesa-like, flat-topped and steep-banked. Standing rather abruptly above the river, it was barren of all vegetation except ground lichens and mosses, intriguing and somewhat formidable. It felt wonderful to get out of the boats to stretch cramped leg muscles and peel off the tops of our wet suits as we climbed the steep, crumbling bank to the crest of the hill. The top surface was uniformly level, almost unnatural, spongy to walk on and covered with a lush cushion of reindeer lichen. We were standing on a raised peat-plateau several meters in depth. The view afforded our first unrestricted look across the tundra; and although we couldn't see much of the actual river ahead as it sliced its way through the deep tundra mat, the overwhelming nature of the open terrain impressed the senses immensely. We ran across the flats like children at a playground. I think more to combat the plague of black flies then to get rid of the pent-up, in-a-canoe numbness. There was a brisk wind, but it did nothing to deflect the persistent waves of flies. The smoke from the fires, maybe the heat, kept the biting flies at bay periodically, but they were now out in legions.

Russell and Hodding were bearing up to the bugs and wore their headnets without complaint. Russ couldn't take photographs through the bug mesh so he left it off more than he should have, but he was getting used to the bugs and the bites. Dawson's bare skin began to turn colour with outbreaks of lesions and blisters, a reaction to the amount of insect repellent he used. None of us wore headnets while running whitewater though the black flies never let up while thrashing down rapids at more than fifteen kilometers per hour. They simply latched on and got embedded in our clothing, enjoying lunch and a free-ride.

We had difficulty finding a suitable campsite along this stretch of river. After running a three kilometer section of easy Class II rapids beyond the peat island, where the river takes a north sweep for twenty kilometers, we started feeling the pangs of both hunger and fatigue and decided to make a day of it. Nerves, adrenalin, pure extreme challenge of endless rapids, the constant harangue of bull dogs and black flies, all taxed the energy reserves.

Paddling further than we intended, we finally found some respite on a rough gravel beach on the west side of the river, lee to the wind and infested with flies. We had scanned the shoreline for miles finding nothing dry, or level, or clear enough to set up tents on the east side of the river, which was still basking in the late afternoon sun and relatively bug free because of the breeze. We made do with a shaded, steep gravel bank, fatigue winning precedence over selective comfort. Dawson and Hodding concocted a mock seafood chowder and cornbread for dinner and by the time we had finished eating the sun had already made its departure. A seal would occasionally slip past, staring at us curiously as they always do, disappear quietly, reappear, followed by another and another.

I was exhausted. We all were by now. The staccato of mosquitoes bouncing off the inside of the tent-fly hummed a frenzied, monotonous chorus. Muscles ached, joints were stiff, but it felt luxurious to stretch out on my sleeping bag, naked and free of biting flies. We could still smell the smoke from the fires. Had it not been for the checkered line of tundra, we would probably be racing the fire all the way to Hudson Bay. Instead, lucky for us, the only remaining mark of the blaze was the incident smoke drift which created the most astounding sunsets cast through the pall into diffused and unusual brilliance.

The highlights of this expedition were exceptional, the experiences extraordinary, but oftentimes pushing extreme to the limit. Exploration is all of that. What can make an outstanding venture work against its success is generally human conflict; disagreements, power struggles, even hardship that drives a less experienced person over the edge. In our case it was those little annoying behavioural peculiarities seeping out of the mire that grated on my nerves. Dawson. If a day went by without some manner of eccentricity or plain weird conduct, it was a blessing. Trouble was, a day didn't go by that my assistant guide didn't challenge my leadership. And most of this was directed at getting under my skin because for Hodding and Russell – they were just clients, often oblivious to Dawson's idiosyncrasies. Had we not been on a wilderness expedition, my complaints would seem trite. Expeditions such as this one demand a very rigid control of the trip environment, from quality of equipment, morale and especially food.

Expedition food had to be organized into daily menu allotments, enough to replace expended calories each day, well packed and waterproofed with a strict adherence to the established eating schedule; all under strict management and scrutiny of the guide. Deviating from this could be disastrous. To over-indulge beyond the proportioned daily stock could mean a shortage later on. People unused to wilderness living and survival often carry with them the same habit of eating as if they were still in civilization, where food can be acquired simply by walking to the grocery store. Some clients, if given carte blanche access to the communal pot, will sometimes take far more than the average serving, even leaving leftovers. If not portioned, per person, an avaricious client may easily over-indulge. Not only is this unfair to the others in the group, causing social malaise (and it eventually will if left unchecked), but will most certainly put food stores in the red. That is why the guide polices over the food, first-aid kit and the whiskey. Especially the whiskey; and only because we had such a small amount packed along.

I had worked out a menu for the expedition and it was working well, except for the coffee. That was a disaster! Dawson was supposed to have picked up regular ground coffee for the trip, to supplement what I had brought for the first week. He decided to pick up flavoured coffee. Bavarian chocolate coffee. Bavarian fucking chocolate coffee! It was not a hit with the Americans. It was not a hit for me either, but Dawson loved it. Serving bad coffee to clients in the morning was tantamount to leaving behind the toilet-paper. I prided myself at making the best backwoods brew in the north. Everyone raved about it, pleaded for more. This little faux pas was a morale game changer; mornings were a little less pleasurable. You didn't mind the bugs so much if you at least had a good cup of java. But that wasn't all. Dawson began to rummage through the food wannigan when I wasn't looking. Before I could intervene he would whip out one of the "special" desserts, or treats normally saved for morale boosters on particularly hard days. He also started to mix up the already arranged meals so that there was little organization to it, making it difficult to know how much food was actually remaining. If it was his turn to cook, the directions were simple – *stick to the menu* – however, he would decide to add this, or that, take away something else, but it was typically adding more than required. I took him aside and reprimanded him about this with the same result as before: a puzzled look of annoyance. He remained defiant.

The next morning, as usual, Dawson sat on his wannigan smoking, talking, waving at the first assault of black flies, while the rest of us broke camp and packed up. We were always waiting for him to get his things together. The more I prodded him, the slower he became. *I wanted to leave him right there.* I felt bad about thinking that but I *had* thought of it. I hated myself for having allowed myself to be put into that train of thought. I hated him for the experience.

Russell and I left ahead of the other two so we could photograph seals. We couldn't wait for Dawson any longer. I told him to meet us about nine kilometers downriver where we would make an early camp and rest up for the last few days ahead. He was surprised I would leave without him. It was the only way to get him moving. I realized too that his slack behaviour was his way of controlling the moment.

There were more harbour seals the closer we travelled towards Hudson Bay. They were often sunning themselves on the smooth offshore boulders, almost impossible to distinguish from the grey-black rock, and they would slip into the water like a bubble of mercury when we cruised by. Although the seals were always curious, of their own volition, whenever we approached to photograph them they would only allow us to get within about fifty meters before dropping out of sight.

According to the Canada Parks survey, there were no suitable places to camp past the point of our chosen island rest site and we still had sixty-kilometers to go to reach the Bay. The river plunged a further eighty-five meters! Considering the supine nature of the tundra along this stretch, the elevation drop was difficult for us to fathom. The Seal, nonetheless, never ceased to move eastward to the sea without an animated spirit. Even here, along this calm patch of river, the current was tenacious. It was a short day. From here to where we planned our last night on the river, twenty kilometers shy of the Bay, the rapids would prove to be demanding. The river would tip off the continental plate at a rate of two-meters every kilometer – a terrific descent for such a voluminous river. The half-day rest would do us good.

The beach campsite looked like a movie set out of *Blue Lagoon* or *Treasure Island*. The natural forces had sculpted and manicured the most fantastic arboreal display over a terraced sand dune of grand proportions. When we landed on the beach, under the scorching sun of the early afternoon, Russ and I felt as if we had been shipwrecked and washed ashore. Had it not been for the affliction of black flies it would have been easy to fantasize a south Pacific seascape. Instead of coconut palms there were large, twisted, stunted spruce with exposed roots erupted in pockets across the dune. The island begged discovery and exploration.

The wind picked up later that day, after camp was set up, and the flies almost disappeared completely. They either gave in to the breeze or it was just too hot for them. I needed space from the others and walked the long beach alone, trying to capture the events of the trip, attempting to block out the nonsense with my assistant. I laughed out loud. The others would have thought I had gone stark raving mad. I stripped off all my clothes and folded them over a rock by the shore. It felt luxurious to be naked and no biting flies, to feel the breeze, sun, cold water on my bare feet, to smell the pungent sweet aroma of the tundra, trace the line of beach with my eyes, identifying the signatures of wildlife in the sand. It was a rapturous escape, paradise removed and undiscovered until now. I left my own footprints in the sand, our overturned canoes down the beach, smoke rising from the campfire. Voices afar. Still paradise.

Sand had been pushed up in long striations at the back of the beach where spring ice plowed up along the shore, not so long ago. I was trying hard to capture the old-feeling I normally had on wilderness trips, usually alone, or at least on a journey where people share in the magic and without the annoying showmanship of a troublesome dupe. I was amazed at how one person can destroy that elation of euphoria. I wondered how Russell and Hodding felt about the trip and whether Dawson had compromised the magic for them. I wondered what Hodding was writing in his journal. I believed that I had done well at salvaging the expedition, more or less 'protected' the Americans from the brunt of the discourse between my assistant and me. It was hard not to notice, though, and although few words were spoken between me and them, I could read it in their eyes that something was amiss, questions they were afraid to ask perhaps, a feeling of bridled anxiousness, maybe. Most conversations took place after hours, in their tent and it was usually just Dawson's voice I heard. My interplay conversationally with the others took place during the day and it was usually more instructive than informal chatter. Dawson dominated any free space for that.

We had made it this far, alive, which I was thankful for despite my aggravating assistant's attempt at scuppering the whole lot. But now there were other concerns, like polar bears along the coast, and the paddle down Hudson Bay to Churchill; real apprehension that could easily be dealt with had Dawson not been along, ready to explode at the most inopportune time. The constant thought of what he was going to do, or fail to do next was on my mind, and in Russell's thoughts too. Russ and I started talking about Dawson and his behaviour, but I was reluctant to share my real thoughts yet. Hodding was indifferent, almost supportive of his paddling partner; but I surmised Hodding had been oblivious of the impact Dawson had on the greater picture. Had I allowed Dawson absolute freedom to do whatever he pleased, not only would our provisions been expended, but some disaster may have already taken hold of our crew. He had no consideration for his actions and their subsequent effect on trip dynamics, safety, or general morale of the group. Worst of all, he showed no remorse for the inconsiderate actions he seemed to do out of personal habit, traits that Hodding seemed to readily accept for a *joie de vivre*, or Canadian spirit characteristic of the average northern guide. I'm sure Hodding saw me as a bit of an autocrat with a chip on my shoulder; too serious, probably, or focused a little too intently on trying to keep order. Hodding's own adventure following Lewis and Clarke's historic route across the west in a motorboat was rife with misadventures and chaos that all worked out in the end. But if a day didn't go well for them, they just had to walk to a phone and call for a ride out. We were stuck with Dawson, unless he somehow disappeared; discomfiting thoughts I had more often than I felt comfortable with.

I walked for as far as the beach would allow, about a kilometer from our camp, stopped and looked back along the beach from where I had come. The two blue *Royalex* canoes strangely blended with the scattered boulders strewn upon the beach, and the bright yellow tents had ducked behind a sand dune where the others were sleeping or sitting by the fire. I felt strong enough even though I was dead tired, weary, enervated by angst mostly, the blisters and sore muscles were honest companions I felt comfortable with. I walked slowly back, picked up my clothes and sat by the fire for a short while chatting with the others. Once in my tent I collapsed without undressing and fell into a fathomless, dreamless sleep.

Chapter Ten

Final Descent

There was a stiff northern breeze blowing and we paddled into it for a good hour before the river swung south in a yawning meander. Russell and I took a narrow side channel, or braid, off the main trunk of the river. I enjoyed sweeping close to the shore where there was always a better opportunity to see wildlife. Dawson paddled straight down the middle, talking Hodding's ear off, no doubt recounting his own often embellished exploits.

The narrow ribbon of water turned out to be a veritable sanctuary for birds, both large and small. Canada geese in small social groups clustered close to the river bank of the channel and scurried into the sedge as we paddled by. There were mallards and blue-winged teal, mergansers and sandpipers, and such a collection of warblers we had trouble naming them all; many of their calls were totally foreign to me.

We met up with the others just shy of the many rapids marked on the topographical chart and agreed to have lunch before making our descent. It was a good call. As we sat on a rock outcrop at the head of the first long rapids and looked downstream there was no end of the wild-water for as far as the eye could trace the river. The Seal turned eastward again for its final plunge to the sea, gallant and grandiloquent. For forty kilometers there would be little break from the tedium of rapid-play. Over the next fifteen-kilometers we would drop over one-hundred feet along a series of contiguous rapids: from Class II to angry Class IV canoe-eaters; Tambany Rapids and Deadly Rapids loomed ahead with hardly a moment's pause in the downward rush.

Gear was packed tight, spray-covers cinched taut and wet suits put on in expectation of a long bout in the canoe.

Along the spillway there were no trees, just tundra and extensive outcroppings of granite. We had entered a surreal world of stone and frost-shattered blocks of Mother Earth scattered about the barrens, edging their way into the river, turning the current into angry white waves and devilish sluiceways that boiled and churned chaotically. We were in the thick of it. *Felsenmeer*, the German word for "sea of rocks", commonly known as a "block-field" in geological terms, jagged, angular and deadly, confronted us with an unforgiving challenge. To the seasoned whitewaterist it could have been pure ecstasy; playing through the gauntlet of sharp-toothed rocks as one would play a game of checkers: moving forward only, cutting diagonal paths through an utter confusion of boulders and false channels, making split-second choices, coursing ahead, correcting, side-slipping, bracing. No time to rest. No place to pull over. Up ahead the river dropped out of sight, completely; the sound of the rapids deepened into a low, rumbling growl. My lunch slowly moved back up my esophagus and the bile burned my throat. I was starting to feel the motion in the pit of my bowels, getting everything moving inside while the world flashed by outside. It did not look good up ahead, a steep pitch out of view. There was a break in the rapids, an eddy, and we headed for it.

Pausing briefly, I stood up in the canoe and scanned the

rapids and determined that there were no ledges. All agreed to take the right course to avoid the two-meter haystacks down the middle. The initial plunge was so steep it forced the air out of my lungs. I needed a quick brace for the rise up on the end of the tongue as it broke into demented waves and angular furls. A dump here would be fatal unless you were lucky enough to scramble to shore in time. Utter chaos. The river took a wild dog-leg bend, pinched together by sinewy stacks of granite on either side of the Seal with no way out except down. As the river straightened out we were propelled into the gaping maw of a tenuous monster rapid; row upon row of vicious back-curling white waves with no end in sight.

"We're in for a ride!" I yelled at Russell. I braced as he yanked up tight on his spray-cover and cinched it tight under his armpits and I could feel him spreading his body weight lower in the canoe for stability. He was getting used to the long runs. This time we stayed to the middle of the river where the flow drowned out most of the felsenmeer nearer the shore. It would have been hazardous to try and navigate through the maze of rocks. Dawson kept his canoe close to our stern.

We were entering Tambany Rapids, a three kilometer Class III boulder garden rapid. With the higher water level the run was easier than we first expected, so long as we steered a straight course and braced through the massive standing waves. Dawson fell behind and it was harder to keep an eye on him. I headed for an eddy at the bottom of the run so I could watch the other canoe come down. As we swung into the pool at the base of Tambany, we looked upriver to see Dawson making a mad dash sideways to the current, heading for a large boulder. As his canoe struck the heavy wash around the rock, the boat flipped over and spilled into the eddy. From our position it was a bad place to execute any kind of rescue. They were too far out from shore.

Russ and I pushed our canoe onto the shore rocks and I was about to get out, rescue rope in hand when I saw Hodding and Dawson scrambling safely to shore, pulling the overturned canoe with them. They managed to get themselves out of trouble.

"Stupid, stupid....*STUPID move!*" I foamed at the mouth. They had it made. They were moments from finishing the run and he had to pull a stupid stunt like he did at Great Island. At least this time nothing was lost but Hodding was not a happy camper. They were both bumped and bruised up from banging around the rough rocks. Dawson just laughed it off. I told him to take the lead for the rest of the day so I could keep an eye pinned to his back. If he made one wrong move I would be on his tail and my paddle would find the back of his head.

Dumping in rapids was dangerous. If the gear packed in an open canoe was not tethered in somehow, the gear would float downriver for quite a distance making it hard to collect, potentially losing important equipment. If the gear was tied in tight to the thwarts and yoke, the canoe could be hard to extricate if jammed against a rock. With a spray-cover fastened, gear stayed in the canoe, luckily, but extremely precarious to rescue because of the weight and having to unfasten the decking to get at the packs. It was messy business, all the while standing in deep, moving current and manoeuvring around sharp rocks.

The course of the river here, as it spewed us out onto a deltaic plain, where the Seal estuary was still rebounding from the ice-age, resembled a confused and disoriented maze of islands and back-channels. We had a few kilometers of easy water to navigate before the river widened again into the delta, and that prompted the decision to camp wherever we could find a suitable place to brush out a site. The large, treed islands appeared like an odd oasis of green, sandwiched between plains of barren rock, sedge and peat moss. Huge fifteen-meter tamaracks, some over two-feet thick and likely more than three-hundred years in age, blanketed the low, gravelly slopes. Deep peat deposits carpeted the floor turf while caribou antlers in numbers lay gleaming in the late afternoon sun; an old crossing place perhaps. There was nowhere to camp. It was going to either be wet tundra flats or a hacked out campsite on one of the treed islands.

After a lengthy search we did find a perfect island and only thirty-kilometers to the Bay from where we would also face the most treacherous water of the entire Seal River. Since Canada Parks confirmed there were no likely places to camp (usually a sand beach or raised peat shelf), we would build a new site on one of the islands. The one we found was level, protected, easy to access and there was a surfeit of firewood available – a bonus anywhere in the barrens. We would have our last campfire of the trip. Up until now, all campsite meals were prepared over an open fire; the primus gas-stove was used solely for making quick tea or coffee only.

In our search for a suitable camping site we stumbled across an old mining camp that was likely established in the 1950s. It was an exploration depot still littered with decades-old trash tossed across the tundra floor; piles of tin cans and bottles, core samples, plywood, rusted machinery. It was typical then and no different now for companies to just leave everything behind, the rationale for such slovenly habits resting on the fact that it would cost too much to fly it out.

A camping area was cleared carefully; just enough of the low sedge and small spruce trees were removed to afford room for a couple of tents and a ring of stones for a safe fire-pit. It turned out to be one of the more pleasant havens of the trip: our oasis of green, comfortably enshrined within a valiant forest in an ocean of desolate nothingness. Other canoe parties could take shelter at the site after us.

Dawson had caught a grayling and cleaned it on top of the wannigan lid, against my recommendation. A polar bear could detect the smell from miles away. He shrugged off the warning as if it were a fly on his shoulder.

"We've got a gun," Dawson retorted with defiance.

"That's not the point. The general idea is to *avoid* any confrontation so we don't have to use it," I countered, trying not to get angry in front of the others. He understood the way I worked and it was mentally debilitating. He provoked me, trying to get me to show my anger in front of Hodding and Russell. They wouldn't understand my reasoning for getting angry at my assistant; they knew very little about bears and neither did Dawson. I did - at least bears other than polar bears, like blacks and grizzlies, but I assumed the smell of fresh fish guts would be ambrosia for any carnivore. Fish were always cleaned away from the campsite, usually on the backside of a paddle and the offal tossed far out into the water for gulls. The paddle was then thoroughly sanitized.

Instead of a display of temper, I walked quietly down to the shore where he was gutting the fish and whispered into Dawson's ear. "If you fuck up on the coast you're as good as bear bait Dawson," I said sternly, and handed him the soap and a scrubber to clean the wannigan lid. Dawson smiled back at me; that crooked, penetrating, leering smirk of a crazy man.

"Sure, whatever," he said, swiping the soap out of my hand. *I hated that smile.* It was always a precursor to trouble. I leaned closer so the others couldn't hear our little confrontation. "No, not whatever; and take that fucking smirk off your face!"

"Alright, alright already...cool off why don't you?"

So, that was it; the last word every time we butt heads. I knew I was fighting a losing battle. There's no way to win an argument against ignorance. I retreated back to the campsite where the lads were setting up their tent and I walked back to a lush thicket of black spruce. From this glade I cut six stout poles, eight feet in length, to be used for rigging the canoes into a catamaran sailboat once we reached the Hudson Bay coast. There were no trees at all past this island so we would carry the poles with us the remainder of the way, tucked in the bottom of our canoes under the packs. Our food packs were now considerably lighter, more compact, allowing extra room in the canoes. After Dawson had started invading the food supplies I had to keep a close watch on provisions to make sure we had enough grub to finish the expedition. Along with each day's rations, which were quite generous, I made sure there was at least three to four days of "safety" rations, mostly compact dehydrated food that took up little space in the pack. If we had an emergency, either a smashed canoe, serious injury or bad weather, the extra provisions could keep us going for another week. It had happened to me once before. Russ had asked me about it one night around the campfire.

"We talked about trip food and taking extra supplies, " Russ inquired, "but have you ever been stranded, late for pick up or lost before?"

"Sure. You spend enough time out here and things happen, sooner or later," I told him, "and you want to be ready for that, for whatever might happen that might compromise the trip."

"So, give me an example," Russ demanded with curious enthusiasm.

"Okay, I think it was in the early 1980s," I began slowly, trying to remember all the details from a decade ago, "I was charting out a canoe trail from Kipawa Lake in Quebec to the headwaters of the Dumoine River, a route used by Keewaydin and other camps and I wanted to add it to my outfitting expeditions. I was paddling solo, along with a husband and wife couple who wanted to tag along. Crossing the many lakes was not a difficulty for the couple, but when we began descending the many rapids on the Dumoine River their lack of skills became apparent."

"What do you mean, what did they do…or not do?" questioned Russ.

"Too proud to listen to my advice," I said, "and they ran a gnarly rock-strewn rapid instead of safely lining their canoe as I had suggested. I saw their canoe broadside a rock in the middle of the river. They did everything wrong, allowing the canoe to lean upstream and it immediately filled with water and wrapped itself hopelessly around the boulder."

"Shit, then what?" Russ asked.

"They got pinned, both of them, between the canoe and a river boulder, went under for a few seconds and then managed to free themselves just before I could scramble up the shore to help them out.

"What about the canoe?" Russ was now leaning forward, elbows resting on his knees. Hodding and Dawson had long since retired to their tent. It was one of those rare campfire evenings when we chose to stay up past the witching hour.

"The canoe was too far out in the river to perform an easy rescue and in very heavy current. It was also late in the day so I shuttled the couple to a nearby campsite where we tried to figure out our next move. They were reluctant to leave their brand new cedar-canvas prospector in the river; we also had too much gear and my canoe wouldn't hold three people safely. We still had four days left to get out. The only thing to do was to try to extricate the canoe using cut poles as pry-bars and work the broken canoe over the rock."

"Did that work? The canoe would be scrap after that, even if you got it out," commented Russ.

"Well, it took all of the next day to unsnag it from the boulder. The canvas was intact but the gunwales were broken along with several ribs and planking. It had to be repaired before we could paddle out with it. We towed the busted canoe back to the camp. The first thing I did was to keep the canoe open side up and pile river rocks inside along the damaged section."

"Why would you do that?" probed Russell. "Why bother with that?"

"If the wood dried while the canoe was humped up in the middle, then it would take on that shape when it dried out. I went out and cut fresh cedar for the other repairs and these would be whittled down and tied in for gunwale braces, planking, and support joists to hold the bashed-in bottom from oil-canning. This little misadventure put us three-days behind schedule. After the third day being late for pick-up, my wife at the time was about to call Search and Rescue. I did manage to make the call before the end of the third day. The damaged canoe was paddled out, albeit thirty-pounds heavier with the field-repairs, and we managed to live quite handily on the extra food provisions I had packed along once our regular supply ran out. This was complemented by fresh caught fish."

"Those people were lucky," Russ commented, throwing another log on the fire.

"Yup, and a good reason to take good stock of your food; something Dawson can get a bit wiser about for sure," I quipped, knowing well Russ knew that I was pissed with Dawson for screwing up our food wannigan.

Dawson had sufficiently compromised the order of our menu, exhausting some of the luxury items early on in the trip when he took it upon himself to impress our clients. We still had a week's supply of food, including the safety provisions and I would keep the remainder of our stock under close scrutiny. He kept prodding me to "dole out some of the goodies" when they were kept for regular breaks or "tough" times when we all needed a lift. Aside from the food issues, there was one more item of contention that would be ironed out very soon.

There was only one day left to reach the Bay and we were two-days ahead of our scheduled pick-up by Jackie Bastone from Churchill. We weighed the options of waiting it out at the estuary for a pick-up or to paddle down the coast to Churchill. Of course, Dawson opted to paddle. His reasoning was primarily financial; he could pocket half the savings by not using company money to hire the boat. The thought of nasty weather, or polar bears never factored into his decision and that concerned us all. It was this kind of thinking that killed the four young canoeists coming off the Albany River some years back. For Hodding, Russ and I, that particular tragedy was still very much on our minds. Waiting at the estuary for a safe haul to Churchill could give us plenty of time to explore the beluga whale calving waters, or trek deeper into the tundra to look for caribou. Paddling the coast was very tempting, but not to save money.

"If we run the coast, we do it my way," I told the others. I did want to see the coast, feel the tide, maybe see a polar bear from a distance. I had no idea what to expect with the tidal fluctuations either; it was never an issue down south in lake land.

"Once we reach Hudson Bay we'll raft the canoes so that we can safely photograph beluga whales," I explained to the others. "If we were to notch the rigging poles to fit tighter to the gunwales of the canoes we could keep the spray-covers fastened."

This was crucial in case the wind suddenly came in off the Bay. We would also take advantage of the high tides, push hard when the water level along the coast was sufficient to clear us of the boulder fields and then rest on-shore when the tide was out. The plan was to follow the lee of the shoreline heading south, hoping for an offshore wind from the west, and under no circumstance attempt to cross-over Button Bay to make the short-cut to Churchill. All agreed, even Dawson which surprised me. I thought he would have disputed the Button Bay issue but instead remained silent. Our eyes never met.

With the last residue of evening light, I worked the freshly cut spruce poles into rigid 'stays' that locked onto the canoe gunwales, test-fitted them with the canoes half-a-meter apart, and adjusted the notches accordingly. I was pleased with the result. It would be a sturdy craft. Whether or not it would stand up to the tempestuous nature of *Tu Cho* – Hudson Bay - remained to be tested.

"Here's how it will work." I sketched out the diagram on a blank page in my journal while the others formed a semi-circle in front of me. "Two poles will lock the two canoes together, anchored with rope to the back of the seats; another pole will serve as a mast, fastened to the front stay by notch and parachute-cord, held aloft by four lanyards, each secured to the ends of the canoes. The last pole – the boom – would carry the sail and can be raised or lowered with a short rope which passed through a carabiner at the top of the mast. Two short ropes, secured to the bottom corners of the large tarp – our sail – can be manipulated to swing the boom in order to catch the wind. I'd rather have used a two-pole mast where the tops are tied securely together while the bottoms are lashed behind the bow seat of each canoe and wedged in place with the weight of the packs; but, in this case, the single pole mast fastened to the center of the front stay, over the void between the canoes will allow us to secure the spray-covers. Any questions?" Everyone nodded, looked at each other, Dawson shrugged and Hodding said "awesome": his favourite expression for just about anything.

Canoes are not designed for sailing. Over the years I had learned some tricks to compensate for the lack of manoeuvrability. Still, any wind not blowing from behind would be imperfect and without a dagger-board of some kind, the craft would be blown sideways. A paddle tied outside of the center thwart would work as a lateral stabilizer had we not planned to fasten down the spray-covers. If the canoes were tied too close together, without the use of spray-covers, a flume of water would quickly materialize between the boats and irreverently sink them in a matter of a few minutes. Even with all the precautions in place, a strong wind and capped waves could easily sink the quasi-catamaran. The spray-covers would help, considerably, as they did while running rapids, but a heavy sea could snap the four-inch spruce poles like matchsticks and flip the canoes. This may have happened to the four paddlers leaving Fort Albany to Moosonee.

The others had gone to bed. Their candle was lit and I could make out their forms through the thin nylon veil of their tent. Dawson, as usual, was doing most of the talking. I felt quite alone. But that was my doing. By sleeping apart from the group I had missed most of the conversation with the Americans. During the day, talk would embrace the industry of the expedition; which channels to run, where to pull over for lunch, where to camp but almost nothing of a personal nature.

"I wish my fiancé were here," Russell lamented one day out of the blue.

"Do you think she'd like the black flies," I laughed. Russell shook his head.

"Don't know for sure. She would tough it out."

"You miss her, don't you Russ?"

"Yeah, I do. I can't wait to phone her when we get to Churchill."

I felt a little nostalgic after that, thinking about my own situation. But I was happy for Russell. His fiancé was a lucky girl. Hodding would be recounting small adventures and escapades, perhaps his fascination with studying animal scat, or what it was like to be a postmaster in Thermond, which would eventually lead to past romances and love affairs, to which Dawson would add his own reidentifications as poet, scholar and lover. I felt my age; the difference in years that set us apart, aggravated mildly by the distance between the two tents.

I missed that part of the expedition, the interfacing with interesting clients. I had been so caught up in reading their moment to moment expressions and moods during the course of the days on the trail that I had failed to notice *who* these two people were. I held a rather marked distaste for labelling the participants as "clients", as it denoted separation and classification, even though as guide you are required to remain somewhat authoritative and aloof. But I couldn't get anywhere near the Americans on this expedition. Dawson stood in the way. I could sense his interference every time I came close to getting to know either Russell or Hodding. I believed he was trying so hard to impress them, to be written up in the *Men's Journal* article as the swashbuckling hero, the Canadian wilderness guru, the bon vivant of the backwoods. It *was* almost comic. I knew that Russ was not impressed by Dawson's actions, but Hodding seemed to take everything in stride. Whether it was borne out of the camaraderie of being his canoe partner, or whether he was enamoured by Dawson's silly antics, it was impossible to tell. I had long stopped thinking about the article. It was all I could do to bandage up my assistant's screw-ups on a daily basis, get us through the fires, to keep the canoes afloat down insane whitewater, threading the needle through a complex grid-work of boulder rapids.

I was exhausted, both physically and mentally. I loved the river, the landscape, the rawness and even the dangerous aspect of the trip. The most enervating component of the expedition, by far, was the constant *looking-over-the-shoulder*, trying to interpret Dawson's next move and devising ways to keep the expedition on track. It was as if I had given up the pleasures of conversation out of sheer exasperation. Not that the Americans would think it anything other than my own eccentricities. But the conflict between me and my assistant guide was beginning to show, seep through the bandages and it was festering. Russ and Hodding had been asking more questions about what to expect up ahead, at the end of the trip, about the most dangerous part of it. Dawson was now left out of these conversations, as if they knew he was a wild card not to be trusted. The Americans wanted to get out alive, to file their story to *Men's Journal*, and to return home in one piece. They had the story; more than they ever expected. Now they just wanted to finish. Get out.

I still didn't know much about them. Not that they weren't asked a lot of questions; it wasn't like they didn't have a lot to share. Hodding seemed to live vicariously through his more famous relations. Most of our conversations focused on the "what-ifs" and the "how-to's" of expedition paddling. A lot of questions I didn't have answers for, just presumptions and educated guesswork. But nature is like that; not everything is written out, time-tested or obviously comprehensible. Nature is chaos with a profound and palpable purpose.

I kicked the last embers of the fire into a pile and poured the last of the un-drunk coffee over them. The hiss and steam charged the stillness with a final gasp of energy and then all was silent. The stars dazzled the void of night in special brilliance and the river flowed on to the ocean. I could see my breath in the starlight. Across the river the half-moon hovered above the serrated vanguard of spruce, offering just enough light for me to pitch my tent. I had been so busy that evening that I had neglected to prepare my own bed. I left the rain-fly off so I could see the stars through the mosquito mesh. I fell asleep before I could even crawl into my sleeping bag.

*   *   *   *   *

The delta region of the Seal River, in terms of fluvial age, is a relatively new and undeveloped stage of river morphology. This new-fledged river course – a by-product of the glacial era – presents an interesting dilemma for the canoeist. The convoluted channels are rife with a bewildering maze of terraced islands, demented rapids, shelves, boulder-trains and ledges – all impossible to scout. Not only does this entail a particularly intimate affair with the river, but also presents the formidable likelihood of being blanketed by fog, inbound from the near coast. If this happens, visibility would be reduced and it would be next to futile to try and read the location on the map. The terminus of the Seal ends abruptly at "Deaf Rapids", so called because you cannot hear it upon approach. In the fog, one could easily be swept into its mouth. The drop is acute – over eight meters. The run is less than five-hundred meters so the pitch itself blocks its own audible or visible presence to the approaching paddler; that is, you can't see the bottom of the rapid from the top. Canada Parks rated this rapid at the top of the scale – a Class VI – not that they had been entirely accurate up to this point, but at least we had some premise as to the danger that lurked ahead. Then there were the polar bears.

We had camped just thirty kilometers from Hudson Bay. Dawson's propensity for adding to the unknown had everyone on edge. Not caring about polar bears and so eager to paddle the coast without caution indicated to the rest of us that his mantra was the same that lured others to their death. Next morning there was a brisk west-northwest wind blowing downriver. It was mutually decided that we would test out our sailing rig, at least as far as Deaf Rapids. It took half-an-hour to ready the boats; the tarp-sail noisily impatient for us to shove off into the current with the wind behind us.

The river was a kilometer across with no rapids for the first ten kilometers, just current. The river-scape spread out as we edged closer to the Seal estuary and Hudson Bay, the tundra broad and sweeping as we cleared the oasis of spruce islands, retreating from the expanse of sky, a thin band of green in a world of blue-grey. Water and heaven balanced on a thread of land so innocuous, the eye strains to make purchase on anything tangible, pulled along by forces unseen but sensed, water and wind. We sailed with the current at such a speed it would be difficult to stop. When we spotted the rock it *was* difficult to stop. Just as Allen had told us.

It wasn't a formidable rock in the middle of the river; it was purported to be a sacred rock to the Dene People, a few hundred meters in from the shore, often missed because of the thick sea fog that plagues the traveler. Today was clear and the visibility excellent. According to the Dene legend, Coppermine woman left several stones across the tundra to mark her way back home after she was kidnapped by the Inuit. After some time, she escaped from the abuse of slavery and rape and found her way back home by following the "waymarkers" she had left behind. This stone was special. It was the largest along the coast and closest to Tu Cho where her captors had come south by boat. For many centuries the Dene left sacred offerings at the rock in recognition of the strength and determination and courage of Coppermine woman. Now, the rock is only a legend. No one had laid eyes on it for decades. Allen had asked us to keep a lookout for it and if we found it, to mark the co-ordinates carefully on the topographic map.

We were cruising far too fast on the other side of the river, opposite the rock. The sail was dropped and the canoes spun around for an upstream ferry. It was hard work with little progress against the power of the river and by the time we reached the shore we were a kilometer past the rock. The boats were hauled up and anchored to a knot of wiry sedge, the loose sail flapping crazily in the wind. Spread out over several hundred meters were the discarded remnants from a prospector's camp; garbage, eviscerated equipment, plywood, sheet-metal, scattered amongst the peat hummocks, moss and crowberry, a testament of man's lack of care. Industry incarnate.

We all walked across the spongy mat of tundra heath to the monolithic stone, thrust upwards at an acute angle towards the sea. There were several glacial erratic boulders strewn over the general landscape but this rock did not look as if it had been transported by an ice field. I was not sure if this was the actual "lost" waymarker of the Dene but I left an offering of tobacco anyway. Russ took photographs, Hodding climbed to the top of the rock, twenty-feet above the tundra, while Dawson paced impatiently nearby.

As it turned out, I discovered the actual rock waymarker three years later while paddling the Caribou River, about thirty kilometers north of the Seal. The monolithic stone had a phallic-shaped rock perched on its apex, positioned carefully as a waymarker . The rock was easily missed while paddling as the river cuts deep into the tundra landscape with no view beyond the apparent shoreline. One of the canoes in our party upset in the rapids and we chose to camp at that location, hauling our gear up the bank and onto the flat tundra common. Looking back across the river I could see a barn-shaped rock standing alone on the tundra floor, about a kilometer and a half off the river. Oddly enough, at that distance it looked like a large building with a chimney protruding through the roof. Upon closer inspection, the waymarker and stone was discovered.

Unbeknownst to us we had actually been in polar bear country for the last few days. Due to global warming trends, bears were wandering further inland searching for food and since the expedition, polar bears have been sighted more than two-hundred kilometres in from the coast. I had brought along my shotgun as I was told that bears like to sleep in the shade behind these large boulders. I also wanted to test-fire the "bear-scare" cartridges, something I had never had to use while on southern expeditions with black bears. I was told that if I fired the bear-scare at an approaching bear and accidentally lobbed it over its head and behind it, the bear would run directly at the shooter. I didn't want this to happen. I loaded a cartridge in the chamber, picked a large white boulder and fired the gun. The cartridge "popped" and sizzled over and past the boulder and exploded with a sharp *bang!* Okay, good thing it wasn't a real bear. At least I knew now that the bear-scare was ranged for about fifty-meters, no more.

The Seal River at this juncture was definitely in a hurry. And it carried with it an uneasiness that crept into us all, and settled upon each joint and membrane and every conscious thought about what we were to find at the coast. The air was clear, the wind from the north kept the sea fog far out on the Bay. We were still nervous of the final rapids that would carry us out into Hudson Bay. The Seal River still broadened out to more than a kilometer wide, splaying out into the rebounding estuary, into countless recumbent islands of sedge and white boulders – rocks that often resembled polar bears. The labyrinth of channels made it difficult to navigate with any sense of place as it was referenced to the topographic chart. There were no landmarks, no high-points shown by contour gradient. Many of the islands shown on the map were also flooded out. All I could do was to steer us along what looked to be the main flow, the wind still filling the sail, our craft being tugged dramatically by the downhill rush of the river.

We were ten-kilometers from the coast. The wind eventually ceased and the sail languished helplessly. As we rolled up the sail and tied it off to the mast, Hodding yelled, "I can smell the ocean!" Looking eastward, our eyes betrayed reality as the world tipped almost one-hundred feet below us to the ocean we could not yet see.

"Ledges ahead, lots of them!" I yelled, but which one was Deaf Rapids? I leaned on the ruddering paddle and steered the catamaran towards the first drop. There was no place to land on shore, either to scout ahead or to dismantle the canoes. Scouting would be futile anyway. From here on it would be "play-as-you-go", take each ledge one at a time and hope to hell to be able to pull ashore before Deaf Rapids. It was difficult to see the ledges until we were right over them, and although the canoes were quite stable, having kept them lashed together they were sluggish to move into the running channels. With luck we somehow managed a clean run through the confusion of rocky sluiceways, over broken ledges and around impassable rock barriers, keeping to the main river, edging closer to the final plunge. The stays holding the canoes together creaked and strained under the variant pressures of the sudden drops and the ropes began to loosen until the whole rig felt as if it would suddenly become unhinged. The whole mess would topple over in the middle of a rapid if we didn't get over to the shore quickly, or we could be sucked down Deaf Rapids altogether, a jumbled mess of ropes, poles, packs, canoes and people.

"Deaf Rapids ahead!" someone yelled out. It was Hodding, now standing up in the bow to get a better look. We all followed suit. Sure enough, up ahead about a half-kilometer downriver, the entire Seal disappeared without a sound. A bold meniscus of water melted into the northern sky. We were in the middle of the river where the current was strongest, the pull of gravity taking almost full control of the catamaran. The boats were turned up-stream and powered against the flow into a dramatic cross-river ferry to the north side of the river. Still, the shore seemed unat-tainable until we launched ourselves clear of the center channel and cruised easily to a beaching site of flat rocks.

The canoes were quickly freed of their bonds and the gear repacked with the five poles being tucked under the loads. We would need them again when we headed out on the Bay coast. Spray-covers were snapped into place and all was set for the run, except us. We sat there somewhat perplexed as the rapids couldn't be assessed from the top. All we could see were the backs of two-meter breaking waves marching down the middle of the run while the shore channels were choked with Volkswa-gen-size boulders. It would be next to impossible to line or por-tage the canoes through or along the shore with such a tangle of tundra growth so we were committed to make the run.

To this point in our journey we had yet to make one portage, managing to play each rapid according to a contrived plan and a bounty of good luck. We were determined to complete the Seal in its entirety without carrying one item of gear. What a glorious moment. What a flash of intractable ambition and purpose. *What stupidity and nonsense!* It could be foolhardy and I wasn't about to throw caution so easily to the sea winds. I picked up the rifle and told the others to follow along the shore. We would scout as much as we could until we felt comfortable about a game-plan. And as we picked our way along the scummy shore rocks, in and out of thick sedge and wiry willow brush, always conscious of the fact that a polar bear may appear at any moment, we paused occasionally to read the play of the rapids.

From our vantage point halfway down the rapids we could see a way through along our side of the river; keeping away from the maelstrom coursing down the middle would be imperative.

It would be a task to keep from being pulled in to the center run as the narrowing of the river, the rapid geology, had formed a slightly sloped inward structure. Ecstatic about the possibility of running the rapid near the shore, we sat on the rocks by the canoes and talked about the run. To the east we could plainly see Hudson Bay. We could also smell it – that pungent, piscine smell of the sea, especially as the tide went out.

"Shit! We have to get going!" I yelled out to the others, "We have to take advantage of the outflow before the coast water levels drop five or six meters. That'll leave us stranded in the middle of a boulder-field."

We were actually looking down at Hudson Bay from our vantage point, three-kilometers away, the river dropping ten-feet every thousand- meters, marked by a procession of ledges, and pocked by inhospitable boulder piles and scabrous islands. We had to hurry. Dawson and Hodding ran Deaf Rapids first while Russ and I spotted for them near the bottom of the run. It was a fine piece of water-play, even for Dawson, and we applauded their success as they pulled into the eddy-pool at the end of the run. I was eternally grateful that Dawson never pulled one of his bone-head stunts.

Russell and I walked back to our canoe at the head of the rapids and I could sense that he was nervous; his actions were jittery and spastic as he pulled up his spray-skirt and cinched it tighter than usual. I couldn't tell him that I was nervous too. That would have totally freaked him out. I did my best to console him, told him that he managed to get us this far and that it was an easier run than it looked. If the others could make it down safely, we should have no problem at all.

"Don't look at the rollers down the middle," I explained to Russ.

"Why not?" Russ turned to me seriously and repeated,

"why not...?"

"They'll draw you into them. It happens, as you pull away from the shore rocks bit by bit and before you know it, you're in the middle run. Just play the boulder garden toward shore and we'll get through, like all the times before."

We pushed off into the excited current. Right away you could feel the energy of the vertical drop in the pit of your stomach, trying to snatch your breath, forcing your heart to beat an unnatural rhythm. It was an angry rapid, lashing viciously at the stanchions of rock that broke the river into vehement, white waves, clear and pure, as if the sanitized water of the Seal was fighting its eventual conjugation with the murky brine of the ocean. To our right we could hear the rolling thunder of the mountainous stationary waves; to our left was a blur of brown rock that broke the ricocheting sound into a multiplicity of scattered notes, rising and falling in pitch with each passing rock-face. Ahead lay a confusion of channels propagated by a perplexing matrix of underlying boulders.

"Draw left," I shouted at Russell. "Good. Now push hard and brace – *too much* - ease up a bit, good, keep it there but watch that pillow rock – excellent!" Crash! The canoe bounced hard against a vault of rock that seemed to move in on us from out of nowhere.

"Shit," we both resounded disdainfully, as a strike against our egos. That was too close for comfort. Before we realized it we were at the bottom, panting, sweating profusely, congratulating ourselves, patting our backs with praise.

"We're not out of it yet," I reminded everyone, "The tide's dropping fast and we've got to finish it through or we'll get stranded high and dry." The collective *oh no what now* look on their faces was priceless. I looked back at Deaf Rapids from the bottom. It was such a bizarre sight that I had to pause momentarily to rub my eyes. The rapid looked like a hill of waves, a winter ski-slope mogul run that suddenly appeared from a portal in the sky. It was hard to fathom that we had just paddled that sloping washboard of crazy rapids and actually made it down unscathed.

Ten years later, while running Deaf Rapids in low water, I waited three-hours at the top of the run for the tide to come in and reach its zenith. The rush of down-slope water off the Seal River plunged into the incoming tide off the ocean with such a force that it created enormous standing waves that spanned the entire bottom of the rapids. We needed the high tide in order to float our canoes out of the shallow estuary and up the coast to Jackie Bastone's goose-hunt shack. To manage the "tidal-waves" at the bottom, I rafted all three of our canoes together, made it through the run successfully, and had plenty of sea-clearance up the coast.

From Deaf Rapids the estuary fans out into uncharitable terraces that shape-shifted with the outgoing tide. In the pools between the steep ledges, harbour seals glided nonchalantly, staring at us with distant curiosity. Coal black eyes. We missed the opportunity to get out to deep water and paddle to the goose shack up the coast. We now had only a few minutes to find somewhere to camp amongst an impossible scrabble of islands, matted thick with two-meter high willow growth. There was nothing. The tide pulled us out farther to the last of the scrub islands. We were forced to back-track upstream in the hopes of finding better tenting ground but it proved futile as the last dregs of the river drained off the gravel bottom of the estuary.

Luckily, there was a knob of high ground barely large enough for our tent. It was an extremely dangerous and precarious place for a camp as the high sedge growth that pushed tight against the tent would allow a polar bear to be right on us before we could react. But we had no choice - we were here for the night; there was nowhere else to go. Our canoes bottomed out as we beached and quickly set about to pitch the tent. To make matters worse, the mosquitoes and black flies were horrific – the worst we had encountered yet. We couldn't get the tent up fast enough. Once it was pitched sloppily over the uneven patch of ground, the others dove in with their sleeping bags while I quickly prepared the usual one-pot masterpiece – a hearty pea soup with ham and a cabbage salad. I passed the steaming bowls through a crevice in the tent screen and told them to make room for me.

Before digging in to our dinner, I told the others to wait while I scrounged inside the bottom of my personal pack. I had hidden a litre of Sapporo beer to be cracked open when we hit Hudson Bay. Now was the time. We filled our mugs, twice, and toasted the trip and each other. We laughed and joked about our situation, perched on the very edge of the world, a patch of grey nylon between us and an endless neverland of gravel, rock, sea water and...polar bears. It was all too precarious, but for the moment we were in Japanese heaven, our head-space slightly skewed from the brew, accentuated by fatigue and gut-spinning adrenalin flow.

Up until now I had kept a bear "blaster" in the shotgun cartridge clip. The last thing I wanted to do was to shoot a polar bear and if I could scare it with the pop of a large firecracker, all the better. This wasn't going to work that night at all; we were the only open, all-night snack-bar for bears roaming along the coast. To lessen everyone's angst about unwanted visitations during the night, I loaded only hollow-nose slugs in the Mossberg 12-gauge and then duct-taped my flashlight around the gun stock in case of close night encounters. The live ammo appeared to assuage some but not all of the mutual nervousness. Before the Seal River expedition I had talked with an arctic guide who had to shoot a polar bear that had ripped its way through the wall of their tent.

That scenario played over and over in my mind while the others slept; I kept watch with the gun tucked beside my sleeping bag. The nylon tent fabric brushing against my shoulder suddenly seemed a whole lot thinner.

The air inside the tent was thick with the smell of sweat, smoke and farts. It was not a quiet place inside or out and in this type of situation the mind challenges all levels of rational thought. A gust of wind causes a dry twig to snap; the wind suddenly shifts and with it brings a whole other array of unknown sounds; somebody snores more like a growl than a snore. It was all too unnerving. I got up and walked around outside, not that I could go more than ten-feet between the tent and the canoes. It was still light. I sat down on one of the overturned canoes, shotgun over my lap. I checked the high-tide mark to make sure our canoes and camp wouldn't be washed into the ocean and secured the boats as best I could with one of the painters tied to a boulder. There was nothing more that I could do.

Jack Bastone – the guy with the barge – maintained a goose-hunting shack up the coast but there was no way we could have made it there with the tide going out. Bastone had made a point that we should "do our damndest" to get there so we would be safe. "Problem bears that get into trouble in Churchill are branded and helicoptered out to the Seal estuary," Jack had said. *That's fucking great!* It would have been far better to pitch camp on the open tundra than to be wedged amongst the tangle of island sedge where visibility was nil. Polar bears were hunters. Not just good hunters but *stalkers!* Humans probably looked like seal meat to a hungry bear; inside the tent we would be an easy meal; and we not only had to deal with the average polar bear, but also the bad boys from Churchill!

Returning to the tent I could tell that the others were trying hard to fall asleep. The air was too heavy with everyone's particulate aroma; three-weeks of living under uncertain conditions had started to define us by our smell. I just hoped it wasn't strong enough to attract a polar bear. I knew one thing for sure – that I wasn't going to sleep at all.

Chapter Eleven

Ghosts

An early Hudson's Bay Company factor reported that the white whale mated in a vertical position, belly to belly, with their heads protruding out of the water. Whales, dolphins and porpoises, which form the order *Cetacea*, are purported to have evolved from terrestrial mammals a long time ago. Evolution has concealed the tell-tale mammalian traits under fibrous tissues but they are still there all the same. They are quite possibly a race of creatures so chaste and perfect that they found solace from a rapidly changing world by retreating to the primordial sea. Aquarian ghosts, mystical, wise and somewhat melancholic, hounded through history by remorseless humankind. *Humankind*, what an oxymoron. One simply has to review the history of whale slaughtering to denounce the implication of "man" as a compassionate, caring and "kind" being at all.

The white or "beluga" whale is actually a primitive dolphin. It has that particular "beaked" snout of a dolphin, that permanent "smile" which expresses its renowned passive character and playful manner; only the beluga lacks a dorsal fin and sports a massive forehead which it uses to break through ice, giving it a unique countenance among its whale brethren.

"Beluga" is Russian for "whitefish", not to be confused with the Russian sturgeon from which beluga caviar is obtained. Beluga are smallish whales rarely exceeding three to four meters in length – just shy of the length of our canoes. Young calves are born in early summer, are dark slate in colour, while juveniles remain in multi-shaded grey coat until four or five years of age. Whalers referred to the beluga as the "sea canary" because of the variety of whistles and squeals that could be heard distinctly as the whale cruised underwater, replicating the sound of a songbird. The sounds are accompanied by a rush of air bubbles from the blow-hole on the top of the head; maybe an ancient language impossible to interpret. Beluga cruise the river estuaries and the shallows along Hudson Bay for a diet of cuttlefish, crabs and char, swallowing them whole. Belugas are often stranded in the shallows as the tide retreats, offering up a bounty of food to the wandering polar bear.

In 1688, the Hudson's Bay Company began harpooning whales for oil and meat. Unlike other whales with thin skins, the beluga skin was thick and tough and the hide could be used for various purposes. Over hunting eventually forced legislation to protect the beluga in Hudson Bay. Today the biggest economic contribution in the Churchill vicinity is derived from the European vacationers who conscript the tourist sloops for a chance to view the famous white whale – arctic ghosts.

The Seal River estuary is home to the largest concentration of beluga whales in the world – three-thousand to be more specific, according to whale scientists. How they actually counted them defies rational possibility and I'm sure the figures are purely speculative. It was the very presence of this mammal that intrigued me; made the Seal River expedition that much more interesting and unique beyond the varied landscape, boreal to tundra, beyond the crazy whitewater. It was part of our conversation almost every day of the trip so far – to paddle our canoes amongst the whales once we reached the coast.

I gave up trying to force myself to sleep. It was useless. It was only 5:30 in the morning, but I had that pervasive notion that a polar bear was lurking just beyond the door of the tent. Several times during the night I had reached out for the stock of the rifle to make sure it was still handy, safety on, barrel pointing towards my feet. There was too much tension just laying there, listening to the others snore and fart. I was used to sleeping alone and the tent was far too crowded. I had to get up.

While the others slept I re-rigged and tested the sail assemblage. We wouldn't trim up the canoes for sailing right away but if we needed to, the mast, tarp and boom were left handy enough for quick set-up. The sea was calm; eerily calm with hardly a breath of air to disturb the morning stillness. It was unnerving. There was plenty of time before the tide came back in. We were obligated to sit on our tiny island until the rising tide could carry us clear of the coast rubble. That wasn't for another six hours. High tide was three-hours later, at 2:00 in the afternoon. The amount of good paddling time was limited; and for a coast that seemed to thrive on the bitterest of environmental conditions we needed to take advantage of every opportunity that presented itself. Because of the off-shore tidal flats – a malaise of boulders, sand and muck – once the tide began to recede we would be drawn seaward with it several kilometers from the coastline, just in order to have enough water to float the canoes. The only other option was to 'ground' the canoes until the tide came back in. The inherent danger, in this case, would be an offshore wind, coupled with the incoming tide; the thought of being dashed to pieces against the coastal rocks was very real. Added to this trepidation was the constant threat of polar bear confrontations in a virtual feeding ground along the beluga and seal-infested coast.

I tried to ignore the knots in my stomach. I could only hope that all went smoothly and Dawson didn't pull one of his usual stunts. The others began to stir in the tent; my cue to ready breakfast: hot oatmeal with raisins and dried apples with a liberal dose of Earl Grey tea. Even the Americans preferred the tea to Dawson's flavoured coffee. There was anticipation on everyone's face this morning; an almost impatient longing to finish the trip, to reach the sanctity of the port town of Churchill - alive! The daily dread caused by the fires and the constant adrenalin rush of the rapid play had left all of us trail-worn and anxious. The most difficult and dangerous leg of the journey was about to unfold and we were sorely prepared for it. I was exhausted beyond my own limits, feeling edgy and not quite in control. It was a chore just to keep things together. The caffeine in the tea finally kicked in, cleared out the sea fog in my brain enough to concentrate. I threw a handful of tobacco into the rising tide. The salt water now girdled the cluster of rock islands at the end of the Seal River and it was finally time to go.

We ran the canoes down the last riffles out to the Bay, stopping briefly in a large pool where dozens of seals were frolicking about, circling our canoes, snouts raised to the sky. One might think it was some kind of welcoming committee. The canoes drifted lazily out of the estuary, and as we moved seaward the immensity of the water-world suddenly became intimidating, even though the depth was no more than two-meters at any one point. There was a slight but steady breeze blowing off the coast, barely rippling the water of Hudson Bay. The conditions were perfect. But where were the beluga whales?

Finally, we spotted them out in deeper water, rising just above the surface, expressing water and air through their blowholes. Hundreds of beluga whales! Before we even realized it, we were suddenly surrounded by white whales, dozens upon dozens of them! They were everywhere, and we were amongst one of the busiest whale sanctuaries in the entire world. The ocean surface began rippling and churning all around us as the beluga whales cruised by for a closer look. They even swam directly under the canoes, no more than a meter below us, gentle, curious and truly magnificent spectres of the arctic coast.

As we slowly paddled across the Seal estuary, mesmerized by their presence, the whales tagged along playfully, careful not to come too close, as if they knew that one thrust of their powerful flukes could easily turn the canoe over in the icy water. But they would follow; almost in formation of sorts, closing the gap until they were right upon our stern, then they would silently drop below the surface and glide effortlessly below the canoe. I reached down and nearly touched one. Our eyes would meet and they would look right into your soul. I could feel some ancient, telepathic message trying to materialize in my brain, not quite connecting. A complex and marginal solemnity passed between us. No words, just a mild feeling of wonder.

The most primordial of earth's creatures sculled around us, singing with enchanting and venerable voices, childlike and penetrating. Mother belugas with their young clinging to their back flanks, grey and smooth, would surface nearby and they would look at us. I could see their eyes move as they cruised by, unflinching and never looking away, as if to show us their living progeny, new life, old life, the genesis of mammalian existence. They would stare deep into our hearts and it felt as if they were trying to read our thoughts and emotions. It *was* difficult not to become emotional. All we could do was sit and drift aimlessly in our canoes while surrounded by ghosts from another dimension in time surround us.

As the day progressed past high tide we could feel that gentle surge outward and beyond the casual nature of the shoreline. For the time, we paddled autonomously, enjoying the disconnection from the other canoe, while beluga whales continued to follow us along the coast, south of the Seal estuary, amongst the boulder scrabble. At no time did Russell or I feel threatened by so much movement around the canoe by such temperate beings, except maybe once when we drifted into a large pod that had been feeding quietly in the shallows and had been startled by our sudden presence, maybe thinking our craft was an approaching polar bear. We had been forewarned about whale stampedes, or surprise encounters with beluga whales. Not that the whales became aggressive, it was their sudden confused scrambling that would transform the ocean surface from a relative serene composure into a stormy maelstrom. And without any expectation whatsoever, having no idea as to the location of the whales until they broke surface near the canoes, did we manage to break into a circle of feeding belugas. The ocean around us, defined in a circle of about thirty-meters, suddenly bore the resemblance of a huge whirlpool with breaking whitecaps embracing the perimeter with us in the middle. Russ and I had to perform some serious bracing as if we were still riding the back of a wild rapid, hoping not to get swamped by the chaotic waves as the whales tried to regain composure.

I had run out of film. As a photographer, that was a catastrophe and I borrowed the only film Russell had left. It was high-speed print film, but at least it was film. In a way, running out of film just before experiencing the beluga was somehow karmic, as if we weren't supposed to take their picture. In fact, after a few shots I stopped photographing altogether and began to enjoy the intimacy of the experience without looking through a camera viewfinder; a common enough conundrum for nature photographers who feel a mechanical separation from the subject, a betrayal almost, of the emotional or philosophical aspect of the encounter.

We realized that by spending so much time with the whales we had compromised the window of time and paddling conditions that coincided with the high tide. We had planned to paddle hard down the coast during high tide, perhaps even halfway to Churchill, the equivalent of about twenty-five kilometers. It wasn't going to happen. The tide was going out and the scant shoreline was disappearing. I began using my compass to align ourselves with the coast which by now was at least three-kilometers to the west. I made a gesture to the other canoe to follow me into shore, or whatever semblance of shore we could gain as the tide went out.

Standing knee-deep in salty water we all pitched in to rig the canoes into a catamaran once again, getting it ready for a sail down the remainder of the coast. We had to walk out with the receding tide as we worked, completing the re-rigging in about half an hour. The spray-covers were secured and I checked to make sure the shotgun was tucked under the skirt in front of my seat, easy to extricate in case of a polar bear confrontation. We had been previously warned about bears loitering along the coast and there were ample enough boulders to serve as hiding posts to launch quick attacks. And it would be dark soon.

Chapter Twelve

Mutiny on Tu Cho

After constructing our sailing rig with the poles we had brought along from the Seal River, we managed to catch the last gasp of water as it drained off the forlorn coast. There was no wind and we were all too tired to paddle. I had left out the camp-stove in order to cook the last few meals on board since there was little likelihood of finding friendly respite on shore anywhere by the looks of it. A steaming pot of mocha was prepared, more to boost lagging spirits than to graduate any increase in energy. After about an hour we gave in to the ocean and allowed the boats to run aground upon a bed of wet gravel – an endless plain of sand, mud, strands of kelp and boulders.

The shoreline was no longer a visible issue; it had retreated as we were pulled farther and farther out to sea. Now, quite abruptly and unceremoniously, we found ourselves stranded with absolutely no cover at all and six hours to wait until the next high tide. If a strong sea-born wind accompanied the incoming tide it could drive us hard into the coastal rocks. For now it was peaceful, surreal, as if we had just landed on the moon.

It was eight o'clock in the evening and the next tide would be in at two in the morning. It would be a long wait. Our ridiculous vulnerability propagated a host of silly antics. As I walked away from the frail island of canoes, perched absurdly on a vacant sea, I turned around to take a photograph only to be greeted by three men with their trousers down to their ankles and their white bottoms glowing like beacons. We all laughed. The simple humour was just the right elixir to break the aura of uncertainty.

I cooked up a tasty pasta for what was purportedly our final meal and we all sat in our respective canoe seats cleaning off every morsel from our plates. The hours went by slowly. Small rivulets continued to drain the coast and it became easier to make forays away from the boats without having to jump from rock to rock to avoid landing in the slick mud. Thick clumps of kelp lay in patches between the boulders and the rich smell of the ocean became ever-present as the coast revealed all its latent treasures. The constant twilight was enhanced by the smoke haze that continued to drift to the coast, setting a blood-ochre atmosphere. In one sense, the surreal nature of our position was totally exciting, captivating, and eerily sublime. On the other hand, the foolishness of being stranded and vulnerable to the worst elements on the planet was audacious but risky.

Our perch revealed an indistinguishable vista in all directions; an identity so desolate and austere as any desert on earth, only more inhospitable for twelve hours of each and every day – a virtual paradox of life. One moment a wretched, languid wasteland, and within an instant, flushed with such a complexity of vibrant life forms. The fact that we were likely the only living being standing upon a tidal desert the size of the Sahara only served to aggravate the feeling of suspense; apprehension even more so. Not that the exposed sea-bed was completely devoid of life forms – it wasn't at all. There were spider crabs, mussels, whelks, bent-nose clams, and brown seaweed upon closer inspection.

We were impatient to get going again. For the entire three hundred kilometers to this point on the map we were in a constant state of flux, moving all the time, towards something or away from it. Sitting still for so long, waiting, was tough on the nerves, worse because we were all dead tired. Movement had a calming effect on the nerves, but this waiting, watching for the tide to come back in was by no means a pleasant game.

I readied the sail and hung a candle lantern from the stern boom-line. I wanted to be fully prepared once we were underway. How fast the tide would come in was a mystery. The light of dusk had been constant, the sky unchanged from its pall of yellow-brown haze, and there was still no suspicion of any wind blowing in off the sea. I spat into the tiny stream of water that ran aside the beached canoe and watched as the raft of saliva drifted seaward. The tide was still going out and six hours had elapsed. I spat into the stream a second time and was surprised to watch the saliva float the other way this time – a change in direction in less than thirty seconds!

"Tide's coming in!" I yelled at the others who were out walking on the sea-bed. The canoes were suddenly lifted by the rush of the incoming tide, the others scrambled to get into the freed canoes and we were afloat once again. Within minutes most of the coastal rocks were under water. The canoes swung around fitfully; without a compass bearing I would have had no idea which direction to point the boats. I checked the topographic map and estimated our location along the coast against the amount of time paddled before being stranded. We had barely achieved a very modest ten kilometers since leaving the estuary. There was too light a breeze to fill the sail and push the canoes along so we paddled in earnest on a 170 degree, south by southeast heading towards the bottom of Button Bay, following what I guessed was the Hudson Bay shoreline. The only indication that we were still within the tidal flats were the rocks we continued to brush against that were just below the surface. The canoes would often lodge against them and we would get hung up, and the canoes would swing a hundred and eighty degrees, pointing us in another direction. It was just dark enough now to need the flashlight to check the compass reading and I would order a "hard left!" or "hard right!" to get the boats in line again with the coast, or what I imagined was the coast, intermittent as it was, and just a slightly more elevated swath of mud and boulders.

I tried to steer the craft just out of range of the boulder-field but it seemed as if we would run aground at least every five minutes. Sometimes we were caught up so tight to the rock that it took several minutes of cursing, pushing, prying and heaving to get ourselves unstuck. It was tiring work that pushed us to a new limit of exhaustion. I constantly checked my watch to estimate our accomplished distance down the coast which appeared to be interminably slow. The candle lantern was lit, not that it would help me see the topographic-map or anything else in the canoe, but more to dispense a cheery incandescence over the canoes.

A breeze began to emanate off the coast, slightly behind us, filling the nylon sail with renewed life and the canoes surged forward slowly; the others lifted their paddles, now almost too heavy to hold on to, while I kept mine in the water as a rudder. Barely moving at paddling-speed, it didn't matter, any kind of rest was welcome. Hodding and Russell settled into a sleeping position in their respective bow seats while Dawson sat smoking a cigarette in the other stern seat beside me. He seemed far too quiet for my liking.

The candle-lantern danced wildly as the canoes bucked the chop. The wind whistled through the lantern and shrouds sounding like Ulysses taunting sirens. There were no stars. No moon. Nothing to navigate by other than the compass. No sign of land,

just the rippling of sea-water against the hull of the canoes under the weak blush of light cast by one small candle.

I thought of Henry Hudson and knew exactly how he must
have felt when his men mutinied and set him adrift in 1611.
Hudson, English explorer and navigator, attempted to locate
the *Northwest Passage* to Cathay, discovered Hudson Straight and
sailed south to James Bay where his boat, the "Discovery" became locked in sea-ice. After surviving a long winter on shore, he
wanted to press on to the west but many of his men preferred
to sail home. There was a mutiny and Hudson, his teenage son
John, and seven feeble crewmen were set adrift in a small shallop,
marooning them in Hudson Bay. They were never seen again...
except maybe their ghosts on occasion.

So totally alone they must have felt with little chance of
survival. Supplies gifted to them by the mutineers amounted
to a paltry supply of meal, powder and shot for hunting that
would not last beyond a couple of weeks, an iron pot for cook-
ing, clothing, some pikes for pushing the boat off ice jams and a
few miscellaneous sundries – not enough to keep nine men alive
until any hope of rescue. The surviving mutineers were tried for
treason but never convicted; the Crown deeming their knowledge too valuable.

And although our situation wasn't as bleak as Hudson's definitely was, the immensity of the ocean, the darkness, the aloneness and exposure could be no different at all. I could only think
of polar bears at this time, lurking behind a boulder waiting for
us to cruise by or get hung up, and while we were busy pushing
off with our paddles, it would pounce on us without warning
and drag us out of our canoes, one by one. What made matters
worse came in the sudden flushing of groups of eider ducks or
Canada geese from their night roost, the cacophony of wings
exploding off our bow would send spears of adrenalin racing

through every fiber. And each time I would reach for the Mossberg expecting to fend off an attacking bear; each time sighing in relief, each time a little more of my reserve being whittled away, almost too tired to rudder the paddle or to watch the compass-bearing.

At about four in the morning we could barely make out the lights of Churchill, about thirty kilometers to our east, across the expanse of Button Bay. It was hard not to take your eyes from the alluring glow as it was the only visible entity around us, aside from the swinging candle-lantern which by now was more of an annoyance than a pleasantry. Dawson immediately pleaded for us to aim the canoes for the town and make short work of the distance, rather than following the safety of the coast. I reminded him of the two dead canoeists who had tried to cross the Bay before us.

"Not only that," I told my assistant with some authority, "the lights might be coming from a ship moving north out of the port. We don't know for sure."

It seemed to make no difference to Dawson at all. The lights wavered and flickered tauntingly. He stared at them, transfixed for several moments as if scheming something.

"Just be patient. We'll maintain the course along the coast until we reach the bottom of Button Bay," directing my instructions at Dawson. Russ and Hodding were in complete compliance to the plan. They wanted to get out alive. After what we'd been through already, they didn't want to push their luck.

"Once there we can swing northeast towards Churchill and use the prevailing wind to push us the remaining twenty-kilometers to Churchill." Dawson said nothing

By now both Russell and Hodding were asleep in the confines of their bow compartments, slumped down into their spray-decks for warmth. The canoes moved slowly along the boulder-strewn coast on a conservative course headed for the bottom of Button Bay, as planned. Reluctantly, I asked my assistant to take the rudder while I stole a few minutes of sleep. I was about to pass-out from fatigue. He was given strict instructions to maintain the heading and I was fool enough to believe that he would.

I've tripped hard in the past, pushed myself until I collapsed but it was all from physical exhaustion. And there is an extraordinary pleasure to it and recovery is swift. The exhaustion that overwhelmed me now was not so much physical tiredness but the mental stress of the expedition. And that psychological tension wasn't all about the difficulty of the rapids, or the threat of being burned alive. It had, in a huge way, to do with the interaction with my assistant guide, fixing his fuck-ups and mitigating abnormal eccentric and dangerous behaviour. I was afraid to fall asleep. But if I didn't get at least a few minutes, I would not be good for anything else and it was my responsibility to get everyone out safely.

I fell into a deep and wonderful sleep; gently rocking, comforted by unconscious dream, peaceful. Slumber nirvana. I must have slept for some time. Even when I was jostled awake by the waves and the rising sea, my brain didn't acknowledge the situation we were in. It took a while to focus but I could make out lights in the distance, fading in and out, moving. I could hear the stays holding the canoes together creaking, straining and voices, not conversation but shouts. " Do something!" I splashed cold water on my face so I could focus. "I don't care, I just want to sleep," I answered still numb with sleep and fatigue. Not the answer Russell and Hodding were looking for. It finally donned on me that we were heading across Button Bay, directly towards the lights of Churchill. ' "What the fuck!" I yelled aloud. How could he do this to us?

Dawson leaned hard on his ruddering paddle, staring straight ahead. I tried to gauge how far from the coast we had come and I figured far enough to make it hard work to get the canoes back on course. We were now running with a brisk wind and the waves were starting to swell. It was impossible to say whether we would have sailed safely into Churchill harbour or not, keeping to the pell-mell course across Button Bay. Given the rising spirit of the sea as we sailed further from land, matched against our weakness from fatigue and the strained creaking of the canoe stays, the odds were not favourable. Hodding and Russell started yelling at Dawson to turn us around.

"Put up your paddle, now!" I screamed at my assistant. He didn't. "Put up your fucking paddle Dawson!" I yelled again. He leaned harder on the rudder. I tried to counter his steering power with my own but with the wind directly behind us we were too heavy a craft and moving forward too swiftly. The canoes were bouncing in the waves now and the whole craft seemed to be coming apart slowly. I looked at Hodding and Russell and saw the look of dread on their faces. To come this far, through so much, to have it end right here was not the way it should happen. As leader of the expedition, as captain of our canoe-catamaran, I took the only measure left to me. Drastic as it may have seemed it was my only alternative. I slipped my hand under the spray-skirt in front of me and grasped the 12-gauge shotgun, thumbed off the safety and began pulling out the shotgun.

Dawson knew what I was doing, was about to do, and he knew that I would have no qualms about doing it. It had gone this far. Too many buttons were pushed and Button Bay was the last one. Before I had the gun fully drawn Dawson pulled up his paddle and threw it down hard on the gunwales, almost bouncing it off into the water.

"It's your ship!" was all he said. It felt like we were re-enacting the Caine Mutiny. Dawson sat back, arms crossed against his chest, tucked in his chin in defiance. We didn't have any time to lose. I told Russell and Hodding to lower the sail while I manoeuvred the canoes around to face a non-existent coastline. "Paddle hard!" I barked and the three of us dug in our paddles against the strong wind and waves and edged our way westward. It was a long time before Dawson picked up his paddle again. It took us more than an hour to gain our old course back. The wind had subsided and the morning light was illuminating a non-descript shoreline. We paddled without resting for another two hours until we reached the south end of Button Bay before finally stopping for a break. Dawson was the first to break the silence, talking to us as if nothing at all had happened, jumping into his usual composed babble. Only this time nobody responded, even Hodding remained silent. I wanted to throw up. The thought of nearly killing someone turned my stomach. I kept asking myself over and over, *what would I have done if he hadn't thrown up his paddle? Shoot him and push his body into the ocean?* Maybe.

We had paddled deep into the Bay in order to take full advantage of the southwest wind. Once the sail was thrown open it exploded into a final applaud of energy that almost lifted our craft out of the water. We cruised along at about eight-knots, keeping about two kilometers off-shore and headed northeast towards Fort Prince of Wales and Churchill. The smoke-haze from the inland fires, a hundred kilometers to the west, curtained the sun creating an uneasy light that did its best to cast shadows. It was light just the same and the end of a long night; a night not easily forgotten, and not overlooked by my American friends. Hodding and Russell were anxious to put ashore, stretch their legs. Dawson remained sheepish. He knew we were all pissed at him so he tried to initiate conversation. Nobody really wanted to talk. Before long we were sailing amongst beluga whales again.

This time we had the security of a more stable craft, visibility enhanced by standing on the gunwales of the canoe, clearly watching beluga's submarine under the boats.

We could finally make out the old stone palace, Fort Prince of Wales, restructured and handsome, set alone on the stark footing of Eskimo Point at the entrance of Churchill harbour. And as the extent of the tidal flats diminished, the shoreline took on a more prominent face, still modestly clothed in whatever such a harsh environment would charter. There were patches of black spruce and *krummholz*, white spruce stunted, hardy survivors of icy winds and salt-spray, branches growing only on the lee side to the wind, gnarled and artistic, also known as "knee-timber" because of its low stature. I think it was at this point that we knew we were going to actually complete this expedition and be able to go home with more experiences than we anticipated.

The canoes were beached on the shore in front of the Fort, secured to boulders, and we stood there for some time relishing the feel of solid earth under our feet. It was a moment of elation. The Americans had their story with no deficiency of adventure, a dash of sedition and a wealth of photo-images that would be priceless. The actual realization that the expedition was over, and that we survived the rapids, the terrific fires and the insane trip down the coast at night was just sinking into our head-space. I wanted to shout at the gods, embrace my canoe partners, thrash the mutineer, put my hands against the sun-warmed stones of the old Fort. Most of all I wanted to sleep in a room with no black flies and enjoy a solid shit in a porcelain bowl. Taking as deep a breath of the salty-air as I could inhale (almost passing out) I let out a very loud *HURRAH!*

"Let's take the Fort!" and we all rushed at the walls, canons silent, staring down at us from gun-ports, we filed past the glowing cenotaph to Sir Thomas Button and Samuel Hearne, and to

where we all took turns pissing against the wall before breaking into the unprotected gate, finally entering the bowels of the rock ramparts that, in the 1700s, took forty years to construct, 'where the English surrendered to the French without resistance', and where Canada Parks staff conduct guided-tours depending on the weather and the tide. I stood beside one of the canons and looked out over the expanse of Hudson Bay – *Tu Cho*. I wanted to cry and laugh at the same time. It hadn't been the trip I expected it to be. I ran my hand down the pocked, cold iron of the dead canon, and I thought of the work it must have taken to get it here.

What foreigners we are to this country, I thought, not solemnly but with an air of satisfaction. We came but we didn't conquer anything; to think we conquered the land would be arrogant and self-serving. If anything, this expedition was a humbling experience; a portrait of our own weaknesses. I had come so close to killing someone, killing Dawson to save the rest of us. The thought made me shudder. *Would I have actually pulled the trigger?* I kept asking myself. I think I would have.

Admiralty Law: 23rd. Article "suppression of mutiny" – *an officer is warranted in employing the most rigorous means – in using a deadly weapon and taking life – for the suppression of a mutiny*.

I gazed over the precipice of rock wall out over the bleak landscape, the sorry scrabble of rock and the incident growth of sedge and lichen that surrounded the Fort. I looked closer. It wasn't really bleak at all. It was actually quite beautiful, remarkable in fact; the tenacity of arctic life. Holding on to that thought I realized I was a part of that resolve. We had been travelling so fast, been so wrapped up in the adventure that we forgot to look at the beauty of it all: the alpine arnica, robust saxifrage growing in clusters in the cracks of rocks, so many orchids...coralroot, lady-slipper, blue-flag iris, and there was Labrador tea, mountain avens and the blush pink alpine azalea, and birds too numerous to count...bonapart gulls, terns, jaegers, sand-hill cranes, willow ptarmigan, plovers, loons back on Shethanei.

The others had gathered at the gate waiting for me. "Let's go home," I announced with nods and high-fives, a short walk to the canoes, past the sign that said "CAUTION -Polar Bear Area", and we pushed off one last time with the sail rolled up, we paddled into the port town of Churchill. A man, part native, working aboard one of the docked boats looked down at us as we pulled in beside him. He said nothing but I could tell by the look on his face he was quite bewildered at the oddness of our sea-faring vessel. I could tell that he had spent his life out there, on the sea, the countenance of his weathered face, rough, large hands, gave away his occupation. For a brief moment our eyes met and he could tell, from our own complexion and appearance that we were not ordinary tourists. He gave us a friendly smile, an honorary welcome with all the same respect he would have given to an old friend. I smiled back. He knew.

Epilogue

Churchill is not a pretty town, sprawled accidentally over the tundra like a spilled barrel of spare parts. The towering grain elevators capture your attention wherever you go, empty and silent for most of the year, while the town of 1,100 souls live within its shadow, seemingly waiting for the bustle of tourists that come in late summer to see polar bears, beluga whales, birds and the northern lights. For the most part, locals endure the long winters in relative harmony, content with the isolation and notoriety as the only human settlement in the world where polar bears can be observed in their natural environment. At a safe distance, of course, camera-toting tourists encased in large "tundra buggies" whisk across the tundra flats to see bears.

If ever there was a tourist Mecca it was right here, in Churchill Manitoba. I suppose one of the few honest applications of the word "eco" prefixed to an adventure component, good enough commerce to pass the scrutiny of the environmental and animal rights watchdogs. Some might think that tearing up the sensitive coastal alpine plants and lichens growing on the tundra, crushed under the wheels of gargantuan all-terrain-vehicles and tourists harassing wildlife is perhaps not an ecologically sound business. Occasionally a polar bear does get out of hand and end up in the Churchill "jail", to be helicoptered up the coast and dropped off in the Seal River estuary. But there are other things to do and see in Churchill. It is here that Japanese tourists flock in to view the northern lights, *aurora borealis*, believed to be an elixir for procreation; and if you don't fancy waving your camera in front of an animal you can always find an outfitter that will help you shoot one. Churchill is also renowned as a hunters' paradise, rife with caribou and snow geese. The passive tourist can hike a short distance along the coast to see the shipwrecked

Ithaca, caught in a windstorm in 1961 while carrying nickel ore from Rankin Inlet to Montreal, or you can take one of the many tourist sloops out on to the Churchill River to photograph beluga whales.

And like every other northern Canadian town, Churchill has its seedy side of life – the shiftless vagrants, drunks and hangabouts who decorate the crude tables at the local Legion Hall. That's where Dawson hung out while we waited two days for the train that would take us and the canoes back to Thompson. And when the train finally arrived, and Hodding, Russell and I waited for Dawson to show up with the train tickets, he was nowhere to be found. One of the baggage handlers finally jumped in his beat-up truck and plied the bars for my assistant guide. He was at the Legion. He was higher than a kite, doped up, hyperkinetic and obnoxious. The three of us retreated to one of the passenger cars to find peace and left Dawson with the polite baggage handler.

Hodding and Russell offered to pool resources to buy Dawson a train ticket from Thompson back to Ontario so I wouldn't be stuck with him in my car for three days. Although a very tempting offer, Dawson was still my responsibility and I felt bad enough that the Americans, all of us, had to put up with such irresponsible nonsense. We talked awhile about the trip even though sleep was weighing heavy over every word in an effort to share last thoughts about the journey. Hodding was excited about writing the story for *Men's Journal*. And as it turned out, he found it difficult to trim the original manuscript from a novella down to the acceptable 3,500 words, so the magazine delayed publishing his story for nearly four years.

I could tell that Hodding was brimming with expletives, long narration and his own brand of philosophical conjecture. He admitted that he was far too immersed in the wonder and awe of the surroundings to really pay much attention to Dawson, until the last few days. It's easy for writers to become self-involved.

For the first time, Russell and I sat together and talked openly about the expedition. When the magazine had asked him to go, Russell said he couldn't refuse. They had agreed to outfit him and pay him handsomely for the photography. Russell said that the more he learned about the river from the editors, the less he liked the idea, regardless of the remuneration. He was afraid. He was in over his head. Initially he thought nothing of the risks involved. He figured that if the guides had their collective act together and he was supplied with a life-jacket, things would be okay. Dawson showing up in the bar in Thompson, stoned on hair-spray, was a slap in the face of reality. He was close to calling it quits. Russ admitted that his most profound experience was his own naivety about risk-taking, calculating his chances of survival, and accepting decisions as possibly the last ones he would ever make. His greatest fear other than dying was being a burden on the group.

"I called my fiancé last night from the hotel," Russ told me. He was excited to share this with me. He was beaming.

"I bet she's happy you made it out alive," I said jokingly.

"Yeah, really glad; she's flying up to meet me in Thompson; we're going on a two-week canoe trip on the Grass River, just west of the town."

"That's surprising. I would have thought you'd want to high-tail it back to New York after this trip." I was a bit perplexed but I could see the glow on Russell's face.

"Naw, I really feel like I can do this on my own now with the skills you taught me. And my girlfriend is stoked too; sort of a pre-nuptial honeymoon I guess."

We shook hands for a long time, slow and deliberate. He thanked me for getting him out alive, and I assured him that it was because of his own resources and will power that pulled him through. Russell handed me a postcard he had picked up in Churchill, shoved it into my hand and walked away. Was he crying? I turned the card over, dated the 20th of July, 1994. It read:

Hap – "It's quite odd to spend that much time with someone you don't really know fifteen or so feet behind you, feeling their force, their rhythm; almost their breath. We didn't chat much but somehow that's even more of a bond – the quiet, interrupted by that vibrant rumble, shared. Learning to trust that eloquent guidance, I am so warmly indebted. I would enjoy crossing paddles again...& again..." Russell.

I read it twice. My hand holding the card was shaking. Tears welled up in my own eyes and I tucked my face into the crook of my arm and tried hard not to cry but the weight of the expedition came out in deep, visceral sobs, emotions born out of exhaustion and conflict. Finally, a heavy shroud had been lifted from my soul just thinking of heading home to my cabin in Temagami. As with any expedition, each journey into the wilderness where the camaraderie and the difficulties ensued and the dangers shared, there is the resultant anti-climax, the engulfing melancholy as soon as you step out of the canoe and back into civilization - the disconnection. The irony of it all.

I stared out of the train window into the boreal. I smiled, thinking of all the crazy things that had plagued this expedition, both noble and unforgiving. I knew I would be back again. I had left part of my soul embedded in the golden sand of *Sheth tie eye tuay*.

Afternotes:

More than two decades have passed since this expedition. Russell Kaye went on to produce award-winning photographs; Hodding Carter managed to abbreviate his article for *Men's Journal Magazine*, from novella to feature; Dawson's whereabouts are unknown to me. I went through a period of withdrawal, perhaps a mild case of Post-Traumatic Stress Disorder (PTSD), which left me anxious, irritable and emotionally numb. The accumulative effect of hard expeditions, rescuing clients from precarious incidents, researching the 30 deaths on the Missinaibi River, the environmental battles, blockades, lost love, topping it all off with the crazy trip through the fires on the Seal with an assistant guide I very nearly killed, pushed me close to the abyss.

On the positive side, I was gifted a tremendous insight into the life and perils of our northern First Nations people and to the land in which they were and still are, inextricably aligned and dependent. I did retreat to my cabin on the Lady Evelyn River, deep in the Temagami wilderness, for periods of reflection and healing. I also returned to the Seal and many other arctic and tundra rivers over the years. Best of all, after eighteen long years apart, I married the woman who had once stolen my heart.

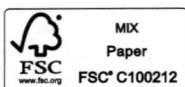

MIX
Paper
FSC
www.fsc.org   **FSC® C100212**

Printed by Imprimerie Gauvin
Gatineau, Québec